NO BULL

The Authorised Biography of Billy Hamill

NO BULL

The Authorised Biography of Billy Hamill

Brian Burford & Billy Hamill

TEMPUS

In memory of Carlos Cardona

First published 2004

Tempus Publishing Limited
The Mill, Brimscombe Port,
Stroud, Gloucestershire, GL5 2QG
www.tempus-publishing.com

British Library Cataloguing in Publication Data.
· A catalogue record for this book is available from the British Library.

ISBN 0 7524 3219 2

Typesetting and origination by Tempus Publishing Limited
Printed and bound in Great Britain

CONTENTS

ACKNOWLEDGEMENTS

I would like to express my thanks to Billy, Christina, his mother Gay and the rest of his family for their assistance in the writing of this book. A special thank you to Greg Hancock for writing the foreword, and for his words of encouragement at just the right time. A special mention of gratitude goes to Mike Patrick who, in the true spirit of all speedway people, took the time to go through his extensive photograph archive even though he was recovering from a back operation and had been ordered not to work. I would also like to express my appreciation to Craig Cummings and Chuck Askland for their contribution, many thanks to Mark Sawbridge for tracking down a tape of the 1998 Polish GP, and all the staff at Tempus, especially James, Wendy and Becky for all their help and for continuing to support the sport of speedway racing. A note of appreciation to my mother for reading the same sequence over and over until I got it right, and John Chaplin, Gordon

Day and Gareth Owen for their continued support and encourage-ment. Finally, I would like to dedicate this book to my fellow whacky racer Phil Handel, for all of his advice, help and good humour over the last few years.

Brian Burford

To thank everyone who has helped me during my speedway career would fill a book in itself, but I would like to express my gratitude to all the sponsors and fans who have supported me. I would like to say a special thanks to all my friends who have encouraged me during my career. However, I'd like to thank Greg for writing the foreword and Brian for tracking me down and keeping the pressure on, but most of all for doing such a good job. Finally, I'd like to dedicate this book to my family who have all backed me through thick and thin, good times and bad, but especially to my wife Christina, my two great kids Margi and Kurtis, and my Mom and Dad who have always supported me.

Billy Hamill

Now you see the challenge rise, victory holds a prize
Who'll know the price you'll have to pay.

– Fastway (Carroll/King/Connor/Reid/Manning)

FOREWORD: 'THE RACER'

It was a privilege to be asked to write a foreword for Billy Hamill in his new book. There is a lot to say about Billy within his racing career. He and I grew up together racing in Europe and chasing our ultimate dreams. It is safe to say that all of those dreams have come true!

Billy Hamill, 'The Racer' or 'The Bullet' as most people know him, speaks for himself when it comes to speedway. His style and character are portrayed very much through his racing. I believe that most, if not all of his fans would agree. Billy has always had the determination to be a winner and there is no doubt about that. He and I had a lot of the same training but we learned in two totally different manners. When I would stand back to take a closer look, Billy would go for it. In a nutshell that sums up Billy Hamill. He is a real chaser and when he finds the opening or the ultimate line he will just point and go. To be a winner takes a lot of quick decisions, but many times those decisions can lead to some very tricky situations. Billy could usually ride himself into that situation and his experience or skill would also ride him out of it. There are not many riders in the world with that skill. Many would call it a gift, but I would also say that it is part of the determination to be the best whether you have the gift or not.

Billy has had a very successful speedway career up to date. He has also had great support from his family, friends and fans. It was a sad day when he had to take the very difficult decision of withdrawing from the Grand Prix in 2003. He has spent his whole career building the best team for himself and then it was like someone dropped a bomb. To lose a major sponsor's support can be the key to your whole season. Racing towards the World title is not cheap, but there is a price for everything. When you want the title, you have to work hard to find the support. That doesn't happen overnight though. He worked hard for a lot of years to get the support that he had and to keep it. The Grand Prix and American Speedway has missed Billy Hamill in the World Championship. I don't know where his future lies, but I am sure that wherever it is he will make it successful. Perhaps you will find out more as you read on.

Good luck Billy and family!

Greg Hancock
1997 World Champion

INTRODUCTION

No matter what our chosen field of interest is, we all believe ourselves to be able to predict the outcome of a sporting event – that is why the bookmakers are so successful! In 1990 Billy Hamill arrived to race for Cradley Heath in the British League and his performances had most people predicting big things for the all-action Californian.

The first time I saw him race was at Swindon and he scored 3 points. Given that he was more used to the smaller tracks in the USA, the big Swindon circuit must have been a new experience for him. But as each race passed he was clearly getting to grips with it. A few weeks later he returned to Swindon as a guest and he put his previous experience to good use and was a different rider. He finished with 7 points, and would have scored more but for a fall while challenging for the lead. It was after that performance that I turned to my father and told him that as long as he steered clear of major injuries he would be a

World Champion one day. Six years later, the man they called 'The Bullet' was crowned Champion of the World in a dramatic final Grand Prix of the year in Denmark.

It was when I was preparing my first speedway book, *The Moran Brothers*, that I approached Billy hoping that he would write the foreword. He was my first choice and I was delighted when he agreed, as I knew that Kelly and Shawn Moran were an influence in his racing career. I discovered that while Billy was an easygoing Californian, he also strived to present himself and the sport with a more up-to-date modern image. His association with firstly Exide and then Kenny Roberts Racing illustrated his desire to move the Grand Prix concept forward.

Billy and I are of a similar age, and we've both chosen a different career path from the one that had been in our family for generations. To go against a family tradition is not easy, because you cannot fall back on the knowledge that you would normally obtain from them when you're making your own way in the world. Therefore, it can be a lonely business. That's not to say that Billy's family did not support him because they did, but, as he bluntly put it, 'They weren't interested – I was.'

This was one of the motivating factors behind my enthusiasm to work with him on this book. By taking to the track he was pursuing a dream and making it a reality. To become a World Champion in any sport is an achievement; to be able to say that 'I was the best in the world at my chosen profession' is a major accomplishment that should never be underestimated by anyone.

Ambition and adventure is determined by the fear factor: fear of failure, fear of injury or the fear of making a fool of oneself. When we sit in the stands and watch riders like Billy performing on the racetrack it's easy to criticise. But no one but the closest to them know of all the sacrifices that riders like Billy Hamill have to make to reach the top: the travelling, the rivalries, the preparations, the time spent away from your family, and the 100% commitment that is required to be the best.

Therefore we should all remember that most of us are just spectators and not experts; but I am one spectator who is proud to have known and worked with someone who has earned the right to call himself an 'expert'.

Brian Burford, February 2004

One

BUCKING THE TREND

People come to California, and they aim to do it right/
Every waitress a performer; you'll be famous overnight.

Only in America (Tony Clarkin)

In February 2003, Billy Hamill announced that he was withdrawing from the Speedway Grand Prix World Championship. He was an ever-present in the series since its inception in 1995 and he had brought much to the sport at the highest level. But his departure from the scene indicated that the financial benefits had yet to reach the riders.

'I have been unable to put together a racing budget to compete in the 2003 Grand Prix,' he said in a press release. 'It has been a very difficult decision to make and a very disappointing one too.'

For Hamill, who had dreamed of being a speedway rider since he was a very young boy, it was the end of an era and a sad farewell to a racer who had come to epitomise the modern Grand Prix rider. While the flames of ambition may not have been burning with quite the same passion, he still wanted to be in a position from which he could win GPs. He didn't want to be involved simply to make up the numbers and as the family saying goes: 'If you're going to do it, do it right, or don't do it at all.' This phrase was born out of years of competition that the Hamill family had been involved in.

At the same time that Billy shook the international speedway world with the above press statement, post-production was well underway on a major new motion picture called *Seabiscuit*. This movie told the true story of a racehorse that had captured the imagination of the American public during the dark years of the Great Depression. At first glance, there is very little to link these two seemingly unconnected events until you learn that one of the exercise riders for Seabiscuit was Billy's granddad, Keith Stucki.

Seabiscuit, starring Jeff Bridges and Tobey Maguire, was an Oscar-nominated hit and it was based on a prize-winning book by Laura Hillenbrand. Stucki was able to provide the author with some back-ground information about the horse and its environment when she was researching her subject. Horses, horse racing and horsepower – of both the animal and mechanical variety – would all come to play a large part in the life of Billy Hamill.

The thrill of competition and the desire to win was no stranger to the Stucki/Hamill family; nor was the struggle to succeed. The Great Depression was a very hard period in the history of America and also that of Western civilisation. People who lived through that turbulent era were all affected by it in some way. This was a time when employment was scarce and men would travel hundreds of miles for the promise of a day's work. This atmosphere of uncertainty produced a breed of men and women who were hard and resilient – qualities that shaped future generations, some more than others.

'It was tough,' said Stucki. 'I left home when I was twelve and went to work in Montana and Wyoming and then came to California. I was riding horses by the time I was thirteen, but when I was sixteen I was already too heavy to be a jockey. I met Tom Smith and he gave me a job and that was how I came to be an exercise rider for Seabiscuit. Red

Pollard was the jockey, and when he didn't show up or he was in the jockey "hot box", I galloped Seabiscuit. The first time I galloped him, Tom Smith took Seabiscuit to the half-mile pole and then we turned to face the infield. He said: "Keep him in the middle of the track toward the outside and just keep your hands down in one hold and he'll gallop real good for a mile and a half" – it felt real good. Times were very tough back then, but the crowds were enormous when Seabiscuit was racing and his presence was a like a blood transfusion for the local Santa Anita racetrack.'

A little light recreation was a welcome relief from the hardships that faced ordinary people everyday. A little horse called Seabiscuit became an improbable hero, and his success maintained the nation's spirit during a period when misery was an unwelcome neighbour. His victories inspired people to believe that the American dream was still alive. The Seabiscuit phenomenon transcended all the economic constraints of the time and his presence ensured large crowds.

On the face of it there doesn't seem to be a great deal of similarity between speedway and horse racing. However, one of the most famous events from the Seabiscuit era was the match race that was staged at Pimlico in 1938 between Seabiscuit and the seemingly superior thoroughbred from the East, War Admiral. Seabiscuit, a smaller horse, won a thrilling head-to-head contest that captured the interest of the country and guaranteed the colt's status as one of racing's immortal icons. 'There may be another horse that comes along greater than Seabiscuit, but none that will have endeared himself to the multitude,' wrote the *Los Angeles Times* in 1940.

Meanwhile speedway racing was developing its own match race championship – more commonly known as the Golden Helmet – that would run with some distinction until the mid-1980s. It was a format that brought glory for many riders, including such stars as Jack Parker, Peter Craven, Peter Collins, Ivan Mauger and Barry Briggs.

Horse racing is a worldwide sport, with races like the Grand National, the Kentucky Derby, the Prix de l'Arc de Triomphe, and the Melbourne Cup all earning international recognition. These are major events that attract the top horses, trainers and jockeys from all around the world. Consequently the horse racing industry is like a global village and each nation that trains horses to race in competition is part of this community.

That community stretches across the Atlantic Ocean to the troubled country of Ireland. There has always been a special link between Ireland and the USA, and there are many in America who proudly display their Irish roots and refer to themselves as 'Irish-Americans'. The pull of the large and glamorous continent of the USA on the inhabitants of the Emerald Isle might have diminished slightly in recent years, but the bonds between the two countries remain strong. During the eighteenth century people flocked from Europe and other continents to the 'New World', seeking to find a better life and to make their fortune. It was not only seen as a land of opportunity, but also purported to be a land of plenty. This glamorous image still attracts thousands of people today, just as it did all those years ago.

Indeed the Stuckis can trace their history back to the pioneering days of the old American West, when they travelled from England and arrived in New York. Here they boarded a train to Iowa City where Keith's grandmother, Sarah Ann Oakey, joined the Willie Handcart Company. Her family walked and pulled handcarts across the high plains of Wyoming. The journey was a most arduous and hazardous one that resulted in sixty-seven deaths and left many with permanent injuries. They left on 18 August and arrived in Salt Lake City on 9 November 1856 after enduring many horrific hardships.

However, Billy's father Gordon was born in Portadown in Northern Ireland in 1943. In 1920, Northern Ireland broke away from the rest of the country to form a state that was allied to Great Britain. This split is a source of much controversy and violence, which has not been helped by the religious divide between Catholics and Protestants. Nonetheless, the political and religious reasons behind these troubles are not a subject that should be dwelled upon in this book.

This nation has a fine reputation for breeding championship race-horses and, of course, the jockeys to ride them. It is a durable country whose charm, beauty and a drop of the black stuff (Guinness), seems to lift it above the rainy days, stormy nights and political turmoil that its leaders are always embroiled in.

It was the thunder of the hooves over the hallowed turf that brought the Hamills and America together. Gordon Hamill was a young boy when his family uprooted from Portadown and moved to a stud called Woodpark Stud in Dunboyne County Meath, Dublin, in the Republic of Ireland (South). This farm is still there but it is now owned by Sheik Maktoum al Maktoum.

Ireland was an underdeveloped country at that time, especially when it was compared to its near neighbour Great Britain. Some would say that it was only when the European Economic Community was established in 1958 following the Treaties of Rome that Ireland was able to make great changes to its standard of living through the Common Agricultural Policy. This eventually enabled the nation to become the envy of some of its European partners. But in the mid-1950s, despite its transatlantic links with the USA, Ireland suffered from a poor economy.

It was during these less than prosperous times that Gordon's father, William, decided on a course of action that would change their lives forever.

'My father decided to emigrate to America,' explained Gordon. 'He left on his own in 1955 to find work and establish a home, and then when he was ready he sent for the rest of us. We emigrated in 1957 to join my father; there was myself, my brother and my mother – and we never looked back.'

William Hamill was also a jockey in Ireland and he found work on a stud farm/ranch called Greentop Farm that was owned by Joe Maggio, who was known as the 'Carrot King'. Greentop Farm is located near Descanso, which is just twenty miles away from the Mexican border.

'It was so different from my homeland,' recalled Gordon. 'Ireland was so backward, especially when you compared it to America. For a start there was plenty of warm sunshine, and I couldn't believe it when I saw all these houses had swimming pools in their back gardens. I was thirteen years old and I learnt to swim in California. It was always so cold in Ireland that as soon as you were in the water you had to get out again before you could learn anything because the water was so cold.

'Joe Maggio used to live at El Centro and he used to come to the ranch about once a fortnight. My father ran the ranch and looked after the horses and I used to ride too. It was great, and I've never wanted to go back – I've never even thought about it.'

As a stranger in a strange land, Gordon found that he attracted some considerable interest from the other kids in school. His Irish accent was a source of much fascination for some and an item of ridicule for others. Furthermore, there was a time when there was some stigma attached to being an Irishman in America, and you weren't considered to be American but Irish – no matter how long you and your family had been there. This was one of the reasons behind the Irish communities and various bars that have sprung up in different cities in the USA. Children's mockery can be among some of the most hurtful, and it wasn't long before Gordon lost his Irish accent in favour of an American one to blend in with the rest.

Billy Hamill recalled an incident when his father slipped back into an Irish accent when he met another man from their home country.

My father doesn't talk much about Ireland, and I think that's because he doesn't really have any good memories. He's never been back, and he never talks about it. He's still an Irish citizen and he still has a Green Card, but he has no trace of an Irish accent. But he can turn it on just like flicking a switch. I remember we ran into this Irish guy and it turned out that they came from the same area. Just by talking to him my Dad slipped right back into his Irish accent. I found that kind of bizarre for my Dad to suddenly start speaking in this unfamiliar accent within seconds of meeting this other guy. I think when he came over here as a thirteen or fourteen-year-old kid and he was in school, they wanted to hear him talk and he became very self-conscious about it so he adopted an American accent quite quickly.

I've never been to Ireland and, although I'm curious, my father has never wanted to go back so why should I want to? I have some British blood in me on my father's side and I have an aunt who lives in Chesterfield. Whenever I go and visit her I am always fascinated by her stories of my father and the rest of the family. Because of my racing schedule I don't get a lot of spare time, so it's hard finding the time to go and see her. I can't go for an hour or something like that, because when we do get together there is so much to talk about. I like to be able to relax and talk to her without the pressures of knowing that I have to be somewhere at such and such a time.

Following his experiences with Tom Smith and Seabiscuit, Stucki used that knowledge to begin his own training stable and soon began building a fine reputation in California for the quality of his thoroughbreds. His daughter, Gaylord, also worked with her father at the stables carrying out various tasks including a role as an exercise rider.

Unlike in Britain, it's possible to house your horses at the racetracks in California. Stucki had his stables at Santa Anita, and this was where they carried out all their exercising and training. The Americans also have a three-month race programme at one track and then it moves to another in the region, for example Hollywood Park. Furthermore, whereas in Britain the stable lad will carry out all sorts of tasks on the horses, such as exercising, grooming etc., in the US an exercise rider is just an exercise rider, while a groom attends to the animal's grooming needs and does not exercise the horses.

It was at Hollywood Park that Gaylord first met Gordon Hamill. They were united by the fact that they both rode horses – although Gordon was beginning his career as a jockey himself – and they began seeing each other on and off for two years before they eventually married in 1968. Unfortunately, their marriage was short-lived and they were divorced by the time Billy was one year old.

On 23 May 1970, Gaylord gave birth to her first child, who she christened William (Billy) Gordon Hamill, in Arcadia, California, USA. From an early age it was clear that it would take something quite special to capture her son's attention. With the family's roots firmly in the horse racing industry, it seemed that a career with horses was Billy's destiny.

During the 1970s there was still some prejudice displayed toward single-parent families in Britain, who were frowned upon by British society. Happily for the Hamills, however, they never experienced any intolerance for being a single-parent family in the US. Although Billy saw his father regularly, Gordon pursued quite a successful career as a jockey in the Vancouver area of Canada, which meant that long periods of time would pass before he would see his son.

I wouldn't say that my Dad was very active in my early life; I know it hurts him to say that but I didn't see much of him. However, he was always support-ive. I remember when I used to race BMX bicycles, I hadn't seen him for what seemed like a year – it's hard to imagine as a five-year-old how long it really was – but I hadn't seen him for ages. Then he showed up and he had bought me a jersey to go racing. But he didn't buy me one he bought me two – one to go racing in and one for practise. With little things like that he was very supportive, but he was never there as a father figure. He has never been a father figure to me; he's more like a best buddy. To this day he's still a like a best friend. Being part of a single-parent family was pretty normal even then, and I never really thought about it and it never bothered me.

My Dad rode in America and Vancouver. He rode for about five years but he was always fighting his weight. He was an exercise rider after that for another five or six years, which is how you start out before you become a jockey. After my Mom and Dad got divorced, he went up to British Columbia to race and that was where he had most of his success. In California, especially the circuit in Southern California, Santa Anita and Hollywood Park are very competitive. It's probably one of the most competitive places in the world where you have the best horses, jockeys and trainers, and they usually come from that circuit. So he wasn't as successful when he rode in Del Mar, Santa Anita, and Hollywood Park because the competition was so tough. But when he went up to Vancouver the competition wasn't nearly as strong and he became a leading rider.

Gaylord Hamill revealed that it was Gordon's late decision to become a race jockey that eventually convinced him to try his luck in Canada.

'Gordon was a late starter as a jockey and because he was older he couldn't take advantage of what was called the "Bug". This is a term that is used to describe a weight allowance for apprentice jockeys who are allowed an extra 5lbs in weight as part of their training. However this was only allowed for jockeys up to twenty-five years old. So because he couldn't take advantage of this he went to Canada to race.'

However, when Billy was four years old, he moved with his mother from Primrose Avenue in Monrovia to a house that was owned by his grandfather in nearby Duarte. Duarte is twenty-one miles north-east of Los Angeles and is located near the base of the San Gabriel Mountains. It is a small town and their home in Baylor Street was part of a community that Billy not only grew up in, but also came to know very well. With the rest of the kids in the neighbourhood he would play football and baseball in the street – even though he was one of the youngest.

The street where I grew up, Baylor Street, there were loads of kids and I was the youngest of the generation. The Cardonas lived opposite me and they were a Mexican family. Their youngest was a girl who was the same age as me, and there were two more boys who were older than me by two or three years. Carlos was the oldest by five years; and we remain good friends to this day.

Meanwhile, Keith Stucki was enjoying some success with his stables, especially with a horse called Ancient Title. It was so named because its owner, Mrs Kirkland, whose family came from Germany, held a title in their fatherland. However, this horse was the second Californian-bred racehorse to earn over $1 million in prize money. The horse retired from racing at the age of eight after winning twenty-four of the fifty-seven races it entered.

Billy's mother continued to help out at her father's ranch and this, inevitably, meant that her son would also be involved. Although it may not have been said in as many words, because the whole family was involved in the horse industry it seemed natural that Gaylord's son would follow the same path.

My grandfather had what I would say was around a dozen head of horses at his stables and he had about three or four riders. Every morning they would take them out and exercise them – and my Mom was one of them. I remember when I was three or four years old, every morning at 3.30 I'd get up and go to the racetrack. We used to go to Santa Anita racetrack, which was local to Duarte. My Mom used to get me a doughnut and she would tell me to hold on to her belt loop because I was half asleep. It was so early for a young kid at that age and all I wanted to do was sleep, so she used to say 'Hold onto my belt loop', because then she would know that I wouldn't get lost or I wouldn't fall down. And then she used to walk me to the stables and she'd put me in the tack room. My grandfather had a little bed for me and everything, which was made up from horse blankets, and I used to sleep in there until whenever I woke up. My Mom would probably get on maybe five, six or even seven horses during that period.

By eleven o'clock we would go to the bar, called the Clown Town, where she would have a couple of Bloody Marys and I'd have a couple of Shirley Temples and then we would go home. In those days there used to be saloons and they would go and have lunch in a bar and it was dark inside – and I mean dark! When you walked out, especially in California, it was really bright, the sunlight was almost blinding after you had been in there for three hours or so. The normal routine was to have some lunch, a Bloody Mary, and then you'd go back to the track for the races to start at 2 o'clock – that was natural for my family. As a young kid it was up at 3.30, go to the racetrack, sleep till around 9, have a bowl of cereal, pass the time with all the grooms – and they could be of all sorts of origin, black, white or Mexican – and then we'd go to the local bar for lunch. When I look back at it now, it was an awesome environment to grow up in.

I grew up on Westerns – mainly the John Wayne movies – and country and western music. Being involved in horses it all sort of came together. I'm still interested in the history of the Old West because it's my heritage and I guess I could recognise that image of the cowboy because of my family's association with horses.

Horses can be unpredictable; they are a living, breathing animal with a mind of their own. One day Billy's mother suffered a fall and broke her back and hip. It was such a serious injury that at one point the medical experts didn't think that she would walk again.

I was only four or five years old when she broke her back and was basically a paraplegic for nearly two years. We always had nurses and people like that living with us, but I was so young I didn't really know what was going on. The nurses were very nice ladies actually, and they took care of her. I knew she wasn't very well, but I just got on with things. I missed her discipline for sure, and I was getting into all sorts of mischief.

I was just creating trouble and raising hell. It was nothing serious; it was just being a kid and doing things that kids do. I used to be a little thief. I would steal from stores – mainly food or toys, because we couldn't afford it. I never stole personal property or anything like that, although some of the kids did. I think I was more disruptive than anything. I always found myself in the principal's office, in front of a blackboard getting my ass whipped at a very early age.

His mother eventually made a complete recovery, but she didn't return to the stables to work with her father, instead she took a position as a legal secretary. But Billy's behaviour was giving her cause for concern. Duarte wasn't isolated from the problems of modern society and, being near to Los Angeles, the influence of the shady side of this large city was never far away.

Billy had a short attention span, and he needed something to capture his interest. He was attending Royal Oaks School in Duarte, but then his mother decided that a more stringent and strict approach was required for his education.

I went to a Catholic school called Immaculate Conception, which was pretty much at my Mom's request. I was in there for two years. My father's a Catholic, but not a practising Catholic. Somehow I was baptised a Catholic, but my Mom has a Mormon background on my grandfather's side, but they don't practice the religion. I was not brought up in a religious environment, so I don't know how I came to be baptised a Catholic — but I was. Maybe she thought that I wasn't paying attention, and could see that the writing was on the wall and thought that I needed a bit of discipline to point me in the right direction. I remember that I didn't know my left from my right, and they carried out a test on me and I guessed — and I guessed correctly! I was in the First Grade and I was six or maybe seven years old at the time. I was there for a couple of years, and when I look back at it now it was tough.

This was the time when they used to smack kids when they were in trouble, and they were sisters of a religious order. They were nice ladies actually, but a couple of them were mean. In a normal school you would get good teachers and bad teachers, and we had good sisters and bad sisters. But they demanded respect — and they could be brutal. One of the punishments that they dished out was the yardstick, which was a ruler that was a yard long and I received that; or a ruler across the hands was another — I used to get all that. In spite of this, when I look back on it now it was a good time. But I was always in trouble though and I eventually got kicked out. It wasn't all down to my behaviour, although a lot of it was. In the end, because my Mom was a single mother and because after her back injury she didn't go back to work with my grandfather, she became a legal secretary. So it wasn't easy for her when she was holding down a 9-5 job, trying to put me through school and my Dad, although he was there in California, he was doing his own thing, and so he wasn't there a lot of the time. The school wanted her to be in the PTA (Parents Teachers Association) and take more interest. She didn't have time to do that and eventually they told her that she wasn't taking enough interest in school activity. She was trying to raise me, working at a job, and she obviously didn't have time to bake them cookies. So that was the end of my Catholic school days and I went back to Royal Oaks.

I was always smart enough not to get into trouble with the law — I always had respect for the law. I wouldn't say that I was travelling along the criminal path, it was just mischief really. But one day, when I was three years old, I stole a packet of balloons when my Mom was shopping at the local store. She had no idea until we were sat in the car and I began blowing up one of the balloons, and she said:

'Where did you get those?'

'I got them in the store.'

She was so disappointed that I had stolen something that she took me to the local police station and made me give them back and tell them that I had stolen them! The cop was stood there and told me off, and it scared the hell out of me.

I was very frightened and I left believing that I was lucky not to go to jail. In fact I was frightened of the police altogether after that experience. I remember once when my Mom was stopped by the police for a speeding ticket or something, and I didn't have any idea of how the law worked because I was so young, I pleaded: 'Don't take her to jail.'

That experience definitely helped with that side of things, and it installed in me a respect for the law. A lot of my friends got into trouble with the law when they were teenagers, but by then I already had an interest. I was heading in that direction, but my interest in motorcycles kept me on the straight and narrow. As I got older, even my friends didn't share my energy and enthusiasm for motorcycles. A lot of them that I grew up racing BMX and motorcycles with, like Damien Batin, his brothers and sisters, George Mandeville, Robbie Stone and David Stumbaugh. But now I am in contact with most of them, and still talk to them because they're my 'homies'.

It was around this time that Billy had his first major experience on two wheels, and his first broken bone. His parents bought him a mono-shock BMX bicycle, and he practised the art of wheelies down the street with his friend Juan Cardona and entered into fiercely competitive bicycle races with the rest of the neighbourhood. It was during one of these races that he broke his thumb – his first taste of the hazards of competitive racing.

He also began to hear about speedway racing and take an interest in motorcycle racing in general. Bike racing was enjoying a boom period in popularity during the seventies. In Britain, it was the charismatic and unconventional Barry Sheene who ensured that bike racing grabbed the headlines on sport's back pages, with a series of spectacular crashes and back-to-back World Championship success in 1976 and 1977.

Meanwhile, in the USA it was Pat Hennen and Kenny Roberts who flew the flag of success. Roberts established himself as a motorcycling legend when he came to Europe and took on Sheene and won three World Championships in succession. His duels and rivalry with Sheene are looked upon as a golden age of 500cc Grand Prix, producing many headlines and some memorable racing. Later, 'King' Kenny would also play a role in Hamill's speedway career.

Throughout the 1970s speedway racing was also enjoying a comeback in America, while over in Europe the sport was enjoying a prosperous time because of the on-track exploits of riders like Peter

Collins, Ivan Mauger, Ole Olsen and Anders Michanek. Speedway was able to capitalise on the press interest generated by riders like Sheene and propelled Peter Collins into the spotlight. Furthermore, Scott Autrey had become America's first World Finalist for twenty-five years when he qualified in 1976, and British promoters began to take an interest in the Californian speedway scene.

To help continue the revival of the sport in America, Ivan Mauger and Barry Briggs regularly brought a troupe of riders over from Europe to race against the American riders at tracks like Costa Mesa and Ascot. Irwindale Raceway was situated close to Duarte and its presence had a big influence on the neighbourhood's young children.

We all wanted to be speedway riders; everybody wanted to be a speedway rider because there was a track nearby called Irwindale Raceway. So we used to organise our own races and we used to get a speedway programme and it used to be, 'Okay who do you want to be, Bruce Penhall, Mike Bast, Rick Woods, Sonny Nutter, or whatever. Okay I'll be this guy.' And we'd start from the yard line that was stipulated in the programme, and we had a little starting gate and we started bicycle races — basically bicycle speedway on the street. Then BMX came up and Monrovia got a track. Well, we were all over that and we were all good because that's what we did. We were already doing it and we already had our own track up in the hills in Duarte, which we had carved out. We were already doing this, so when BMX came around some of the kids got sponsors. We formed a team called the Duarte Sprockets, which was named after the Los Angeles Sprockets speedway team when they had team racing for a year. Team speedway has never taken off in America, and they have never tried it since and stuck with the individual competitions.

The BMX racing was a properly organised event by an association called the Bicycle Racing Association. The track was in 'the Low End', as we called it, and you wouldn't want to go down there now. It was bad then, but it's worse now. In the first race you would sign up and they would give you a paper plate with a number on it to stick to the front of your bike. My number was 104, and it's still my number at home to this day. I wasn't that good at it, especially not to start with. And although I won trophies it was mostly for seconds and thirds — not many firsts. At that age I was just having fun and I wasn't that bothered about being first. It was something that kept me out of trouble. I don't think that I was ever really that good at it — it just captured my attention. I loved it, and I loved being on my bicycle.

So as soon as we got out of school, we would get on our bicycles and ride until your mom said that you couldn't ride anymore that day and you had to come in. But when I had to come in I still wanted to ride. It was just natural and it felt like an escape. I just wanted to get on my bike and ride; go wherever I wanted. At an early age I would just jump on my bike and go!

Nonetheless, despite his growing interest in speedway and BMX, his family still encouraged him to follow the family tradition of a career in the horse industry. But his happy-go-lucky and laid-back nature masked a fear which was probably increased by the fact that he preferred to be on a two-wheeled machine.

I did a little bit of showjumping. I remember when I used to get out from school I used to have to attend horse riding lessons and learn how to ride the English way. We had an English saddle, not a Western saddle, and I used to have to stand up on the horse, turn around, and do all kinds of different stuff.

For my family it was natural because that was what they did. My Dad was a jockey and my Mom grew up riding and exercising horses while working for my grandfather. To them it was like, 'We'll show you this way.' I remember being made to ride in horse shows and so forth, but I was probably like, 'Oh yeah, I'll do it – no problem.' And my Mom was probably trying to do something to keep me out of trouble – to capture my interest.

I was afraid of horses then and I still am. It never felt natural to me to ride a horse. To be a horseman it's got to be a natural feeling. If it's not, those horses sense that and you're not going to make it. It was totally unnatural for me and I found out when I was probably seven or eight years old – possibly even younger – when I got my ass kicked by them. I thought, 'Fuck this, I don't like this – I like riding my bike.' Even at an early age when I fell off my motorcycle it didn't scare me, it was like, 'Why did that happen?' I could understand it was my fault. Whereas it was more personal when a horse bucks you off, it was like, 'This horse doesn't like me.' So my attitude was something like, 'Well, I don't like you either you bastard!' I could comprehend when I had too much throttle, or I didn't put the brakes on my bicycle when I was going down a hill, I could rationalise it in my head. But with a horse, I just believed that horse didn't like me. Now I know that horses sense things. When I got on a horse again about five years ago we didn't even take two strides before I jumped off the other side – I was just scared.

Life in the saddle with the reins in his hand was out of the question for Billy. He had interests elsewhere, in particular speedway racing, as his mother recalled: 'Billy was so excited and he begged me to take him to Irwindale Speedway. He was about six or seven years old at the time and I thought it was very exciting. It was a surprise that he wanted to go into motorcycle racing, but he was scared of horses. He was very keen to get started in it and I have supported him ever since.'

There was Mike Bast, Sonny Nutter, Rick Woods, Bruce Penhall, and the Moran brothers, Kelly and Shawn, were just coming into it – all the top riders were there. It was our local track; I used to go every Thursday night when my Mom used to let me – if I hadn't been in trouble or whatever. It closed in the late '70s. We were all hooked on speedway racing. There were ten to fifteen kids that were totally sprung on the sport. We didn't have any money and our parents didn't have money, so we used to sneak in through a hole in the fence when our parents couldn't take us. We didn't have enough money to buy a hotdog, so two or three of us used to chip in and buy a box of cereal, which was like a full box of corn pops or coca puffs and we used to sit there and watch the races. It was enough to feed three of us and it was awesome to be able to sit there and watch the racing.

One of my favourite riders was John Cook – the Cowboy they called him. He was a showman, and at the end of the night's racing he used to throw his goggles into the crowd. During one particular night at San Bernardino, I positioned myself where I thought they would land and I caught them! Man I was so pleased with my prize, and later Cookie helped me when I was trying to get going in the sport.

We all wanted to be speedway riders. To begin with I wanted to do it because my buddies wanted to do it. I was only six years old and yeah, I wanted to do it. I thought: 'Why can't I do it?' It was just like I wanted to be a jockey, or a police officer or whatever. I grew up in an atmosphere that I could be whatever I wanted. And then, I think, when I was about eleven or twelve years old, I thought I could be a speedway rider – but I wasn't very good. I was horrible to begin with and I wondered if it could happen. But I thought, well, just try and do your best because that was all I could do. There was nothing to lose. It wasn't like 'I wanna be, I wanna be', it was like, 'Yeah, okay, let's do this.'

One of the advantages that American motorcycle racers have in Southern California when compared with their European rivals is that the climate and environment make it possible to practise all year round. Around Los Angeles there are desert areas and dry lakebeds that regularly roar to the sound of motorcycle riders at all stages of their development.

This has been illustrated time and again, and during the 1970s and early 1980s this was especially the case. Speedway riders like Sam Ermolenko, Kelly and Shawn Moran, and Bobby Schwartz, could find themselves rubbing shoulders with racers from other disciplines such as Wayne Rainey, Rick Johnson, Jeff Ward and Eddie Lawson. Indeed famous road racing stars like Rainey and Lawson, and even Kenny Roberts, have all made use of the local deserts and dry lakebeds. Furthermore, to this day many of them begin their careers racing on the dirt-track circuit in the US as part of their progression toward a career on the tarmac.

Places like El Mirage, the Indian Dunes and Saddleback Park have become legendary names in the history of motorcycle sport. They are not just areas for ambitious motorcyclists, but also playgrounds for families and the rich and famous. The real beauty of these areas is that there are no real crash barriers or fences – something that became very useful for Billy Hamill.

I got a Honda XR75 on Christmas Day 1978. I think it cost $800 back then and my Mom and my Dad kicked in with $200 or something, and my grand-parents also chipped in. I couldn't even touch the ground because I was so short, but they said I would grow into it! It was just like when your mom buys you pants which are two sizes too big, 'Oh you'll grow into them, and your shoes too!' It was the same thing with a motorcycle. It was a handful for me because I was way too small for the bike at the time. I remember on Christmas Day, the Cardona's had a little oval in their backyard with a couple of trees and they had a slide. I was riding around with my Dad on the back, and he was saying stuff like, 'Okay, just go easy.' Somehow we ended up riding up the slide! I didn't know what I was doing and I couldn't steer the bike and I ended up on the slide. I was a bit scared and didn't know what to do so I just gassed it! And my Dad, being a jockey, he doesn't have very long legs either and he just said 'Holy shit!' We nearly did an Evel Knievel launch off the slide! He managed to hold onto it and held me up, although I think I did fall off but it wasn't anything major. That was my first experience riding and that thing beat the hell out of me.

I had to grow into it and I probably couldn't ride it for a year. My Mom used to keep a big padlock on it while she was at work because she was afraid that I would get on it and ride it up the road – which was true! I couldn't even hold myself up on it because it was too heavy and I was too small, but once I got going I was okay. Once I got the thing started, and if I had someone to hold me up before I began moving, then I was fine. It had a clutch so I had to master that which was pretty tough, which even to this day is hard for a young kid. You have to know when to give it a little gas and when to roll off the throttle. I was also interested in motocross, but speedway was my passion and it was all my friends' passion as well.

At the time, to me it wasn't two different sports, but now it is. When I was a kid it was just motorcycles: speedway or motocross. But even when I got on my motocross bike I just wanted to get it sideways like speedway, but if there was a couple of jumps, then I would think well, let's do that too. The only time I ever considered doing motocross was when there were a lot of insurance problems, in California in particular, and they weren't going to let us ride speedway until we were eighteen years old because, in the eyes of the law, we were minors until then. So at that point I did consider riding motocross because they didn't care. But I never did, and I never really considered it again because they got over that insurance problem.

But just as he was getting to grips with the Honda XR75, Billy's mother suddenly became seriously ill. As his mother was a single parent, Billy had become very close to her – and he still is.

Fortunately he could call on the help of the Cardona family, who were very supportive, as the various doctors tried to discover what was wrong.

I was about eleven when she contracted a rare lung disease. I knew she was deathly ill for a couple of years. I remember it, but I didn't realise how bad she was at the time because she would keep that away from me. I didn't know it was a life-threatening disease and she didn't want me to have that pressure. I knew she was sick, and it was just me and her. She spent a lot of time in the hospital and having lung surgery. And when she was at home she was very sick and I had to take care of her. They are not fond memories for me. When she wasn't in the hospital she was bed-ridden for a large amount of that time. I had to empty bedpans and stuff like that, but she was my mom and I cared for her as she had always cared for me.

I was lucky because I had the Cardona family across the street, which I would go to. They basically took me in, fed me, sent me to school and I virtually lived with them when my Mom was in hospital. The situation affected and bothered me and I was pissed off. I was getting into fights because I was angry that my Mom was sick. I went through a stage, because she wasn't there to discipline me, when I just raised hell. My behaviour was pretty ludicrous at that time.

Billy's mother was suffering from a very rare lung disease, as she explained: 'My lung disease was called Cryptococcus and it's a fungal disease that is carried through the air. It comes off of bird droppings and when a bird flies over, the flapping of its wings puts this fungal dust into the atmosphere. It only infects people who are rundown and their immune system is low. This happened to me not long after I had broken my back from my horse riding accident because I was still a bit weak from that.'

Interestingly, from her own subsequent research, Gaylord found that Cryptococcus was originally discovered during the first opening of the pyramids and tombs in Egypt. The first men that went down inside the catacombs all died from Cryptococcus poisoning where centuries of this fungal disease had infected the atmosphere. The 'crypt' part of its name is taken from the death of those unfortunate men, almost as a morbid tribute to those people who lost their lives for the sake of history – or greed.

Once they had discovered the problem it was treated successfully. But together, Billy and his mother spent nearly three and a half years fighting off this potentially life-threatening illness.

Irwindale closed in 1979 so the enthusiastic kids from Duarte had to travel to the Inland Motorcycle Speedway (IMS) at San Bernardino to catch some sideways action. In 1980 Carlos Cardona began racing speedway and his younger brother, Juan, and Billy were eager to tag along.

He didn't have a truck to take his bikes to the races but Robbie Stone used to pick him up. He would tell us that if we could fit in the back alongside the bike then we could go with them. We used to make sure that we could squeeze in alongside the bike and off we went.

Carlos was doing okay but he didn't have the best equipment. He had an old two valve but he had a good time. It gave us an insight into speedway racing and I wanted to do it even more.

The first time I got to ride a speedway bike on my own was in the Indian Dunes with Carlos. I was way too excited and I grabbed a handful and just crashed. I hit a bump on the track and the bike straightened up and took off. There were no crash walls, just a mound of dirt, so when I hit the dirt the bike spat me off and I went over the handlebars. The bike got tangled up in the wire fence that was separating the track from the road. I did a somersault and landed in the middle of the road on my backside. Luckily I was only shaken.

Carlos Cardona had a Kawasaki KD100 and that was the first time that I rode a motorcycle and we went out to El Mirage – a dry lakebed. My Mom's boyfriend at this time was Butch Fish and he had a couple of speedway bikes and sponsored a rider, Steve Vandeveer, or 'Kiddo' as we called him. Butch used to take Carlos and Damie out. They were fifteen then and they were riding a speedway bike, so Carlos let me ride his little KD100 and I was so happy to finally know how to ride a motorcycle. By the end of the day I wanted to get it sideways, so I screwed it on and this thing just spat me off and I high-sided. I swear it felt like I flew a hundred feet and I landed on my head. It knocked the wind out of me and I recognised what that felt like from BMX riding days. It was pretty frightening and that was my first experience on a motorcycle.

But when I was riding Carlos' Kawasaki KD100, afterwards I had my very first ride on a speedway bike. Butch Fish gave me a ride on my first speedway bike. I think I was six and I was sat in front of him on a two-valve Jawa with no helmet or anything. I remember him grabbing a handful and the front wheel came off the ground about twelve inches. It was awesome. The first time I did a power wheelie. I can still picture the feeling with the wind rushing through my hair and it was so exhilarating for a young kid. I was holding onto the handlebars and we only went in a straight line but it was a phenomenal feeling – it was something that I never forgot.

It was during another trip to San Bernardino to watch the stars in action that Billy had his first sight of junior speedway racing – and in particular, Greg Hancock.

When I first got involved in speedway what captured my attention was that there was a mini Mike Bast and a mini Bruce Penhall, with the same leathers, and that's what we used to call them – but they were kids. I thought it was so cool, and I wanted to be a mini whoever. I wanted to do that and that was how I thought about it. Greg Hancock was the first one I saw, and I remember seeing Greg in his Penhall leathers and Bobby Cody had Mike

31

Bast leathers. I thought, 'Oh man this is so cool', and I was really keen to get into that.

But it wasn't going to be easy. Hamill's parents didn't have a lot of money available, and unlike his future rival, Greg Hancock, they didn't have the connections within the sport to know where to go. After all, all of his family were involved in horses of some form or another. If you asked them for a seat they would instinctively go into the tack room, instead of the Cody Jawa Racing establishment. Motorcycles were a largely unknown quantity for them and this put Gaylord's son in a disadvantaged position when compared to some of his future rivals.

At this stage it seemed that Billy would have to wait a long time before he could take to the track. However, he wasn't the sort of person to let such matters get him down because he knew how difficult it was for his mother to make ends meet. Indeed, young Billy had been working in a variety of jobs since he was nine years old when he had a paper route.

Juan Cardona and I both had paper routes and you had to if you wanted new shoes or something different. I did a variety of things: washing cars and mowing the lawns – the kinds of things that kids do. When I was thirteen I worked as a bus boy in a local restaurant and I earned some good tips from that. I would clear away crockery and cutlery from the tables. When that closed down I worked in a pizza place doing the same thing and it was called the World's Best Pizza Parlour.

On one occasion I remember going into McDonalds with a few of my buddies and Eddie Van Halen, the guitarist with the rock band Van Halen, was in there and I thought that was cool because he was a big star then. I guess that was one of the perks of living near Los Angeles.

The politician, diplomat and inventor, Benjamin Franklin, once said that there are two things that you can rely on in life: death and taxes. Therefore it seems unlikely that something positive could come out of such a negative statement. Filling in the dreaded tax return to the Inland Revenue in Britain, or the IRS (Internal Revenue Service) as it's known in the US, is a task that many people carry out with feelings of apprehension and dread. Occasionally, though, those faceless people at the tax office grant you a rare rebate, which is a cause for much celebration and joy.

Gaylord Hamill, probably reluctantly, filled in her return for 1982 as usual and carried on with the usual day-to-day activities. Billy continued to be disruptive in school and dreamed of a career as a speedway rider. As soon as the school day was over, he took the first chance he could to get on his motorcycle, or bicycle, with the rest of his buddies and cause some mayhem.

Although he realised that finances were tight, this didn't stop him from badgering his parents about purchasing a speedway machine for him. They were left in no doubt as to where his interest and ambitions lay. It was the motorised version of horsepower that caught his imagination, while the four-legged kind scared the living daylights out of him and, as far as he was concerned, the rest of his family were welcome to it.

His family didn't discourage his interests, but many felt that it was a passing phase that he would eventually grow out of.

I wouldn't say that speedway was big in California, but it was big to us. It was huge to me. It was our life from a very early age, which was odd because it wasn't something I grew up in. I grew up riding horses and doing horse shows, which was what my Mom used to make me do. That was something that came naturally to my family, but it wasn't something that felt natural to me. Motorcycles, and speedway in particular, was different, it was just like, 'This is great.' It was something that was fun to do and I could share the experiences and enjoy it with my buddies. When I look back at it now, it seems strange to want to ride motorcycles while the rest of the family was involved with horses in some way or another. But it interested me and captured my attention, which was what I needed at a young age.

Luck swaggered the Hamill's way when, to his mother's great surprise, she received a $1,000 tax rebate. Fortunately for her son, she decided to use the windfall to fund the purchase of a junior speedway machine. Once they had found a bike, she discovered that the seller wanted $1,300, but she only had $1,000 and, if he wanted to sell it, it was at that price or nothing. The seller took the money and, for Billy, suddenly a career on the shale-covered oval tracks didn't seem such an unreasonable dream after all.

My Mom supported me and she basically said: 'Hey this kid is getting serious about this and he wants to do it.' I think my Dad thought that it was a phase and he probably thought that at the age of twelve or thirteen years old I would get into girls and it would all blow away. But my Mom said we must get him a bike and leathers, and said to my Dad: 'You're going to help out – do as you're told!' I don't think my Dad took too kindly to being told what to do, but Mom said: 'No, you're gonna do it – for my son,' and so on. Eventually, I got the bike, leathers – my dad bought me my first set of leathers – crash helmet and it progressed from there. But my Mom was the backbone behind it. She's a strong-willed lady, and she's the kind of person who believes that if you're going to do something, do it right or don't do it at all.

The bike I had was a Honda in a scaled-down Hagon frame and it had a gearbox and an XR250 motor in it. I believe my parents tracked down this bike in Newport Beach and it turned out to be an old bike that Greg Hancock's older brother, Dave, had once used.

Now he had the bike, he needed the necessary accessories to enable him to go racing. During one of his outings with Carlos to San Bernardino, he bought a steel shoe and some boots from Tom Cirello – his son Trinon was already racing in junior speedway.

When Billy arrived home at one o'clock in the morning and tried on his new footwear, the steel shoe made a distinctive crunch and scrape on the concrete patio at his home in Duarte. For a while he walked up and down listening to this unique sound and imagined that he was a top rider making his way to his waiting machine. This fascinating noise evoked all the excitement of the sport and his imagination began to play out his ambitions. For a short time the scrape and crunch became the soundtrack that announced that Billy Hamill was about to make his mark in the world of speedway. He was very excited that he was going to be able to take to the track and race against all these other youngsters that he had seen during his trips to the Inland Motorcycle Speedway. Nothing was going to stop him now and he wanted a piece of the action.

Two

'CRASHWALL HAMILL'

All the parents tried to get me banned because they thought
I was too dangerous! They were afraid for their kids.

Billy Hamill

Billy took to the track in July 1983, which was at the height of speedway's popularity in the USA. The Americans had swept the board in 1982 by winning a Grand Slam of all the World Championships: Bruce Penhall had retained the World title in the Los Angeles Coliseum, America had won the World Team Cup for the first time, and Bobby Schwartz and Dennis Sigalos won the World Pairs Championship in Australia. Furthermore, they also won every Test match series that they competed in.

However, all was not roses in the garden of American Speedway, because Penhall retired after he won the World title to pursue a career in Hollywood, and former World no.3 Scott Autrey also decided to hang up his steel shoe after several seasons as America's top rider. The number of Americans competing in the British League – traditionally *the* place to be for riders who were serious about making it big as an international performer – had drastically been reduced due to the English pound's weakness against the dollar.

Therefore, riders like Kelly Moran, John Cook and Brad Oxley all chose to remain in California. This decision, by the spectacular duo of Moran and Cook in particular, proved to be a massive shot in the arm for the sport in California following the loss of Penhall. According to the US *Speedway Magazine*, crowds were so good that the most successful riders were taking home more than $1,000 a night. At Costa Mesa, the country's leading track, the riders were entitled to 30% of gate receipts. For Hamill, it was incredibly inspiring to not only watch these riders in action, but also to find himself sharing the same pit area.

It was awesome as you can imagine, because I was pitted next to these guys who were my heroes. It was unbelievable and the racing was brilliant, especially in 1983 and 1984 when Kelly Moran was at home because he was unbelievable to watch. He was doing stuff that nobody had ever seen in California. Along with Cookie [John Cook] as well, those two riders in particular, they were just doing things on a bike that no one had ever seen before. And there I was, a young kid, watching these guys and thinking, 'I want to do that, I want to be that good.' They were a huge influence on all of us. It was just good racing and showboating, but I think you would see it more on the smaller tracks because it was slower and it was close contact. Kelly would just carve through people from the back during handicap racing – Cookie too. Inside, outside, they just carved through riders and it was raw racing. That was something that I did as a kid on my bicycle in Baylor Street, so to see that at 50-60mph was just awesome. They were changing lines, pulling wheelies and waving at the fans, it was a great time for American Speedway.

The Junior Speedway programme was well established by the time Billy took to the track. When the experts sat round to try to dissect how America had risen from a backward re-emerging speedway nation in 1968 to world domination in just over ten years, it was their junior programme that they pinpointed as being responsible for their success. And it was expected to continue to be the vehicle with which to discover and develop new American talent.

There was an infrastructure in place that enabled young riders to race in relative safety. Although crashes were inevitable and the junior riders did sustain some broken bones, there wasn't a spate of injuries that one would come to expect from a bunch of youngsters whose enthusiasm often overcame their ability and experience. This was due to the reduced power of the machines, which had a top speed of approximately 30mph, plus the tracks in California used to be very wide. Furthermore, practise facilities at Saddleback Park, the Indian Dunes and Maely's ranch at Corona had little or no crash walls – which was just as well for the inexperienced Hamill.

The bikes varied somewhat in frame sizes, from half, three-quarters, or seven eighths the size of a standard Jawa frame of that period, depending on the height and weight of the rider. The engines were either a Triumph 200cc Tiger Cub or a Honda XR175 with engine displacement increased to 262cc. There were other makes – John Bemis actually rode a Ducati engine – and later a British Weslake engine was developed for junior racing.

Carol Topping was a journalist with *Speedway Magazine* and she recalled: 'These motorcycles made over 25 horsepower – they were definitely not toys! And they had some nice-looking motorcycles in speedway racing.'

Many of the riders that Billy faced on the junior scene could be classed as seasoned, junior veterans. Greg Hancock had been riding for five years by the time Hamill made his first appearance, and Ronnie Correy was on the verge of turning professional. There were enough young riders around that they used to stage a Junior National and California State Championships as well as other tournaments at places like Ken Maely's ranch.

Hamill described Ken Maely as 'The Godfather of American Speedway', but he was also influential in motorcycle racing in general. Unfortunately he died in 2003, shortly before discussions began about this book. His story is worthy of a tome of its own, and his contribution to American Motorcycle racing is almost immeasurable.

Maely was known as 'the Shoe Man', because he was the man who created and made steel shoes for motorcycle racers in the USA. At the time many racers used one end of a 1934 Ford bumper, because the end curled up which roughly made a toe. They were cheap and plenti-ful as there were many junkyards close by, but they were not ideal because they weighed 8lbs and the metal wasn't strong enough, which meant that they would wear out quickly.

Ken used the bumpers himself, but his engineering and blacksmith background got his creative mind thinking about something better. In one of the last features that appeared about him before he passed away, he revealed in *Cycle World* magazine how, after watching boats skim-ming across the water, he was inspired to make a steel shoe of his own based on the shape of a hull: 'Of course! Why don't I shape a shoe like that?' he recalled. He experimented with various metals, and came up with a shoe that almost every top rider in the US has used. In 1950, Harley Davidson asked him to fit their entire team.

While that may be his biggest claim to fame, he also developed his own speedway machine during the boom period of speedway racing called the Maely. Amazingly his skills were also employed by both the South African and Red Chinese governments, and he also played an important role in the development of Kenny Roberts – during his dirt-track racing days. But perhaps his biggest and most significant role was making his ranch available for riders of all stages of their career to practise and race on all year round.

'Hotshoe Manor' had the facilities and benefits that became very useful to Billy Hamill and other young riders. He also staged 'The Gumball Rally' which is an event that Billy has recently resurrected and was won in 2003 by a promising youngster, Ricky Wells.

My first competitive speedway race was at Ken Maely's ranch. All the kids prac-tised and grew up at Maely's. You couldn't practise at Costa Mesa, but you could at Maely's. Until his death, it was a place where you could pay $20 and ride a speedway bike all day if you had enough fuel and oil. He was an engineer and he made his own engine and he was an old racer who got into making steel shoes. He did all kinds of things. He provided a track, but we weren't racing inside a stadium with bleachers, it was just an oval track on his ranch.

The bike I had was a Hagon frame and I flipped it over once and broke the diamond. He made me a Maely frame, which was my second frame, so he took an interest in that way. He did that as well and he used to chop them down to get them lower. He was the Godfather of American Speedway. As kids, he could provide everything for us and he had a workshop as well – a one-stop workshop.

I did my rider's test at Maely's ranch, so I didn't have to have a rider's test for the 500 because I had already done it. John Cook gave me my test and he was hard because usually you had to lay down your bike when the man on the infield dropped a flag or a rag. But with Cookie he threw out the rag and you had to lay it down and stop before you hit the rag. I think they should do that now.

The Gumball Rally was an organised junior speedway evening. They might give Ken Maely $5 to cover costs, and we had hotdogs, hamburgers, drinks and most of the people that were there were family and friends, but we encouraged people to come and watch the racing. We rode at half-time at Costa Mesa and San Bernardino, maybe once or twice a week, and we would ride one heat race and one main event. So you would only get two races because we were the interval entertainment, and it is still that way. So the Gumball Rally was an organised event run to a championship formula of 20 heats; so it was the next biggest thing to the Junior Speedway National Championship. There were no other titles and it was a big gumball machine full of red, yellow, green and blue gumballs. That's why we brought it back. Maely started that and I thought we should restart it.

His roots were in dirt-track racing and he got involved with Mike Bast. He used to make steel shoes that were used on the Flat Track circuit as well as speedway. I had one of his steel shoes and still do, and they are of a very good quality and they last. He was with me when I won the World Championship in Vojens and I was so glad that he was there to see me win it. He was in the pits with us and everything.

He was such an infectious character and there will never be another Ken Maely. He was full of enthusiasm. He could be a crabby old bastard though, but then he would be your best friend. There was no bullshit with him, if he didn't like you he would tell you. To the day he died he was as sharp as a whip, and because he was old there were some guys who would try and scam him for a bit of fuel or something. But he never missed a thing and he counted every nickel. He was such a genuine man and he would do anything for you. He's done so much for so many us. Not only by providing a ranch and steel shoes, but he was always there to offer you advice – not only about speedway, but life too.

Thus Billy had his first competitive speedway race at Maely's ranch, which was during a training school run by John Cook, and where he defeated none other than Greg Hancock. He was supposed to have also faced Kelcey Gordon as well but he was unable to get his bike to start.

Therefore, Billy faced Greg in what was to all intents and purposes a match race.

The more experienced Hancock made the gate and stormed off into the distance, but crashed and gifted Billy a maiden victory. According to Gary Roberts' book, *Hamill & Hancock: World Speedway Champions*, Greg received some very choice words from his father after he lost the event to Jesse Finch. Therefore, when Billy made his first approach to Hancock he didn't receive the best of receptions!

Perhaps one of the most pleasing aspects of the junior scene at this time was the amount of interest that riders like Cook, Bobby Schwartz and Penhall took in helping the juniors. As a result these youngsters could also be seen in the pits helping out their heroes and Billy could be seen helping Keith 'The Snakeman' Larsen, Doug Nicol and the all-action Bobby Ott. However, it's not clear what 'help' young Hamill was to some of the senior riders because his mechanical knowledge was not that great.

When I started racing junior speedway, Butch Fish used to try and teach me maintenance and stuff and I think he got quite frustrated with me! He was very pivotal in getting Carlos and me racing. He did dirt-track and TTs (Grand National) but he never raced speedway. He sponsored another rider so that's why he had speedway bikes and he used to run Monrovia Diesel. I'm not mechanically minded at all; I'm a lot better now and I know when things need to be changed and something isn't right, but back then I didn't have a clue. Butch tried to show me the basics, but I just wanted to ride and I've never been interested in that aspect of it. However, I used Butch's facilities and, although I would frustrate him, he did manage to teach me some of the basics.

The senior riders at that time had a big influence on the juniors in speedway and they took an interest. Probably half the stickers that appeared on the juniors' body colours came from John Cook. He would give them away and also stuff like goggles because he was that kind of guy. I remember that I was having all sorts of problems getting control when I was racing and he took a look at my bike and said that the frame was bent. I was heartbroken, but he did what he could and with the help of another man called Jeff Hoyt – a huge guy – they jumped on the engine cases which made it better. Cookie was a big inspiration to all the junior riders and he was such a character too and had loads of natural ability.

Billy may have won his first race but he was gaining a dubious reputation – not helped by losing a race to Amy Alvarez – a girl!

It was my first race in front of a crowd at San Bernardino, and on the last lap she passed me and beat me. I made a good start and I was in the lead, but I was going too fast on the straights and going wide on the turns. I didn't know at the time because I was pretty green, but my bike wasn't set up properly. So, one by one the others passed me – and Amy got me on the last lap.

I respected Amy Alvarez as a racer and she was out there with a bunch of boys, and while she didn't win a lot she would occasionally pop out and take a victory. She was more calculated and she was out there crashing with the rest of us. But I took a lot of shit from my buddies and it became a sore subject as I was 'the guy who lost to the girl'.

In reality it wasn't a disgrace because Amy was more experienced than Billy as she had been riding motorcycles since she was four years old. But because she was female it was hard for her when she was surrounded by so many boys. And like many others who were participating on the junior scene, she had a father who raced as well. Nonetheless, there can't be too many female riders who can say that she defeated a future World Champion!

Billy's enthusiasm and aggression was there for all to see, but his finances, or his parents' finances to be exact, were limited. Greg's father, Bill, was the unofficial head of the junior speedway programme and his connections through established stars like Penhall and Schwartz meant that his son had access to more advice than some of the others. Riders like Bobby Cody, David Busby, Scott Brant and Trinon Cirello also had fathers that were in the business and this all helped with their racing programmes.

Being the new kid on the circuit among 'experienced' juniors wasn't easy for Billy. This group had been together for a while and they had established their order of friends, and it's always hard being a new face and making new friends. Billy's cheerful nature endeared him to most people, and this worked in his favour and he got along with most individuals.

However, to begin with his equipment was limited to say the least and consisted of just a wire brush and a fuel can, plus a couple of enthusiastic friends as mechanics. But this didn't stop him from taking the race to his rivals. He wanted to win and he wasn't afraid to go where angels feared to tread to pull off the victory. Unfortunately, this aggressive way of riding was not making him very popular with some of his rivals – or more importantly their parents! In fact, if he didn't win the race, it was usually because he had crashed into the wall while trying to get his machine under control. Therefore, he was dubbed 'Crashwall Hamill'.

I broke seven foot pegs in one season, and that was probably out of ten races! So you can imagine how hard, and with what force, I was hitting the walls. A lot of it was because we bought this bike and we didn't know anything about the gearing and it was just a case of 'let's go racing'. They used to call Carlos Cardona 'Crashwall', even though he didn't hit many walls, and I sort of adopted the name because I was always on the gas.

Greg's dad was involved with Bobby Schwartz and Bruce Penhall and he had a head start over me. He started competitive racing at the age of eight, and he had a dad who had knowledge of speedway that put him on the right path. But my family didn't have a clue, and Carlos was trying to figure it out for himself – although he would help out. Butch, my Mom's boyfriend, sponsored a rider, but he was a diesel mechanic for big trucks so that was different to what I was riding. But Greg's dad knew what was going on from his association with Penhall and Schwartz and he passed it on to Greg. He passed it on to all of us really because he got the junior speedway programme up and running. When I started racing he was running it. Greg always had the best stuff, and along with David Busby they had a company called Grin Racing Products – and they just seemed to have everything.

I never had the kind of sponsorship that Greg and Trinon Cirello had, but that was probably because their fathers were involved with the senior riders, so it was an 'I'll help you if you help me' type of situation. That was where they got that connection.

All the parents tried to get me banned because they thought I was too dangerous! They were afraid for their kids and they banded together. I was wild and I was bouncing off walls. Part of that was because of my aggression and my want to win and, of course, my bike wasn't set up properly. Plus I wasn't afraid; I was just grabbing a handful and holding on. Sometimes the bike went where I wanted it to and sometimes it didn't – and when it didn't, it was usually pretty ugly! Looking back on it now I could see why the parents felt like that, but at the time I was very pissed off – I couldn't believe they were doing that to me.

Every time you get parents involved in something like that you're going to get bullshit. It's still the same there now.

Billy's father recalled their efforts to ban his son: 'There was a lot of rivalry between the parents,' he said. 'I'd been involved in horse racing and I couldn't believe what they were trying to do. The thing was that when Billy got in front most of the time he was way ahead of the rest; it was just that he couldn't control the power. I told them that they were afraid that my son would get it together and just beat their kids. The point was that he was young and he was learning – as were the rest of them – and they just had to let them get on with it, because it was the only way they could learn.'

Although disappointed and a little upset, Hamill was still determined to continue riding. His mother never became directly involved with the racing in the same way as Hancock's father and other parents did. But she did encourage her son to continue attending training schools if he was really serious about the sport.

It was Jesse Finch's dad, John, who helped me out with my original speedway bike. He basically changed the gear and jetted the carburettor. It had a transmission and you'd put it in first gear for Costa Mesa and second for San Bernardino because the track was a bit longer. But the thing was way over-geared and that was why I was hitting the fences. I think he helped me because he was afraid that I would end up hurting somebody, and probably hurting myself in the process. So I think he probably thought that he had to help me because no one else was going to. He got me set up by changing my gear.

No matter how hard I tried I just couldn't slide that bike until the gear change. All I was doing was going across the corner and hitting the fence all the time. It was just a gear change, and if you don't know and no one shows you, then how are you going to know? It was ignorance really, but then what would I know coming from a horse family?

I went to several training schools run by John Cook, Mike Bast and Ivan Mauger – I went twice to Mauger's. I remember watching him race at Irwindale and he was the only rider that could beat Bast. He stood out from the others because he had a crash helmet that was painted in black and white chequers and I thought that was cool.

There was a junior rider called John Bemis and he had a couple of sponsors and I met them at the races. For some reason or another he quit racing, and these guys were sponsoring him. As he wasn't racing in 1984 I called them and asked them if they would help me. Basically I solicited myself and one of them said, 'Let me think about it', and he talked to his buddy. And then they said, 'Yeah, we'll help.' His name was John Brett and he took me under his wing. He passed on his knowledge and took me to Maely's and really looked after me as a youngster and showed me the ropes. We learned a lot together because he didn't know a lot because he was a lumber salesman, but he just loved racing. He would pick me up from school and I think he looked at me as the son he never had. But I believe my Mom must have felt a little threatened or something because I was spending so much time with him and then it just dissolved. She didn't feel good about it, but I always backed my Mom whether she was right or wrong. I think she thought that they were running my life and my education was suffering.

Eventually that relationship fell by the wayside and I was sponsored by FOM [Fast Old Man]. They were Bill and Opal Collins, and Opal used to make a lot of the bike covers, like engine warmers, and give them to the kids for nothing. They were really nice covers too with your name on it and everything. Bill was an engineer by trade and he had built a junior speedway bike. He sponsored Bobby Cody and he sponsored most of us at one time or another. I didn't have a bike at the time so basically they said that I could ride their bike which was a Yamaha. And that was a big help in itself. They were really helpful and they did a lot for the juniors and then they played a bigger part later in my career.

At this time Billy was combining his education with his racing and also his other jobs to get some money together to fund his riding and to help out. Unsurprisingly he didn't enjoy school; it didn't 'capture my attention'. Whether that was down to the standard of teaching or, as it would appear more likely, the fact that he was only interested in motorcycles, he knew that if he didn't put the effort in then he wasn't going to get any support from either of his parents.

His mother recalled that it was always difficult to get him to do his homework, but on one occasion she mistakenly thought that he had finally knuckled down to improve his education and expand his academic mind.

'I had a lot of trouble trying to get Billy to do his homework,' she said. 'I used to work in Los Angeles which was quite a drive. When I came back one evening I was very surprised and happy to see Billy was sat at the table doing his homework. He was concentrating really hard and scribbling away and I was feeling really proud of him. But when I got closer and looked down at what he was writing, it wasn't his homework; instead he was writing letters to Oakley goggles and other motorcycle racing manufacturers for sponsorship. I didn't say too much because I thought, "Well at least he's writing." And they were good letters too, and I still have some of them today.'

Proof, if it was ever needed, that the best way to educate someone is to combine it in some way with what interests them. Hamill was thirteen years old then and, while a career as a speedway rider on the World Championship circuit hadn't entered his mind, he already knew how important it was to have good sponsorship backing if you wanted to be successful in motor sport – of any kind.

I did better in 1984, but I was still horrible. I broke a collarbone that year at a practise track, but generally there weren't too many injuries in junior speedway. That was my first broken bone while riding a motorcycle, and I didn't know where my collarbone was – but I soon found out! I consider myself to have been lucky in my career with regard to injuries. I was never a major player in junior speedway; you would never find me being associated with Greg Hancock, Jesse Finch, Bobby Cody, Scott Brant and all those guys. I was mid-to-lower pack, but I wouldn't say that I was the worst because I showed potential and I had balls. Technically speaking I was terrible when I was compared with Greg, Jesse Finch and Billy Felts – who was younger and had great technical ability.

Billy improved in 1984, but you would still be hard-pressed to find a mention of him in the American Speedway press – except maybe for when he got it completely wrong! The stars of the junior scene were Greg Hancock, Jesse Finch, Bobby Cody, David Busby and Trinon Cirello. These were the names that were expected to make their presence felt in Europe in the near future.

Billy Hamill had yet to show that he had successfully channelled that aggression and gained control to such an extent that people were starting to take notice of him. He did enough, however, to make the Junior National Championship at San Bernardino, but finished with just 3 points in a meeting that was won by Trinon Cirello. But his fearless and 'hardcore' approach to his racing was illustrated when he went into the third bend three abreast alongside Hancock and Scott Brant. However, a combination of his over-enthusiasm and inexperience saw him harmlessly tumble out of contention – although it wouldn't be long before his rivals would be backing off from the pressure that he would generate on the racetrack.

In 1985 he was starting to show more of the qualities that would make him one of the most exciting and entertaining riders of his generation. While Hancock and company were still winning the main events, Hamill was starting to make some serious progress. But the crash walls still seemed to have their magnets set to stun when Billy took to the track, as a concerned Jesse Finch noted in a column he wrote for *Speedway Magazine*: 'My good friend Billy Hamill went into the wall hard enough to bring out the ambulance. Everyone was glad to see that it wouldn't be needed when Billy finally walked off on his own.'

Nonetheless, Billy won his first main event as a junior at Ascot's South Bay Stadium and he deservedly qualified for his second Junior National Championship at Ascot. He put in a solid and consistent display to score 11 points – winning his final outing – to finish in fifth place. Greg Hancock won his first junior title, and both Hancock and Hamill were looking forward to 1986 on a proper, mean-spirited 500cc machine as senior riders.

At the end of the year, Speedway Magazine *voted me as the 'Most Improved Junior Rider', and there was a lot of room for improvement! I was never a top junior rider like Greg and Jesse Finch and all those guys. It was a lot of fun and it was good experience for getting me ready to ride the 500cc machines. I was very bad at juniors but as soon as I jumped on a 500 everything clicked.*

Especially during the early part of his junior career, his father wondered if he was going to make it.

'He did struggle, and he was so poor that at one point I wondered if he was ever going to get to grips with it. But he wanted to do it so bad, and he persevered with it. But as soon as he got on a 500 there was no turning back. It was like night and day. When I saw him on a 500 bike he was a completely different rider, he knew instinctively how to use the extra power. I remember thinking 'Holy Shit, this is more like it!' when I first saw how much better he was on a 500 – it was an incredible transformation.'

It's interesting to note that his first Hagon Honda junior bike was considered to be very heavy compared with the machines that his competitors were using. Author Gary Roberts reported that an ex-junior rider still considered the machine to be difficult to ride even fifteen years since their junior days.

Therefore, having to master this 'difficult' bike probably did more to help, rather than hinder, his longer-term progress. Although, as he admits, he was never a star performer at junior level, having the lighter Yamaha underneath him did bring about some progress.

Gay Hamill passed on copies of the letters that Billy wrote as a junior when he was attempting to gain some sponsorship. One of which was dated 1985 and is addressed to Circle Industries – who sponsored Ivan Mauger at one time and the unpredictable American Steve Gresham. This letter not only reveals the ambitions of Gay's only son, but also shows that he wasn't that bad on a junior speedway machine. Titled a *Resume of Billy Hamill*, I have reproduced this letter below:

Dear Circle Industries:

My name is Billy Hamill. I am 15 years old and race junior speedway. My first race in speedway was July 9, 1983, and guess what I won three out of five races and was placed third overall. Last year I won two main events. July 23, 1984, I won the Arizona Championship and July 18, 1984, I won two main events at San Bernardino.

In 1985, I am leading in the Junior Speedway points. I am the most consistent rider this season and have made it to most main events. My goals in speedway are to be a World Class rider and be World Champion.

Sincerely yours,

Billy Hamill, #104

Throughout the 1985 season there were grumbles coming from the various promoters about the junior speedway programme. On one occasion the riders were not permitted to take to the track because their exhausts exceeded the legal decibel limit. There was also talk that some promoters were not happy with the in-fighting that was going on between some of the parents who had become their kids' managers and agents. The track promoters had enough on their hands with the senior riders, never mind having to deal with parents of youngsters who were not even the drawcard for the public.

But perhaps more worryingly there were insurance problems looming and the various track promoters didn't want to run junior speedway anymore for fear of litigation. At one point the juniors were not scheduled to race anywhere in 1986, but more importantly for Billy, who was going to be sixteen in May, the AMA (American Motorcycle Association) would not sanction a licence for any rider under the age of eighteen.

Suddenly it looked as though his career would be put on hold until he was eighteen! At this point Billy did consider the possibility of racing in Motocross instead – but speedway was where his heart was and that was where he wanted to be. Amazingly, it would be his mother who provided the solution for not only her son, but also for the sport in the States.

Three

ENTER THE BULLET

His bike was an animal and I was trying to show people that I wasn't afraid, but I was shitting my pants.

Billy Hamill

Speedway racing in the USA is quite a different beast to the one that has been appearing in Britain for over seventy years. As with most things in America they do it their own way. The sport's governing body is the American Motorcycle Association (AMA) whose understanding of the sport is, to say the least, limited.

To make matters worse, speedway racing is largely confined to California – mainly Southern California. There is racing in the New York region at Owego and Greene, and they have also practiced the sport in other parts of the country with limited success. Nonetheless,

America's powerbase in speedway is the State of California. The country's best riders come from this state, the most professional of tracks are also based there and the sport's main distributors, such as Cody Racing and Brant Engineering, all reside in the Golden State. The short-lived, but entertaining publication *Speedway Magazine* was also produced in this area while *Turn One* is now giving the sport a voice again.

Therefore, you can understand why a large governing body which is used to dealing with motorcycle sport on a national scale should decide not to devote too much of its time on its problems – in spite of how successful the speedway riders from California have been.

It would be fair to say that the licensing and insurance problems that reared its ugly head during 1986 were more of an indication of the nation's mentality than that of the sport's administration itself. America was, and still is, 'lawsuit happy' and the question of liability is one which causes just as many problems now as it did then. The AMA's decision was a quick fix answer to a complex problem and they certainly didn't look too closely at what was at stake here: namely some of the country's most promising prospects were going to be prevented from continuing their careers for two years because of red tape.

But none of this was helping Billy Hamill, or his young rivals. Put simply: they wanted to race.

There was a problem with the insurance and my Mom, who was a legal secretary, found a loophole in the law. Everybody was saying that they had to wait until they were eighteen to ride, but no way – she found a way that I could race. We were the first ones to do it and then the others followed.

'There were a lot of problems in California with liability that prevented sixteen-year-old riders from going on to be senior riders,' began Gay Hamill. 'I did not want to "emancipate" Billy so that he could ride because if he were "emancipated" he would be considered an adult in the eyes of our legal system. That meant that if he got into trouble with the criminal justice system he would be tried as an adult and not as a minor – the punishment for adults was much more severe than for a minor. I did not think that Billy would get into trouble, but one never knows.'

Ascot Speedway had put on what was called a 'Sportsman Class' of racing for sixteen to seventeen year olds, but they all wanted to ride with the seniors. Ronnie Correy, who was a little older than Hamill, had been riding under the clause called 'emancipation', which meant that he was treated as an adult for the purpose of speedway racing only, but this seemed to be no longer acceptable.

'I spoke with a lawyer, Cary Agajanian, [brother of Ascot speedway promoter Gary] about my concerns,' Gay recalled, 'and he suggested I try a "Minor's Compromise". It was a seldom-used document and had never been used in this context, but he thought it might be worth a try. I engaged an attorney by the name of Philip Barbaro to prepare the document and set a hearing date. I then notified Cary Agajanian of the date. Mr Barbaro and Mr Agajanian appeared at the hearing, and Cary argued the case in front of Judge Xanthos, Pasadena Superior Court Judge, who then approved it.'

As we have already mentioned, there is almost no team speedway in America like there is in Europe. Two attempts were made to run team racing during the early to mid-1970s – both times it failed miserably. The only exceptions are the USA *v.* Rest of the World matches and what is termed as the 'Civil War', where riders from Northern California take on a team from Southern California.

In the USA there are three levels of senior racing which are graded by division. To begin with, Billy had to start in the Third Division, which was where everyone started whether they were a junior rider or not. This meant that at times there was some pretty wild, or some would rightly say dangerous, Third Division guys who had very little experience and were as much of a danger to themselves as they were to their rivals! The aim was to progress to the Second Division as soon as possible and then get into the First Division, which is where all the best riders are –it's these riders that the public pay to see.

At this time there was a maximum of eighteen riders in both the Third and Second Divisions. This number meant that there was a surplus of riders at each meeting so they had a rider on stand-by, engine running, helmet on and ready to go, just in case one of the riders on the programme had to drop out before the race for some reason and then he could step in. There were normally three six-man handicap races held over five laps and the first two riders would transfer to the main event – or final. Their yardage was determined by their previous performance. For example, when Billy made his first appearance he would start on the 0-yard line, or scratch, while the more experienced riders would start further back with the best starting 50 yards behind the start line.

The top sixteen First Division riders would be able to take part in the scratch races where they all started from the start line. Therefore, the goal was to be good enough to enter these potentially lucrative races. These riders also rode in the handicaps too, but it was the scratch races that proved that you were a top line-rider on the American circuits.

At this stage in his career Billy had no real hankering to go to Europe and ride in the British League, he just wanted to become a top American rider. However his closest rival, Greg Hancock, because of his connections with Penhall through his father, was expected to follow that route. His progress was halted by the insurance problem which meant that he missed the 1986 season while all this was being sorted out. Billy had none of these pressures and even less was expected of him following his mediocre junior career.

Because of the insurance problems I had a month's head start and that got me on the board really and put my name in lights. It was a month that I needed to get ahead of these kids like Trinon Cirello – his dad owned Cirello Racing; David Busby – his dad owned Cirello Racing before that; Scott Brant was Brant Engineering; Bobby Cody was Jawa-Cody of Bill Cody fame; and then of course Greg and Jesse Finch. We were all within a year or two of each other and relatively the same age, so you can imagine all these kids going into 500s. It gave me a window of opportunity, so I had a month on them and I gained in confidence. So they had to live up to what I had done, which were twenty-four straight wins and I progressed from the Third Division to the Second Division. Whereas in the juniors they were all so well connected and ahead of me, but now I was ahead of them.

Bill and Opal Collins sponsored me with my first 500cc bike, which was a Jawa. For some reason, as soon as I got on a 500 I was good. I think it was because my bikes were always crap in the juniors and I didn't have a clue. I wouldn't say that riding a 500 was totally different to a junior bike – a lot of it was set-up. When I got on a basic stock Jawa, which was accessible and it was already set-up and half decent, it was so easy! I probably weighed 90lbs when I got on a 500cc bike and I thought, 'Man, I should have been on this the whole time – this thing is so easy to ride compared with junior speedway bikes.' It was,

I felt, easy and they are to this day because you've got the power to help you. It just clicked from the moment I got on it and I was winning straightaway. All of a sudden, this kid who hadn't even won a Junior National Championship was beating all these kids and smoking everybody. It felt natural to be on a 500.

Apart from Mom and my neighbours, who thought it was cool, I never really had any support from the rest of my family; it was what I was interested in. I was so excited and enthusiastic about the sport and motorcycles and about riding my bike, but nobody else shared that enthusiasm. I was getting myself into trouble, and I needed something to capture my attention – and speedway did that for me. But until I discovered it, there was nothing because I was out of control. I was so enthusiastic about it; it was hard for me to share that. Even when I talked to my friends about it they would just go like, 'Yeah.' I would keep going on about it and they would just go, 'Okay, whatever', they just didn't share the same degree of enthusiasm as I had. It was what I needed at a young age because if I didn't have that I would have probably found something else to be interested in which wouldn't have been good.

Out of all the Duarte kids, Carlos and I were the only ones who went into speedway. His brother Juan had a brief stint but never really raced, I don't think he liked being in front of a crowd. But Juan was my best bud, and we lived across the street from each other and we would always talk about doing this and that, and being speedway riders. He was a good rider, he got a bike and leathers, but he didn't want to take it to the next level. I guess it just didn't feel natural for him to do that, but for me it was like the most natural thing to do – it was just like progression.

The presence in 1985 of such talents as Sam Ermolenko, Lance King and Kelly Moran as well as the usual First Division flyers like Mike Faria, Alan Christian and Mike Curoso, enabled the sport to attract some much-needed TV coverage. But in 1986 Ermolenko, – who finished third in the World Championship in 1985 – Moran and King all crossed the Atlantic and returned to the British League.

Billy Hamill's sudden and spectacular progress caught the attention of everyone. He soon won his first handicap main event at Ascot South Bay Stadium and he was attracting plenty of interest and attention. It was because of this that Billy was saddled with a nickname that has become synonymous with other star performers like Kelly 'The Wizard of Balance' Moran, Shawn 'Mad Dog' McConnell and Alan 'Crazy' Christian.

Larry Huffman called me 'The Bullet' and the line was: 'Billy "the Bullet" Hamill, this kid is hotter than a two-dollar pistol.' It was a TV meeting, and I was just making my way up through the ranks, and I think I had done twenty-six races without a defeat. That's what Larry Huffman came up with and it has stuck with me ever since. It's cool; a bit like the ones that some of the other riders had like the Morans, Cookie (John Cook) and 'Boogaloo' Bobby Schwartz and all that kind of thing. We used it for the business later in my career and even now, racing over in England, the TV commentators still use it – it's a pretty unique trademark I think.

While racing was becoming a larger and larger part of his life, Billy still had to finish his education. His parents were keen that he graduated in case speedway didn't quite meet his expectations. Although he probably resented it at the time, he is grateful that his parents continued to pressurise him to finish his education.

Meanwhile with riders like Ermolenko and King racing in Europe, this opened up a few doors for some of the US-based riders. Although Billy was showing everyone what talent and potential he had, he was still learning his trade – sometimes with spectacular results.

I was racing at Victorville and I was on a Weslake engine at that time. I lifted coming out of the turn and my bike just flipped over the fence and into the crowd! Fortunately it didn't hurt anyone but I got banned for two weeks. Greg's dad never really forgot that and for many, many years he would call me 'Hazard Hamill'.

I was trying so hard and I wanted to win so bad. There was no finesse about me at that stage, and there are kids out there now that are doing the same thing. It's all part of that learning curve. Jay and Vikki Wright, who were the promoters at Victorville, helped me by buying me an engine from George Wenn which was from one of Ivan Mauger's old bikes. My Dad thought that we should buy our own bike and I was taking my engines to George and he used to work with Ivan Mauger. So now, because I was showing everyone what I could do on a 500, I was beginning to get the support from people within the sport like Greg, Cirello and Cody had all along when I was racing junior speedway – and it was making a difference. Wenn was really good with Delloroto Carburettors and he was another one from the old school of racing. He had a lot of experience which was what I needed at that point.

Mike Lord was a high school friend and he used to come along and mechanic for me. We had a lot of fun on motorcycles but he never raced seriously at all. We had a lot of fun together and Carlos Cardona would also be with me in the pits too. Mike's a pretty flamboyant character and most of the American riders know of him and he was helping us out during the World Team Cup Final at Coventry. He's a rodeo rider and he's a typical cowboy really. When I go back to ride in the US he's nearly always helping me as my mechanic with Carlos. We go back a long way.

Having riders like Kelly Moran and Sam Ermolenko return to the British League in 1986 didn't really help me that much at that time. It opened up more doors for riders like Mike Faria and Steve Lucero, but it made more of a difference to me in 1987 when I was beginning to figure it out. But when those riders came back to race on rider return the racing was so competitive. In 1987 Bobby Schwartz came back to race in California and then Phil Collins also decided to spend a season in the US and he brought a new edge to racing at home.

Phil Collins was the third brother of the famous Collins brothers of which the eldest, Peter, won the 1976 World Championship. Phil had retired from the British League after many seasons with Cradley Heath, and had been a team-mate of American Bruce Penhall.

Although he didn't enjoy quite the same level of success as his elder brothers Peter and Les – Les was runner-up in the 1982 World Final – he qualified for his one and only World Final in 1983. However, he was one of the most charismatic riders that ever wore a Cradley Heath 'Heathens' body colour. Like most of his family, on a racetrack he was very exciting and his ability to come from the back had the crowd on their feet.

Collins had raced in America for England and a Rest of the World team over the previous two seasons. He had grown disillusioned with the ever-increasing costs of racing in Britain and said of his decision to ride in the USA: 'I know people will be thinking that I am going to America for the money but that's not the case. I'm not even sure if I will be better off financially out there, but the idea appeals to me. It is a chance that I cannot afford to miss.'

Bobby Schwartz also returned for a full season of racing in the US in 1987, and it was these two riders that Hamill enjoyed racing against.

Phil Collins was over and he brought a lot to American Speedway. I learned a lot from him with his racing style and the things he would do, and I would basically emulate him. Just by watching and analysing him, he showed me racing lines that I didn't even know were there. He was a better rider than most of the guys over there at that time, so he brought a lot and he made me a better rider. I used to just watch him in his first heat and I used to think, 'Well, if he can do that then I could do that.' He's a pretty infectious guy and I think he was a legend wherever he raced. I had some great battles with him.

When Bobby Schwartz came back he was just awesome, and he had a fantastic season in 1987, but those two and Mike Faria pretty much dominated racing in America at that time.

Billy was indeed starting to get to grips with the sport and really make an impression. One of the reasons for this was the help he received from one of the unsung heroes of American Speedway, Ken McGoldrick, known in the sport as 'KK'.

A former racer, McGoldrick's famous initials first came to the attention of the sport when they appeared on the leathers of Kelly and Shawn Moran. Later, the famous KK would also be seen on Chris Manchester, but it was the Morans and Hamill that were three of his most famous riders. Very little is known about the man and he is a figure that appears to sit contentedly in the background and away from the limelight.

I had good support from KK. He was good at spotting raw talent. He rode with his brother, but not to any degree of major success. He was a paint and body guy and he just loved racing. His talent was that he could analyse things in a different way to most people – even to this day. He would have a different perspective to anybody I would know, and it would be deep and it would often be the right way. Many times I would be astounded because I had never even looked at something in that particular way. It would usually be thoughts not for today, but where I needed to be tomorrow. That was what a young kid like me needed at that time and that was why he was so good for Shawn and Kelly. He was their manager for a spell, but he wasn't a manager as such for me, although I guess he was in a certain way. KK wouldn't say you gotta do this, or you gotta do that, it was up to me to do it. I would talk to him on a regular basis, and he sponsored me by putting some money into my racing – and it was usually when I really needed something too. Sometimes when I didn't even realise I required it myself.

The experience that he gained with Kelly and Shawn was invaluable to me, but the way I like to describe KK is: 'Give me your broken toys and I'll fix 'em', and that's the way he was.

The British magazine *Speedway Mail* used to cover speedway racing in America on a regular basis. When the American Final of the World Championship was being staged at Long Beach, they sent their journalist Suzy Fox over to cover it. While she was there she also took the opportunity to take a look at some of the domestic action and described the up and coming Bullet as 'impressive'.

Ronnie Correy had signed to ride for Wolverhampton in the British League alongside Sam Ermolenko. It was the beginning of a productive partnership at Wolves, and one that Billy and Greg Hancock would later face in fierce local derbies. Nonetheless, Correy was considered to be the first of a new wave of American racers that were poised to come over to Britain. In an interview he gave to *Speedway Mail*, he confirmed that a new era was beginning in the USA.

'I came up through the juniors, and there are a lot of guys I was riding with who would do good over here,' he said. 'People like Greg Hancock, Jesse Finch, Billy Hamill and Gary Hicks. The Americans that are over here right now are getting older and sooner or later they will start dropping out, and I think you'll see a new group who are every bit as good as they are.'

Billy's performances were attracting interest from all quarters, including the scouts that the British promoters had in the States who were charged with spotting new talent. But at just seventeen years of age he wasn't eligible to hold an international licence until he was eighteen. Furthermore, he was still finishing his high school education – something that he viewed as a necessary evil.

I didn't really like school, I wanted to ride speedway but I wasn't going to get the support from either my Mom or my Dad unless I went to school. The teachers I had never really captured my attention or interest, but I wouldn't really blame their teaching because I was a pretty horrible student. The arrangement with my parents was that I had to keep up a certain grade average, which I wasn't too happy about and I didn't always achieve it. It was hard, but I did it. I ended up graduating from high school and I had to put in some work to do this.

Now, of course, I'm thankful that I did. As soon as school was over for the day I would get on the bikes, so it wasn't easy for my Mom as she knew where my passion was. Basically, my Mom made me go to school and I am very grateful for her perseverance. Of course I didn't appreciate it much at the time and it must have been hell for her – it was hell for me!

His progress in 1987 can be illustrated by the fact that he raced in some of the big individual events of the season. He appeared in the Ascot Track Championship which was won by Mike Faria and he scored 2 points. He was excluded from his last race for a tapes offence.

He did better in the California State Championship at San Bernardino where he finished with 6 points. In an event that was once again won by Faria, he made quite an impact in one of his races when he finished in second place ahead of Championship contenders Schwartz and Shawn Moran.

I was only seventeen then and I qualified for my first US National Championship at Costa Mesa. I finished way down in thirteenth place and I was pretty disappointed with my performance. Brad Oxley won that year and there were a lot of people who thought that I did well to get there considering I was such a young age. But I was out there to win!

Looking back on it now I can see that it was pretty good for a young kid who was still at high school to get to the Finals. I didn't have the experience at that point and all the top riders just stepped up a level that night and I wasn't ready for that – mentally or physically.

However, his determination meant that he was one of the most popular riders on the US circuit. When Billy 'the Bullet' Hamill was on track, the spectators were guaranteed to see a young charger whose determination to get to the front ensured that they would get their value for money.

Just how far he had come was illustrated when he was included in the line-up for the 1988 American Final of the World Championship. If he thought that the competition was tough in the Nationals, the World Championship was even more competitive – he would soon have first-hand knowledge of how much harder the competition became as the title chase began to gather pace – and he finished way down the order with just 3 points. But it was another useful experience for the rider who was still only eighteen years old.

The pay scales and prize money were not quite so lucrative now as they were shortly after Penhall's retirement in 1982, but it was still possible to make a good living – especially for a teenager. With KK at hand for advice and guidance, he was making considerable progress. He continued to work as a pizza delivery man during the off-season and he collected a few sponsors.

I was making good money while I was racing at home. At sixteen/seventeen years old I was bringing home $800 a week. It was only six months of the year and I was earning more than my father was at the time! I had to put all my money into a bank account and it was part of the deal that you had to put 60% of your earnings into a bank account. So when I was eighteen I had a little bit in the account to buy a car. I was able to buy a car outright without having to make payments, which for an eighteen-year-old was good.

I bought a 1972 Ford Courier from a guy we called Kiwi – because he came from New Zealand. I had to meet him at this place called 'The Drinkers Hall of Fame' (my Mom and Dad got engaged in there!) which was all part of the Clown Town area. I went along with my $500 to buy this pick-up truck and I was having a good look at it before parting with any money. It seemed fine mechanically speaking so I walked round it and kicked the tyres and generally checked over the condition of it, when I came across these dents in the side and I asked: 'Hey, what are these dents?'

'What dents?' he replied.

'These dents here,' I pointed them out to him.

'I can't see any dents.'

I just looked at him and thought that this guy was just wasted. And then I pointed them out again, 'Look here, these bumps and scratches…'

'Oh they're not dents – they're just whiskey bruises!'

I didn't have a lot of time to spare because of school, racing and working a job – I was pretty busy. So I wasn't doing the same kind of things that other teenagers were doing at that time. But I made time to experience all the good things!

Billy also had the mechanical expertise of Ray Enriquez – known as 'Sugar Ray' – who used to be Mike Faria's mechanic. It was Ray who had hooked up Hamill with KK as he could see that he needed the help. Mike Lord and Carlos Cardona were at the same stage as their buddy in that they were still learning the ropes on the mechanical side of things.

Sugar Ray had been with Faria who had been one of the top riders on the California circuit for some time. He had twice qualified beyond the American Final of the World Championship, but in 1988 he too headed for the British League where he raced for Belle Vue.

However, during the 1987 season he made another useful mechanical contact, and one that would play a major role in his future as his career progressed. Scotsman Craig Cummings, affectionately known as 'Craiger', hailed from Edinburgh and had previously been a mechanic for Shawn Moran. He was helping Bobby Schwartz in the US when he met an inquisitive Hamill for the first time.

'After one of the very first meetings that I did for Bobby everybody went to this Mexican restaurant and bar called El Rachito that wasn't far from his house,' recalled Cummings. 'Bobby obviously had a lot of friends there that he was chatting to and stuff. I didn't know many people, maybe one or two, and I was just standing around. Then this guy came up to me and said: 'Hey, you wanna come and sit at our table?' And I replied, 'Yeah, okay.' So I went and sat beside him and had a beer, and this guy turned out to be Billy. He basically grilled me for about two hours on British Speedway – he wanted to know every little detail about speedway in Britain. That was the first time that I had met him. I had heard of him before but not actually met him, and we got on really well.'

Hamill's mechanical expertise was developing slowly, and most of his knowledge came from Butch Fish, but in 1988 grave news greeted Hamill.

Butch was into aircraft and he used to build his own airplanes. He had built an acrobatic plane and he flew off into the desert to get some hours into the machine, and the canopy blew off. He was wearing glasses at this time and they blew off as well so he couldn't see, and the plane malfunctioned and he crashed into a field and he was killed. I remember I was working on my bikes and my Mom came over to tell me that Butch had had a crash and I couldn't believe it – it was very difficult to take in.

I used to go over to his aircraft hanger and pass the time with him. He would let me do my bike in his shop because I never had the right tools or whatever, and he used to get frustrated because he could see that I never had a clue. He was a hard guy, but he played a major role in my early development. He used to sponsor me with his company called Monrovia Diesel, and then ever afterward I would carry the initials MD as a tribute to him on my leathers. He played a big part during my early years as a racer and his death was a big shock to me.

The Inland Motorcycle Speedway at San Bernardino, whose catch-phrase was 'The only reason for Wednesday nights', closed after the 1987 season. Its closure confirmed what many people had been suspecting for some time: that the boom period for American Speedway was over. IMS was a well-established track in Southern California, but another new track opened in the region to soften the blow and that was at Glen Helen.

Unlike many tracks in this area at that time, it wasn't located in a fairground but at a motorcycle recreational park, and it had a 280-yard circuit. One rider that was seen practising at this venue before it opened for business was Jim Fishback. Fishback, known as 'the Animal', was one of the most popular riders to have appeared at the IMS and he announced that he was making a comeback for the 1988 season.

No doubt the people behind the Glen Helen location were hoping that the return of 'the Animal' would have a positive effect on the attendances at the new venue. He earned his reputation, and nickname, for his uncompromising style of riding. A big muscular rider, he was making a comeback at the age of thirty-four and, as Billy discovered, he hadn't forgotten that hard-as-nails approach to his racing. It made an impression on the youngster that he had been in a race with 'the Animal'.

Earlier in the evening I watched Fishback take out Bobby Schwartz, he just railed him in what I thought was a pretty stupid move really. I had watched Jim 'the Animal' Fishback race before, but he'd been in retirement and he had just made a comeback. I guess he was pretty determined to beat Bobby Schwartz because he was winning so much and the only way he was going to beat him was to rail him.

I was a cocky kid and I had just seen him take out one of my heroes, and I wasn't going to let that slide. I happened to be in third and saw this and I thought, 'What an asshole', and I thought, 'I'm going to pass this guy', so I went underneath him. But he was having none of it and he leaned on me. He was doing lefts and rights on me as I was on the inside while Bobby was on the outside. When we clashed his chain came off and I thought, 'Yeah, that's what you get for being an asshole!' I went through turns 3 and 4 and down the straightaway and my right foot started tingling. I had another lap to go so I just put it to the back of my mind, but when the race was over I looked down and I saw that my foot was just flayed. There was what looked like spaghetti hanging out of my boot, but what it turned out to be was my tendons and they were just spurting blood!

I'm the biggest chicken when I see blood. I can break a bone or do anything, but when I see blood it just freaks me out and my son is the same way. I saw this and I thought, 'Oh shit', I couldn't believe it. At that point I knew that I must have caught my foot in the sprocket, and I wondered what to do. So I just laid down and the paramedics came and when they took my boot off, where the sprocket had caught my foot, the small toes on the very right were right over, almost at a right angle with my foot while the rest of my foot was where it should be. The sprocket took a big chunk out of the side of my foot, so when they took the boot off my foot just fell open!

My Dad is the same as me and he happened to be there, and he was trying to reassure me before they took the boot off by saying, 'Oh you'll be all right.' But when they took off my boot he just turned away and said, 'Oh fuck this!' and he couldn't handle it. He was trying to be all macho about it, but he was nearly puking. By now I had passed out after I saw it. This slowed me down and it was a couple of days before my graduation so I couldn't go because I was in the hospital having my tendons all tied up and repaired. I lost a nerve as a result of that crash and even now my toes don't work too well.

I was out of action for six to eight weeks, and I came back just before the Nationals. I ended up fifth in the Nationals with 10 points and Steve Lucero won his first and only National title that year. It was a hell of an effort for me at that time to do that well after coming back from what was a pretty serious foot injury.

I can't handle the sight of blood. That's why I don't run out onto the track when someone gets hurt. I just turn away and sit in my pit. Years ago, at Wolverhampton, I was off gate four and Paul Thorp was off gate three, he lifted and we ended up clashing and he went over the handlebars. Naturally I just wanted to check to see if he was all right, and when I got there he was choking on his tongue and he was doing the fish out of water thing just trying to grab some air. I just felt ill and I puked in my helmet right there and then. From that moment on I decided that I can't go out there, I won't, and I don't like that side of the sport. To see one of your friends in trouble, someone who you race against and probably have a drink in the bar with after the meeting, is upsetting – and I can't handle it.

One of the big events in America during the 1988 season was the staging of the World Team Cup Final at Long Beach. In 1985 the Americans successfully staged the final for the first time and lost marginally to Denmark in what was arguably one of the greatest finals ever staged. During this time the event was staged as a four-team tournament and the title of 'World Champions' was decided during one night of racing held over twenty races. America faced the reigning champions, Denmark, Sweden and England.

Much was expected from the American team because they had their best riders available for selection: Sam Ermolenko, Lance King, Kelly and Shawn Moran and Rick Miller. However, they couldn't contain a dominant Danish side that ran away with a comprehensive victory while the US finished a distant and disappointing second.

Denmark was at the peak of their domination of international speedway at that time and provided the top three in the World Championship, with Erik Gundersen winning his third World title. However, Gundersen's British club was Cradley Heath and it just so happened that one half of England's managerial duo was the Heathens' boss, Colin Pratt.

It had not been a happy final for England as Kelvin Tatum had lost a run-off to Sweden's Per Jonsson for third place. Nonetheless, while he was in California Pratt sought the opinion of ex-Cradley rider Bruce Penhall.

'Bruce had already recommended Greg Hancock to me', recalled Pratt, 'but he made a point of meeting me at that stage and he said, "I've got another for you, but one will have to come over one year and the other a year later!" I said, "That suits me fine as long as we do a deal that both come to Cradley Heath and nowhere else." I was doing my job. We arranged for Greg and Billy to come to England on a special trip, just to get the feel of the place and so we could have a look at the boys in action at the stadium.'

This was arranged for late October 1988, but for Billy the thought of a British club being interested in him was still a dream.

As soon as I first got on a 500cc bike, all I wanted to be was a good American speedway rider. The only time I used to see Sheffield or Eastbourne, who Shawn and Kelly rode for, was when I used to go to H-Salt, which was a fish and chip shop chain in California. They had a little map on the wall and you could see where these towns were situated in England.

One day Bruce Penhall asked me if I wanted to go over and check it out, and it was like, 'Wow! Bruce Penhall's asking me if I want to go to England and ride at Cradley Heath', which was his team. It was unbelievable for a kid from Duarte, California, who'd been dreaming about being a speedway rider. It wasn't something that I thought was realistic. So here was the dream.

I went with Greg Hancock, who had been over before so he knew what to expect. But I remember on the flight over I kept him up during the whole flight because I was way too excited. He wasn't sharing my enthusiasm because I was way too sprung, and I think he was getting a little bit pissed off with me because he's a pretty mellow guy. I couldn't believe that I was actually going to England and staying with Lance King.

I didn't know all the details until I got there but it was also arranged that we would be riding Erik Gundersen's bikes at Cradley Heath – I had no idea until I arrived in England. It was just a case of winging it; it was unbelievable. To this day, to have an opportunity as an eighteen-year-old kid to come over from California, or for any kid to come over from say, Sweden or Denmark, and to ride Tony Rickardsson's bikes at a famous club, but not only to ride them, but to have a practise day and do a demonstration after a meeting or whatever – what an opportunity. It was an awesome experience. Erik Gundersen had just won the World title for the third time after a run-off in Vojens, so he was the reigning World Champion too!

I can remember getting off the plane at Heathrow Airport and all I saw was black taxis. I couldn't believe how many of these taxis there were and they looked so weird. We jumped into Lance King's van and all the houses I saw were made of brick, and you don't see brick houses in California. I thought that was cool and it must have been expensive. I realise now that because of the weather if you don't have bricks then you're in for trouble. You can't have dry block like we do in California because it just wouldn't stand up to the climate, but I thought it was weird at the time. And I couldn't understand why everybody's houses were so small and I wondered why they didn't have an open plan in the houses. Now I know it's because of the cold and you have to keep the heat in. It was green everywhere too which was a lot different to California where everything is dry and burnt from the sun. They were vivid things that made me realise that England was a lot different.

We travelled to Cradley with Erik that night and he picked us up from Lance King's house because he was riding for King's Lynn at the time. He picked us up in the van, and I had never seen a van that was kitted out specifically for speedway, and it had 'Erik Gundersen 3 times World Speedway

Champion' written on the side, and a coffeemaker – all the stuff that a top rider of that time had.

I was sitting in the back and he hardly talked all the way to the races. I was so nervous, but I was still excited because I was sat in Erik Gundersen's van! All I wanted to do was talk to the guy, but it looked as though he didn't want to be disturbed. He had his race face on, which I understand now, but at the time I just wanted to talk to him.

Wolves were at Cradley in a challenge match and after the match, which was 15 heats, we jumped on two of Erik's bikes and we did a four-lap race. We thought we did great and we put on a good show – everything was cool. His bike was an animal, and I was trying to show people that I wasn't afraid, but I was shitting my pants – and I'm sure Greg was too. We were eighteen years old and we were scared, because we had only ridden Weslakes at that point, but here we were riding a GM which was geared and set-up for Cradley. I remember coming off the corners and the bike just lifted every time and I had never done a wheelie like that while going so fast. It was such an experience. I couldn't have asked for a better opportunity and I consider myself to have been very lucky.

We were both excited and we were going into the changing rooms and Sam Ermolenko was in there and he said: 'Hey, how did it go?'

'Oh it was awesome man, it was so cool and the track is great.'

And he replied: 'I knew it was you guys. I didn't see you but I could hear you shutting off the throttle going into the corners and no one ever does that over here, so I knew it was you guys.'

It was a total dig, and I thought 'What a thing to say', and it totally blew our high. I remember thinking, 'Oh right, we shut the throttle off too long, but don't ruin it for us.' But for me, a kid from Duarte, staying in Lance King's house and riding Erik Gundersen's bikes, I didn't take that stuff for granted and it was a dream that had come true.

It was impressive, the whole thing impressed me. Everybody had heard of Greg Hancock because of his association with Bruce Penhall so he got all the attention – which was fair enough. I was pretty much travelling on his coat-tails through Bruce, and it took the limelight off me and I just enjoyed myself. Everybody was so friendly and inquisitive. Craiger (Craig Cummings) took Greg and I around and he transported us and we went to Oxford, Belle Vue, Wolverhampton and Swindon.

I remember watching Andrew Silver at Swindon who was unbelievable; he was coming off the back straight and diving under people. I was very intimidated by the size of the tracks. I was a bit scared and I didn't know if I would be able to ride them and I wondered if I would be afraid of the speed because I had never gone that fast on a speedway bike – let alone been on a bike that fast. I couldn't believe how fast everybody was and that's why, when Sam said that to us, we realised that we weren't good enough. I was just impressed, and we were going to speedway every night of the week. What more could I ask for when speedway was my whole life? It was more social than in the US, because afterwards you could go and have a beer in the bar. But in California you'd just sit by the van and talk with your buddies or whatever and then go home. But in England it was more professional, and it was everything that I had imagined it would be.

I couldn't understand an English accent. When I came over in 1988 I didn't know that there were different regional accents, I thought everyone sounded the same and I couldn't understand anybody! It wasn't only the Cradley accent, which I understood quite quickly, but because of the way that Colin spoke I didn't understand half of what he was saying. I remember speaking to George Hunter who had a broad Glaswegian accent, and he was very hard to understand. And the Dudley accent seemed impossible at that time.

Lance King showed us a lot too because we were staying with him. He talked to us about contracts and told us not to sign a thing at that point. So when we went into Prattie's office we were on the defensive because Lance had said that they would get us to sign for them and he warned us not to sign a thing.

I think we were both hoping to eventually get contracts. We were impressed with the team that had Jan O. Pedersen, Simon Cross and Erik in it and we both wanted it. Colin Pratt sat us down in the office, but I didn't really understand it at the time because I couldn't understand him! Basically he told us that we didn't have to sign for them at that point, but they had paid for the flights for us to come over to England. The deal was that if we ended up signing for Cradley then we didn't have to worry, but if we signed for another club then we had to give them their flight money back. He asked us if we had an agreement and we did – it was a 'gentleman's agreement'. I thought that was cool: they paid for our flights, we got to ride Erik Gundersen's bikes and they didn't seem to care whether we signed for them or not. There was no pressure whatsoever and that was a pretty good deal.

By the time I went back home I was dead excited, but KK told me that I wasn't ready for England yet. After my trip I knew I wasn't ready. There was no way, and I knew that if I did go over I would be flung to the wolves. I knew I had a lot of things to do and we worked on it all winter for 1989. Greg had different ideas because of his dad and Bruce, but I knew I still had a lot to learn before I could go racing in England.

Four

BE FAST, OR BE LAST

I could see straightaway that he had such great potential. He had brilliant balance and you could see his want for success in his eyes.

Erik Gundersen (Triple World Speedway Champion)

That trip to England set me up for 1989 at home. I just tried to emulate what Erik had showed us with his workshop and all that. I had never seen a workshop like it; it was clean and tidy, meticulous, and ridiculously clean. That's what the Danes did that no-one else did and it worked at the time. As soon as I got back I gutted my whole workshop, or garage, and built workbenches and just copied what I had seen to help with my racing programme.

I just paid more attention to detail. I took a lot more time with my bikes and the preparation and just took a lot more interest in it. I had a good working environment and a good set-up. I was living with my Dad at the time at his girlfriend's house and she had a two-car garage, which was more than I needed so I was able to set myself up really nice. I had good engines from Dave Brant, of Brant Engineering, which were short-stroke Weslakes that just flew, and I dialled the clutch in a bit more and all that kind of thing. It was just the little things, and the trip to England made me grow up and I matured a lot as a result. I did all my bike preparation by myself and KK was there to help me. In 1987-88 Sugar Ray was my mechanic and he was a good mechanic, and a guy called Mike Kelly also helped out along with the rest of my buddies.

I was out of school and I managed to graduate from high school and I was racing four nights a week, which I also did when I was in school. My week was Glen Helen on a Wednesday, Ascot was Thursday, Costa Mesa Friday and Victorville on Saturday. Imagine doing all that and graduating from high school – it was very busy. I didn't really have time for girls like other kids did at that age, but I made time.

KK was so influential and the big difference was that he directed me to Dave Brant and that was when I really started to come up. KK was stand-offish in a way but when you got to know him he was okay. He's still that way, he's a behind-the-scenes type of guy and he's clever. He doesn't go to speedway anymore and while I keep in touch, we don't speak on a regular basis. But you know he's a good friend because we always pick up where we left off. I'll always be there for him and I know he'll be there for me because that's the type of guy he is. And he was such a big influence at a vital time in my career and he earned my respect.

1989 was the year when the Bullet stopped showing glimpses of his potential and began to leave his rivals in his wake. During one eight-day period he won six main events: four scratch and two handicap. Among the riders who were left trailing his fumes were Mike Faria, Bobby Schwartz, Steve Lucero and Phil Collins. He was third behind Faria and Schwartz in the table for the most main event wins when it was first published in July.

I was winning week in and week out and I had some tremendous battles with Phil Collins. He wasn't the best gater out there, but he was so exciting and he would pass from the back by creating different lines. When we were out together I loved racing with him, but I don't expect he liked racing with me because I was a young kid and a bit dangerous.

In '89 I seemed to come of age and I had some good engines and I started smoking some of the good guys. It was a good year and even when I went to England I used to look back at '89 with a lot of satisfaction. In 1994 I was looking back at that year and I remembered how awesome it was to feel that good and to have good bikes. I knew what I was doing by then and I knew where I was going – and it showed.

I did a lot better than I thought and I raced a lot more on the outside and I just got more confident. But I had a big crash with Charlie Ermolenko. I broke my helmet cleanly in half, broke my two front teeth, and my goggle lens popped out and slit the corner of my eye and I had to have three stitches. Dukie ran over me and I was a real mess and I had his tyre marks up my arm and across my face. That was the first time that my wife Christina – although she wasn't my wife at the time – met my mother. What an introduction: an ambulance ride to the hospital.

It was some way to introduce two of the most important people in his life to each other, and also a preview of what life could be like for the wife of a speedway rider! In a memorable year for him, Billy had met Christina at the start of the season at the Veterans Stadium, Long Beach.

I first met Christina at the beginning of the 1989 season. It was at a Spring Classic meeting. I knew who she was because we grew up in the same town and she had a twin sister. One of my buddies, Denny, who eventually married Christina's sister, used to race BMX with me. He was going out with her, and I had heard about these two beautiful twin sisters. We both graduated from Monrovia High School, but Christina is two years older than me so we just missed each other. I had a girlfriend in high school – which was off and on – but nothing serious.

I met Christina through Denny Noonan, because he came to watch me race at Long Beach and he brought Christina, and I was intrigued straightaway. I thought she was beautiful and I made a point of talking to her, but although she was pleasant, she was a bit stand-offish. I didn't hear anything for a couple of weeks and then Denny called me and said: 'We're going to Disneyland and we've got a spare ticket. There's three of us and we need four, so do you wanna go?' And I said, 'Yeah I'll go.' It turned out to be a date, although it wasn't planned or anything like that, and then we became friends and I took her out the next day.

Well before I knew it we were in love, and we never looked back. I was eighteen years old, and she was two years older than me and she pretty much seduced me! She was the type of girl that I wanted to be serious with, and she was a 'keeper' – she was for keeps. I think she was intrigued by the racing and she had heard about me as a local kid who was a speedway rider. She grew up in a motorcycle/hot rod environment, so she had a racing background through her family. And she has always supported me in my racing.

Billy appeared at Long Beach for the American Final of the World Championship. The format that was used for this round of the Championship was at odds with the other qualifying rounds in Europe. They had five riders in a race in this meeting and the field of riders was twenty instead of sixteen. In 1987 the sport world's governing body, the FIM (the Federation of International Motorcycle Racing), told the AMA that this round had to include two riders from Canada. Harry Oxley, who was the promoter of the event, decided to change the format so that he wouldn't have to reduce the number of Americans in the final and could still accommodate the two Canadians.

Nonetheless, the politics didn't bother Hamill, who improved his performance from 1988 to finish with 10 points and in tenth place. Only the top four progressed to the next stage in an event that was won by Sam Ermolenko. However, a year later and it was a very different story.

Eventually Greg Hancock linked up with Cradley in the British League and was making steady progress. But Hamill's early season form was attracting the attention of British League bosses who were eager to strengthen their teams at the first opportunity.

Belle Vue, known as the Aces in Manchester, is arguably Britain's most famous speedway club. In 1989 they had both Kelly and Shawn Moran in their team and were eager to include the highly-rated Gary Hicks. However, John Perrin, the promoter of the Aces, had noted the form that Hamill was displaying in the US and he made some enquiries.

I got a call from Jimmy Van Dyke who was working for Shawn Moran. He said that John Perrin was interested in me. Greg went over in May and I thought, 'He's gonna get a head start on me', and I thought, 'Why's he over there and

I'm not?' I thought that I should be over there because I was as good as he was then. But I tried to put that at the back of my mind and concentrate on my racing at home because I was still winning races. But then I got a phone call from Jimmy Van Dyke and he said that John Perrin wanted to talk to me, and I thought, 'Wow, Belle Vue – great!' I was a bit torn between completing my season in the US as I agreed with KK, or to head over to England. Jimmy gave me John Perrin's number so I decided to give him a call, but he thought it was a wind-up.

'Who is this?'

'It's Billy Hamill.'

'Oh come on Jimmy you're having me on, don't fuck with me.'

'No sir, it's Billy Hamill.'

But he didn't believe me, he thought I was Jimmy taking the piss out of him and finally he said, 'Oh fuck you Jimmy.'

And I replied, 'Well fuck you too! Call me back if you wanna talk to me!'

I thought, 'What an asshole', and I called Jimmy and said: 'This guy's a dickhead; he won't even talk to me. He thinks I'm you!' So that was my second experience with an English promoter and, needless to say, that didn't go anywhere because we both told each other to fuck off. And then I rode for him in 1997!

Gary Hicks did eventually ride for Belle Vue that season and had a successful debut year. So successful in fact that, such are the intricacies of British Speedway, the rules meant that he was released in 1990 to a rival club. The constant rule changes, lack of co-operation and general uncertainty of speedway in Britain is an unwelcome cloud that constantly hangs over the sport in the UK. As you will discover, success or not has nothing to do with it, and Billy would be no stranger to a winter of uncertainty.

Despite the interest from Belle Vue, there was only one club that he really wanted to ride for and that was Cradley Heath. But in 1989 the Heathens experienced one of the worst years in the club's history. Jan O. Pedersen and Simon Cross both picked up injuries which stalled the club's progress in the League Championship, but the very heart of the club was ripped out when their number one rider, club captain and triple World Champion Erik Gundersen, suffered life-threatening injuries at Bradford in the World Team Cup Final in September.

Gundersen, who had made such an impression on Hamill during his trip to England at the end of 1988, had just lost his World title to arch-rival Hans Nielsen just a fortnight before his date with fate at Bradford. The talented Dane was the victim of a four-man crash during the first race that left him in a critical condition and fighting for his life.

It was a horror smash, and one that sent shockwaves around the speedway world. Little Erik's speedway career was at an end, and the race to save his life was on. The injuries to his spine were so severe that there were doubts about whether he would ever walk again. News of the accident spread across the Atlantic to the USA – Lance King was one of the other riders involved in the crash – and to Billy Hamill.

I was shocked – I was just glad that the guy was still alive. It sounded so terrible, and you know how rumours go, that by the time it got to America the full horror of it all was out. I think it affected the whole of the speedway world and it did affect me, but it didn't put me off the sport at all. I didn't really want to ride at Bradford after that because I was afraid of Odsal for a long time. I went up there once and it was rained off and then the next time I had flu and I couldn't even get out of bed.

But because Erik got hurt there it had a psychological affect on me. And later, because I lived with the guy and saw what he was going through everyday, I had a mental thing about the track. But once I got on it and attacked the track I loved it – it ended up being one of my favourite tracks.

During a magnificent season in America Billy finished the year at the top of the AMA points championship, had won more handicap main events than any other rider and only Phil Collins had won more scratch mains that season. He finished second in the California State Championship behind Steve Lucero and this time he was a major player in the US National Championship. He put on a magnificent display to finish runner-up to Schwartz with 13 points.

In the 1989 Nationals I had to pull some stuff out of the bag. I thought I was going to win it, but I ended up second. I had one race where I found myself in last place, and I had to win this race to have a shot at the title. I just railed it around the outside and I just passed Faria and Lucero and the pressure was on. It was a major achievement for me. Not only winning the points chase that year, but I more or less established myself as a true player in American

Speedway. To begin with that was all I wanted really. At that point I was think-
ing about England, but I didn't think it was possible to go over to England and
be World Champion until I had such a good season in 1989. That was when I
started thinking that maybe I could really do this.

Britain was where he wanted to spend his 1990 season. But while he
was waiting for the British League to get their house in order and
decide what the rules would be for the following year, Billy packed his
bags and headed for Australia to race during the winter.

It was a move that wasn't normally associated with inexperienced
Americans. Established riders like Schwartz and Shawn Moran made
regular trips Down Under to ride during the winter months, while
others chose to winter in South Africa. This was the life of a successful
international speedway rider at the time, but for an American who had
yet to turn a competitive wheel outside of the US and was still only
nineteen years old it was, well, different.

I met a friend at the races, Rodney Bourne, who was with Bobby Schwartz and
they had met through Trevor Harding – or Ghostie as we called him. This guy
had a conversion company and Trevor had a business called Kwiksnax, and
they used to buy lunch trucks in America and then ship them back to Australia
and convert them to right-hand drive. Rodney was partner in the conversion
company that used to do the trucks for Trevor Harding. So they flew him over
and he would buy trucks and ship them back and he was that link. So through
Trevor Harding he hooked up with Schwartz, and I met him at the races and
we became friends.

He was living in a hotel and it was costing him $1,200 per month, and I
said 'Why don't you come and stay with us?' I was living with my Dad's girl-
friend and she had a big house. She had five kids and everybody was in and out
and I asked her if he could stay there and she said that it was fine. He stayed for
a couple of months and we got to know each other and he suggested that I
should go over to Australia and race during the off-season. I knew riders like
Schwartz and Shawn Moran used to go out there, so I said yeah sure.

He said that he would sponsor me and I had a new set of leathers with Varasa
Conversions on them, and I was supposed to have fourteen meetings, but I think
I only did seven. There was a tour taking place by an English team, but when I
first spoke to him about it he didn't know if the tour was actually going to come
off. But it did, so I didn't get the meetings that I thought I was going to get.

I shipped my own bikes over there and rode all my own equipment. All I did was wash my bikes, clean my clutch plates and change my tyre. Looking back, I don't know how I even did all that because I just didn't know enough. But I was racing against guys like Leigh Adams and Todd Wiltshire and I did okay. Todd was already established in England and Leigh was a young up-and-coming rider, and from the start he was a fast rider and I raced against him on his home track at Mildura – I didn't beat him very often round there. The other riders were Shawn Moran, Ray Morton, Steve Schofield and Kelvin Tatum, but because of this big English tour I wasn't able to ride in some of the meetings. Dukie (Charles) Ermolenko was out there too and a Canadian named Jason Rock.

I found Australia was a lot like California as it was really laid back, but England wasn't so easy. For me, Australia was almost like living in a different state. Unfortunately, because I didn't get a lot of meetings I didn't have enough money to support myself so I had to get a job. I worked in an auto parts warehouse on an assembly line just boxing up parts and shipping them out. That was a good experience because it was right in the middle of Sydney so I had to catch a train to get to my work.

I just attacked while I was racing out there. I made a big mistake when I went to Newcastle and I just wiped out Sean Willmott. The track was huge and I didn't really know what I was doing except that I knew I had to stay on the gas with the throttle wide open. I wiped him out so hard that I ended his career. I didn't mean to do it, I just hit a hole in the track and I hooked up and put him straight into the concrete fence. It's not something that I feel good about, but it was just one of those deals. When I went on a tour there in 2000 he was the referee and we were talking about it so there is no problem between us.

The track surfaces were made of clay. While you were racing you would get shrapnel coming up from the track surface that had been deposited by the cars that also raced on it. You would get pieces of metal that were only the thickness of a piece of a paper and they would come flying up at you. If that stuff hit you in the face, it would hurt. I was nineteen years old then and I didn't even think about it. My attitude was 'I'm out here and I'm doing it', I didn't think about the danger and I just went out there to have fun.

Fun it may have been, but Billy was racing very well. If his form in the US had people taking notice, then his success in Australia just captured everybody's attention. The tracks are bigger in Australia because, as Billy has said, they run car racing on them as well, while the tracks in

California are tiny. Faster and longer, the Australian tracks required a different bike set-up, especially if they were running the Aussie mufflers which the riders called suitcases – because that's what they resembled.

On 30 December 1989, Billy won the Yamaha Invitation International at the wonderfully named Wagga Wagga in New South Wales. Dukie Ermolenko was second with Todd Wiltshire taking third place. It was an excellent way to end what had been, to date, his best season as a speedway rider.

In the New Year he raced in the Australian Masters at Mildura and qualified for the six-man final. He faced none other than Shawn Moran and Leigh Adams who led the qualifiers with 14 points. Moran's experience came to the fore and he won the race and took the trophy with Billy finishing in second ahead of Adams.

I didn't really know any different, because a big track was a big track to me – I never really knew any better. The way I would think about it was that America had short tracks and everywhere else had big tracks. I didn't think that one track was 300 metres and another track was 500 metres – I didn't even know what a metre was because I was taught imperial measurements in school.

Wagga Wagga is Aborigine for 'the Place of Many Crows'. It was a gnarly track, fairly large, and there was a bigger track on the outside and a quarter-mile track on the inside – we rode on that. I remember racing Jimmy Nilsen and he was a big name even then and I smoked him at Parramatta Raceway, and I thought: 'That was easy, that guy sucks!' But I just caught him on a bad day because when I came to England I saw the real Jimmy Nilsen and he wasn't that bad at all. I saw Kelvin Tatum in Oz and I thought he was fast. I had such a good season in 1989 that I thought that I could beat anyone now. It was good for my confidence to do well in Australia. Australia was a launch pad for me because it prepared me for bigger tracks and that was the whole reason why I did it because I wanted to go to England. I tried to hone my skills on the bigger tracks. Todd Wiltshire and Leigh Adams were the same age as me and we were coming up together, but they just smoked everyone over there so I knew what I was coming up against and I realised that I had to get my act together.

Meanwhile, Cradley were putting together a team for the first time since 1978 that wouldn't include Erik Gundersen. They seemed to be looking for more strength in depth with Jan O. Pedersen taking over as the club's number one and Simon Cross backing him.

Greg was all set to return and it seemed almost a foregone conclusion that Billy would join them. However, Colin Pratt kept his cards close to his chest and refused to acknowledge that signing Hamill was just a matter of time.

But in mid-February it was announced that Billy Hamill would be a 1990 Cradley Heathen. Pratt admitted that he'd had his eye on Billy for a long time and stated: 'All our American scouts say he has the ability to become a very big star in Britain and his results in Australia this winter seem to confirm that he is something a bit special. He fits into the category we are always looking for in new signings – he's young, he's talented and he's got a lot of personality. He's a signing for the '90s.'

I was definitely going to England in 1990. It was a hard decision for me to remain in the US in 1989. KK wanted me to ride one more year in the US, but there was no way that I could spend another season in America. I knew that I would go stale because it was the same tracks, the same riders, and I couldn't see that there was anything more for me to do there.

'If that's how you feel then you've got to go with what you feel. You know better than I do', said KK. 'But I think you should do another season here.'

But I told him that I couldn't do it, that I would go stale racing here and he supported my decision.

Colin Pratt called me when I was in Australia and at that time Leigh Adams and Mikael Blixt were on the market – so it was between us three. Bobby Schwartz was staying with us in Australia and I asked him what I should do. He basically told me what I had to do. He said that I needed the basic necessities.

'Get a guarantee and then you don't have to worry too much about the points money', he said. 'Get as much as you can: tyres, fuel, oil, all the necessities paid for then everything else is a bonus. If you do well then you'll earn money, but if you don't do well, then you're not gonna.'

So that's how I set up my first contract, which was £25 a point, and that was decent money, but it wasn't that great. But I had a £150 guarantee, which was not set against my earnings, and my rent was paid for and I had a van and insurance. Colin told me that every time I got paid it would always be when I was riding in a Cradley Heath body colour, because every now and then you'll do a challenge match and they wouldn't pay me as much because it was a chal-

lenge. It was all new to me, coming from California, and I had VAT [Value Added Tax] *to contend with, and I didn't know what that was when I first came over here. I didn't understand it at all to begin with. Bobby showed me his contracts and how they were structured and I have continued to base my contracts that way ever since. I never really made money, though, until maybe five years into my British career.*

My family knew I was serious about it but I never really took much notice of what they were thinking. I don't think they ever really thought about it until I came over to England to race, then I think they thought that was pretty cool. If I was struggling and not really getting anywhere, then I think I would have heard more about it! I remember being a little bit afraid when I was coming to England, and it was really hard saying goodbye to my Mom. But if I was going to do it I couldn't be scared, just attack; my attitude was, 'If you're gonna do it, do it right or don't even bother.' I tried to do it as right as I possibly could, and I wasn't in England for a holiday: I was there to win races and to be World Champion. That was my approach.

Cradley Heath, the Heathens, was based in the West Midlands, in an area known as the 'Black Country'. It's called the Black Country because of the colour of the ground, which was black because of the famous ten-yard coal seam which outcropped there. The club first opened its doors to speedway in 1947, just as the sport was booming in Britain following its forced closure during the Second World War – only Belle Vue continued to operate regularly during the hostilities.

The track was situated at Dudley Wood and the circuit measured approximately 336 metres in length (367 yards). According to author Peter Foster, the inspiration for the track was taken from Wembley, the spiritual home of British Speedway. They first opened their doors for speedway on 21 June 1947, with a match against Wombwell which they won in front of a reported crowd of 12,000. Although the venue never enjoyed the same kind of facilities as Wembley or Belle Vue, this never dampened the crowd's enthusiasm, which would remain passionate for the rest of the club's history.

For many years Cradley was looked upon as a Cinderella side, a team that, despite the passion of its supporters, never really posed a major threat to the sport's more successful clubs. The Midlands was the hub of British Speedway for a long time, with tracks at Birmingham, Coventry and Wolverhampton; in particular there was a fierce rivalry between the Heathens and the Wolves. Other venues at Leicester, Stoke and Long Eaton provided a sound infrastructure for the sport to thrive in the area.

However, by the time that Billy arrived to race in England, Birmingham and the wonderful track at Blackbird Road in Leicester had gone and, although the sport remained strong in the area, it didn't retain the same influence as it once did.

Before the formation of the British League in 1965, the Heathens had won the 1961 and 1963 Provincial League Knockout Cup, but had yet to win a league title. Riders like Alan Hunt, Harry Bastable and Ivor Brown were their big stars, and they were followed by Bernt Persson and John Boulger, who spearheaded the charge for Cradley in the late 1960s and early 1970s. The turning point for Cradley's fortunes came in 1977 when Dan McCormick took over the running of the club.

McCormick set about giving the unfashionable team a new image. Up until this point the club was known as Cradley United, but he changed the nickname to a more aggressive 'Heathens' – no doubt inspired by a useful play on words. This image was portrayed on their race jackets as a barbarian character and would later be seen wielding a hammer. The face of the barbarian was eventually dropped in favour of just a hand holding the hammer. This image was particularly appropriate because of the area's industrial heritage. Dudley was considered to be the 'Queen of the Black Country', but other towns in the region were characterised by the phrase 'Red by Night, Black by Day', due to the number of foundries, lime kilns, collieries and other similar places of industry.

McCormick's first major signing was that of 1974 World Champion Anders Michanek. However, his contract was terminated in mid-July when he failed to turn up for a match at Leicester. Nonetheless, this proved that the burly Scot McCormick was eager to bring success to the Black Country side.

In 1978 he signed American Bruce Penhall and almost overnight the Cradley team were transformed from also-rans into potential winners. Penhall was a massive hit, his film star looks combined with a talent for riding a speedway bike were the ingredients that made him the club's first World Champion. It was his success that set up a unique link between Cradley and the Californian riders – Bobby Schwartz would follow in 1979 and then Lance King in 1983. Other star riders such as Erik Gundersen, Phil Collins, Alan Graheme, Simon Cross and Jan O. Pedersen all became exciting performers which gave the Heathens' fans riders to be proud of. But more importantly, silverware began to gather dust on the club's sideboard when they won their first league title in 1981 and were known as the Knockout Cup Kings during the 1980s.

When Billy appeared for Cradley the club was still in a state of shock following the near fatal accident of one of their favourite sons. But the sport as a whole was also in the doldrums. The magic of the Wembley World Finals had gone forever and there was indecision at all levels of the sport – costs were rising and crowds were falling.

Gundersen's accident seemed to plunge the sport into a deep depression and there were many who felt that the good times were well and truly behind them. Even the prospect of the World Final being staged at Bradford that year didn't seem to lift the gloom. Speedway racing in England was a wounded animal, and its organisers seemed to be content just to let it lick its wounds and feel sorry for itself.

When I arrived everyone was talking about the good old days, and that pissed me off. But it didn't worry me because I thought that the sport would come back, and I was pretty determined to do what I could to help it come back – and I think it has to a certain extent. It wasn't my fault that I had arrived in the wrong era and I just dealt with it. I just blew it off, I used to stick up for the sport I loved and I used to tell people that it would come back when they used to moan about it. I would see certain things that could have been improved – and still do – but you have to be careful with what you say and how much criticism you give, because that team is employing you.

Billy and Greg Hancock stayed with the recovering Erik and his wife Helle Gundersen at their home in Austrey, near Tamworth. It was an excellent move for all concerned as the young Americans would have access to advice, help and good workshop facilities, while for Erik it helped fill the hole that was left when he realised that he couldn't race again. In his book *My Two Lives*, Erik revealed that he enjoyed having them charging around the place.

'The sound of them pottering away in the workshop made me happy. And when I've gone out there and watched them taking a carburettor apart, I still feel part of the life I love. So, in the end who cares if my phone bill has trebled? I haven't found out if Billy and Greg still believe calls across the Atlantic are merely local.'

Erik's wife, Helle, later agreed that having the two young Californians made a big difference to their lives: 'When I look back, it was the right guys at the right time,' she said. 'It kept us busy and we were still in speedway because of them – but they were both nice guys. I look back and thank God that did happen. It really did help us. They were sent from heaven in many ways, and it helped ease us into the next phase.'

'He [Billy] was an unspoilt kid, and he was so easy to get along with,' Erik later recalled. 'Everything was so exciting to him and he had an attitude like a kid. I really liked that and I saw a bit of myself in him – the way he went about everything and he had an excitement within him which I liked.'

To come over and live with him was something that I could never ever replace. They were valuable years when you need to do the right thing and for someone to be there and just guide you. It was the little things that people in England took for granted that made all the difference, like giving you directions to Joe Hughes International. Because I came from California I knew nothing. Just driving on the other side of the road was a big dilemma. I hated it at the time, it's no problem now but I found it very difficult. It was so intimidating.

I got to see the other side of the sport too because Erik was recovering from his accident that he had at Bradford. I saw a lot of his physio he had at Pinderfields and in Sweden. It was hard for him and quite sad to see such a great rider and a really great guy in such discomfort. We had a lot of fun living with the Gundersens, and we were always having parties and stuff. Tommy Knudsen would come over, and John Jorgensen and Peter Ravn, and we'd have a big party. They were really fun times. And Erik was getting back on his feet after his accident, and mentally he was getting stronger too.

It was a good set-up for a young kid because I had the right people around me like Eddie Bull, Erik, and Joe Hughes wasn't far away for spares and Morgan Hughes – Joe's son – was helping me too. Towards the end of the year, I knew what I wanted and I knew that I had to organise myself if was going to succeed.

Helle did all the cooking and we were eating well. We weren't eating out, we were eating home-cooked meals. It was breakfast, lunch and dinner. As I came from California I just used to go to a fast food outlet called Taco Bell, but at the Gundersens it was home-cooked pasta, meats and vegetables. I remember Helle getting really frustrated with me because I hated peas and I would never eat them. She liked peas and she would have peas and carrots with every meal, but I didn't want them. But now I like peas, and she can't believe it and she says: 'After all that, now you eat peas!' I never ate peas or mushrooms because they just looked disgusting, but now I like them. When I first arrived I thought the food over there in England was like dog shit! I hated the food over there.

There were McDonald's but not to the extent that we had in America. Fast food is huge in America and that is why there is such a problem with obesity. I remember eating burgers in England and they were horrible. After a meeting at Swindon there was just nowhere to eat and we used to stop at a place which was like a truck stop, but it was more like a Portakabin/trailer. And if you got a burger off that it was rancid, so I was lucky to have Helle.

To me all the food seemed bland. It was just meat and potatoes, no sauces, and I like my sauces. And salads without salad dressing, I mean how the hell do you eat salads with no salad dressing? To me it was just bland, and it was a big eye-opener and a culture shock. For the first five years I would get very, very homesick.

I missed the summertime at home – and even now I still do – because you wear shorts for nine months of the year in California. But in England it was often wet, and there were so many overcast, cloudy and miserable days, and it was cold. I remember years later I raced in an indoor ice meeting at Telford during the off season, and I had never been so cold. It was in February and it had been snowing and boy it was cold. I couldn't wait to get back to the sunshine at home. Overall England was a lot different in many aspects.

Billy Hamill made his debut for Cradley on Saturday 17 March 1990, in a challenge match at Dudley Wood against King's Lynn. His team-mates at Cradley were Jan O. Pedersen, Simon Cross, Greg, Gert Handberg, Alan Graheme and Mark Robinson.

He scored four third places for 4 points as the Heathens started the season with a home defeat at the hands of King's Lynn, 46-44. Seven days later, Billy won his first British League race while on his way to a 6-point score in a Gold Cup match against Bradford at Dudley Wood. He won heat 5 defeating Andy Smith, team-mate Alan Graheme and Paul Thorp, but once again the Heathens lost the encounter 47-41.

It wasn't an ideal way to begin the season, but team manager Colin Pratt wasn't worried as it was early days. The first opportunity for the club to win some silverware came in the Premiership. This was an early season competition that brought together the previous season's League Champions, Oxford, and the Knockout Cup winners, Cradley. It was a two-legged affair with a meeting taking place at each track, and the winners would be determined by the aggregate scores over the two legs.

Oxford was led by Hans Nielsen and the Heathens held the Cheetahs to a 45-45 draw at their track at Cowley. This meant that they just had to win the return match the following night to win the first piece of silverware of the new campaign.

In a tightly contested match, Cradley won 50-40 and Billy scored a hard-earned 9 points that included a memorable victory over Oxford's Martin Dugard.

Morgan Hughes helped me toward the end of 1990 and Darren Boocock helped out and other people like that when I was learning the ropes. I was just getting my bikes running with Eddie Bull who was tuning my engines. I was living with Erik, and all my ducks were in a row off the track. I had good machinery and I was doing the right things in the workshop. I was organised, and I was getting more and more confident. I turned a corner in that meeting against Oxford, when Martin Dugard passed me and I passed him back. We had a great duel and I passed him on the last bend of the last lap, and the crowd just went crazy and I was really pumped up. Dugard was a hotshot then because he was riding with Hans (Nielsen) and he was one of the most promising riders. That was the turning point, and on that particular night I got more confident and I felt that I could do well.

It was also a turning point for Cradley too, as they began to run into some form. They did the double over Coventry and also defeated Wolverhampton and secured a draw at their track. In the end though, they were narrowly beaten to an appearance in the Gold Cup Final by finishing second behind Bradford in the northern section of the mini league.

Hamill settled quickly into British League racing and scored 10 points in the club's defeat of Wolves, and then followed that with a paid 13 in a league match against Reading which they also won 52-38. His form had not gone unnoticed and he was invited to compete in the Peter Craven Memorial Championship at Belle Vue the next day.

Craven was England's double World Champion who was tragically killed in a track crash in 1963. Therefore, there was some prestige attached to winning the trophy and it often attracted a field of riders that were worthy of Craven's memory. Billy's opponents included the defending champion Shawn Moran, his brother Kelly, Simon Cross, Neil Collins, Paul Thorp, Peter Ravn, Gary Hicks and Greg too.

I had no idea who Peter Craven was and I had never heard of him. I didn't realise how prestigious an event it was. The only international meeting that I knew was big was the Golden Hammer at Cradley. I didn't know any better and I just thought I'd go and if I won I won.

I didn't sleep the night before because I was up all night in the workshop just getting ready. It was a Sunday meeting and I had been racing at Cradley the night before. I was so tired because I didn't get a wink of sleep because I was pretty excited to be racing against riders like the Morans, Peter Ravn, Collins and all these guys. At that point I had never ridden at Belle Vue before. I discovered that, with the tight turns, it was like racing on a track at home and after I won my first race I thought that the place was cool. I found myself in a run-off for the title with Shawn Moran and Neil Collins, and I thought that if I could beat Shawn that would be cool. We all finished with 12 points and suddenly it was there to be won.

I made the start on Shawn and he was an awesome gater at that time. I hadn't honed my gating skills at that point – I was pretty terrible really. I won the majority of my races from the back. So to beat him out of the start was great, and I remember thinking, 'I'm here, its here for the taking, its wide open and it's yours', and I won. That was a good achievement for me at the time.

If there were any doubts about the potential or the talent of Billy Hamill, that result signalled to the international world that the Bullet was in Europe and he was here to win races and trophies. As the season progressed he became a popular choice as a guest for some of the other clubs – especially the title-chasing Reading.

Although he was finding it strange to adapt to the different lifestyle and culture of England, staying with the Gundersens helped him a lot. But there was only so much that Erik and Helle could do. Having Greg living there as well, plus the added bonus that he had already experienced one season in England, helped him to cope with his new environment and lifestyle. As a stranger it's not easy finding your way round England, especially when some of the venues are situated some way away from the towns and cities. Driving on the other side of the road, combined with the different laws governing road travel in Britain, was something that he found hard to get used to.

I remember that I spun out when I was driving along the M6 motorway. Greg Hancock was in the left-hand lane and he was motoring in this transit van, but the van didn't have any brake lights. Greg just carved out into the next lane and I was right behind him in a small Ford Escort van. We were going to Cradley and Lance King was with me and I told him before we left that I wouldn't ride with me because I was so dangerous, but he just said, 'Oh you'll be all right.' So he jumped in alongside me and he was drinking a beer.

In California you can just pass left and right, there is no rule saying you can only pass on the right like there is in England. We were just carving through traffic and I was just trying to keep up with Greg in this little Escort van. We were cruising along the M6 at about 80mph and Greg pulled out, but all of a sudden there's this car in front of me doing 30mph! And we're in the slow lane at 80! So I just slammed on the brakes, but the van wasn't in the best of conditions, so when I hit the brakes one side grabbed harder than the other and it just put me in a spin! We were spinning along the M6 and this big truck just went by – whoosh – and it just missed us by inches. I was shaking so badly and we were both scared but Lance just said: 'Shit, I didn't even spill my beer!' I was so shook up and shaking so much that I couldn't drive. Lance drove the rest of the way to Cradley.

Greg carried on and we didn't see him until we got to the stadium at Cradley. When we arrived he said: 'Where have you been?' Well I didn't want to say anything because I didn't want Prattie to know that I had just wiped out because Cradley had given us those vans, so I just said: 'Oh we were behind you', etc.

After that I didn't want to drive in England and I avoided getting behind the wheel as much as I could. It was my fault, but it really did scare the hell out of me.

On another occasion I went to Bradford and Erik came up with me, but Helle was meeting him up there because she was staying with the Boocock family. After the meeting I was in the bar, and Erik was travelling back with Helle. They asked me if I wanted to follow them, but I said, 'No, I'll be fine.'

But I wasn't.

I was close to Junction 11 on the M42, but I wasn't sure which one I had to get off at. I knew Tamworth so I figured it was either one up or one down, but I couldn't remember although I knew it was the next one — I didn't know the number. The services were not there at that time. So I passed Tamworth and I went to Junction 10, and I thought it must be the next one which was Junction 9 for Sutton Coldfield and the A38. When I got there I thought it was the other way then. By this time it was 12-1 o'clock in the morning and I just ran out of gas. I stopped in between Junction 10 and 11.

It was a dark, cold night and I believed that a cop would be along any minute. So I waited for an hour, but I was really cold because I couldn't turn the heater on or anything because I couldn't start the car. I got out to have a look around to see where I was, but I couldn't see anything to give me any idea. I saw the cops passing me while I was stationary and I thought one would stop eventually to check if I was okay or to see if I needed any assistance. But they just kept on patrolling by and none of them stopped. There were no mobile phones much in those days and I couldn't see a pay phone, and it was so late that I didn't want to wake everyone up because I felt sure that a patrol car would stop and help me out.

You always hear that story that if you piss into the gas tank you can get a few extra miles, so I thought I'd try it! So there I was, 2 a.m. in the morning, stood pissing in the fuel tank in a vain attempt to get home... but it didn't work. I was freezing cold and tired, and I was wearing a big coat so I just wrapped it up around my legs and over my head and tried to get some sleep.

Finally, at about 4 in the morning a cop was pounding on the window, 'What are you doing? You can't sleep in your car on the side of the motorway.' And I was like: 'Well where have you been? I've been here for five hours and finally someone pulls over!' I thought there should have been someone there within an hour, and here they were screaming at me when I had been waiting for them for hours and watching them passing me by! These two policemen were yelling at me and I just told them that I ran out of gas. They asked me all kinds of questions like where I'd been, where I was going, and all that kind of thing. Eventually they called the Gundersens and Helle answered the phone, and they said that they had Billy Hamill there and he had run out of petrol. She was more like a mom and she was worried because I hadn't come home yet, so she was up worrying about me.

Once I got talking to the policemen I discovered that they were Coventry fans. Greg came to my rescue and I could see him on the other side of the motor-

way as he passed by to get to me. He had to go to the next junction, turn around, and then come back on the other side to get to me with the gas can.

Where I had broken down was in between 10 and 11, and Austrey, which was where Erik's house was, was about a mile away from the M42 and I could have walked across the field to his house! I had no idea. If I could have seen where I was I would have walked across the field and I would have been in Austrey. I couldn't believe it when I realised, so I had all that trouble and I was only a mile away from home. I was quite embarrassed to be the cause of getting everyone up, but Erik and Helle were really good about it.

Erik would later recall another incident that illustrated how thoughtful and conscientious Billy could be.

'I remember a time when we'd been away in Sweden or somewhere, and on the way back from Birmingham Airport Billy called us on the mobile and you could just hear that something was wrong. We had this wooden table in the kitchen, really light wood, and he had bought an Indian curry and put a takeaway bag on that table. I've never heard him so worried in my life, and we were saying, 'Oh no Billy, you haven't done that!' We just took it outside, sanded it down, no problem.'

The English sense of humour is also somewhat different to that of the Americans, and they sometimes have a little joke at the expense of their inexperienced team-mate.

England, Scotland and Wales are part of the island known as the United Kingdom of Great Britain. Although all three countries are recognised as separate nations, they all come under the UK banner and it is only in recent years that some of the power has been shifted away from Westminster in London to parliaments in Scotland and Wales. Therefore, one can pass between the three countries without any immigration or passport controls.

However, when Billy was asked to race at Edinburgh his fellow riders convinced him that he needed to take his passport because Scotland was a separate nation. He didn't know any different so he took his passport along! Naturally this caused a lot of amusement among his companions. Colin Pratt didn't let this go unnoticed and he presented Billy with a Scottish passport on the centre green at Cradley – just in case.

Billy Hamill was riding very well and in June he travelled back to America to ride in the American Final of the World Championship.

Shortly before leaving he defeated the reigning World Champion Hans Nielsen at Dudley Wood.

Only the top four would qualify for the next stage which meant that there was some serious cut-throat racing on the track. Billy had a big crash with Hancock and Correy, the full repurcussions of which would not be felt until later. At the end of the programmed races, Billy Hamill had qualified with a splendid all-action display to finish on 18 points. Furthermore, he found himself in a run-off for the title as well. He was in a four-man run-off where he met Shawn Moran, Rick Miller and his old rival and team-mate, Greg Hancock.

But the run-off ended in disaster for Greg and for Cradley. He crashed heavily and broke his right arm which put a downer on the whole night. Shawn won the rerun with Hamill in second and Miller taking third. But Billy was quoted by one journalist as saying: 'No matter what I do in the World Championship, I'll do it for Greg.'

The next round was the Overseas Final at Coventry where the American riders would join riders from Britain, Australia and New Zealand who were all chasing a top nine finish to qualify for the next stage. Predictably, Greg had to withdraw because of his broken arm, and his place was taken in the line-up by Ronnie Correy. But it wasn't a happy afternoon for Billy, who found the competition too hot and scored just 4 points and was eliminated from the World Championship.

I thought I was going to be World Champion that year. I believed in myself that much; that was what I was here for and that was what I wanted to achieve. So going out at the Overseas Final was devastating for me. I couldn't believe it – I just rode awful, like an idiot. But I was out of my depth and I wasn't ready, but I didn't realise it at that time. It showed too, because it was a big mental thing for me even in 1990.

The following year it was held at Bradford and it was a big mental thing for me then too. It was like, 'Can I get over this hump, can I get past the Overseas Final? Can I make a World Final?' It was a major thing and I wondered if I could do it at that point. That fear of not being able to accomplish what I wanted was a big motivator for me. But I couldn't let it get the best of me, I had to calm myself down and relax and do my job.

However, the Overseas disappointment was followed by an injury blow. The Cradley Heath doctor ordered Billy to rest after his knee ligaments became so painful he couldn't carry on anymore. It was the latest injury setback for the Heathens, whose season had experienced another earth-shattering shock when Simon Cross sustained a serious back injury in a crash during the World Pairs Final.

The injury to my knee ligaments actually happened before I came to England. I had been racing in Australia and I did well. There was a Spring Classic race at Long Beach, and it was meant to be my farewell race before I went to Europe to compete. I was pumped up because I had already been on the big tracks in Australia and I looked at Long Beach as a race that would be a good build-up for going to England. I had only ridden at Long Beach once or twice because they only held the top races there like the American Final or the World Team Cup Finals.

I had a good engine that worked in Australia, so I was expecting to do well. But there was a hole in the track going into turn three and I just caught my left leg in it. I nearly kicked myself in the back of the head! When I put my foot down I just got it stuck in this hole. But I couldn't let it affect me because I was on my way to England a week later.

Eventually it settled down and it didn't really give me any aggravation. But when I went to the American Final that was held at Long Beach, I had a crash with Greg [Hancock] and Ronnie [Correy]. We tangled going into the bend and it was basically just assholes and elbows. I got way out of shape and went flying through the fence feet first. I hurt my knee and it was like, 'Ouch, my knee's a bit sore and my elbow, but it'll be all right.'

I raced at San Bernardino the following Wednesday and it didn't give me any problems at all, and I thought, 'Cool, it'll be all right.' But when I returned to England I kept having problems with my left knee. It would be all right one minute, but the next minute it would be going in the other direction. My ligaments were torn and I had to babysit it. I was thinking, 'Okay, concentrate, go easy on it, don't hurt the knee and I can get through this – it'll be okay.' But in the end it was just too much. I was nearly in tears with the pain. It was so inflamed, my ligaments were torn and it was basically ripping my kneecap out of its socket and it would pop out! It would be all right in one race and then I would do something weird on a bike, or catch some dirt on the track or something and that would set it off and it was just popping out. I think I rode with it for about two months and I just tried to get through it by thinking that it would be all right.

In the end I was in that much pain that when I came in from a race I was in tears. I think it was at Cradley and I just said to Prattie [Colin Pratt]: 'I can't ride anymore, I can't handle it.' And I was devastated that I was injured. So I was ordered to rest, and they put it in a cast. Luckily we had Doctor Terry Pinfold who was the Track Doctor at Cradley and also ran Russell Halls A&E. He has been involved with all the Cradley team at one point or another. He said that I had to take three weeks off and when I did ride I had to get a brace. And I needed physio too, and he put me in touch with Droitwich knee clinic, which is where I go to this day for any injuries. There is a guy there called Jim Williams who has helped me out with numerous injuries over the years.

Bobby Schwartz helped me to get a sponsorship from CTI Knee Braces. To this day I have to wear a knee brace every time I ride. If I don't, the knee will just blow out. A lot of riders wear them now, but back then it was a new thing. The inside ligaments go on your left leg because of the force from the track or whatever. Your foot is being dragged back at an angle to your leg, but your leg is still there and eventually the ligament just goes. If the track is mega slick then it's no big deal. But I can't ride without it — there's no way.

However, Christina came to stay with him and her presence helped a lot with the feelings of homesickness that Billy was experiencing.

She stayed with me at the Gundersen's for two months, and Helle was dreading it because she didn't know what a girl from California was going to be like. But they got along really well, and Christina has a pretty magnetic personality so she can get along with most people. She was only going to stay for a couple of weeks, but ended up staying for two months.

Christina came back with me after the American Final and Greg had broken his arm in that meeting. When we flew back in, I realised that Greg had the house keys and Erik and Helle had gone. We had been up a long time, we were tired and it was her first time in England, so I dropped by Eddie Bull's to get the house keys.

I decided we would go to McDonalds and get something to eat, and then we could rest. We went to McDonalds and I ended up parking behind a Woolworth's store which was basically no parking except for employees. It was a weekend and there was a nightclub nearby. When we came out from McDonalds my van was boxed in — totally boxed in and there was no way that I was going to get out. I had no idea who these cars belonged to or anything and I wondered what I could do.

There was a tiny gap but I needed a little more room, so I tried to pick up the cars and bounce them along and try and get a little bit more space. The van was due to go into the body shop the following week. Even after trying to bounce the cars around I still didn't have enough room to get out so in the end I just stood on the accelerator pedal and just gassed it! I drove right through the cars and buckled both sides of the van. And that was Christina's first night in England!

Christina also found the local Black Country accent difficult to understand at first, and also noticed how seriously the fans in England took their sport.

'I was sitting in the van, because you could watch the races from the van at Cradley, and one of the St John Ambulance guys came up to the van and started talking to me,' she recalled. 'But I couldn't understand the thick Black Country accent, and I said: "Excuse me?" And he repeated it, but I still couldn't understand him and I said: "Excuse me?" In the end I said to him, "I'm so sorry, I just cannot understand a word you are saying." He just looked at me and walked away and I could see that he was so fed up with me. But I just couldn't understand a word he said. He just gave up on me and walked away.

'It was so different, because in Southern California they don't even keep a programme at speedway, but in England everyone had their programmes and they were filling them in and keeping score.'

As if it wasn't bad enough that both Hancock and Cross were injured, Jan O. Pedersen also broke his arm which ended his hopes of riding in the 1990 World Final. Billy made a successful return and for the remainder of the season Cradley could only field four regular team members: Hamill, Gert Handberg, Alan Graheme and Mark Robinson. It was another year that was wrecked by injury.

Hamill's form had attracted the attention of the American team selector John Scott. Ronnie Correy had been struggling a little and it was decided that Billy should take his place. He would join the Moran brothers, Sam Ermolenko and Rick Miller in the team at Pardubice, Czechoslovakia where they would meet England, Denmark and Czechoslovakia. It would be Billy's first appearance for the USA and also his first trip into Eastern Europe – and it would be a very fruitful one too.

I thought it went remarkably well, and it was my first trip into the European continent and it wasn't that long since the Berlin Wall had come down. I travelled with Sam Ermolenko and Carl Blomfeldt in a Sherpa van and we stopped off at a track in Landshut, Germany and I saw Mitch Shirra ride – it was the first time that I saw him ride because he was banned from England for failing a drugs test. It was another experience and Sam raced and then we jumped in the van and headed for Pardubice for the final.

It was a late call and I don't think Ronnie Correy was very happy but what could I do? I wanted to do it and I was ready. I was quite excited because I was going to be part of the American team, which was another part of the dream. Mario Jirout was just a kid at the time – maybe twelve-thirteen years old – he was my mechanic, and later on we were racing against each other. He got stuck in and helped because I only had one bike and no mechanic with me.

Shawn and Kelly flew over but their leathers never arrived, and I remember watching Kelly practising in Sam's leathers. But after the practise, Kelly just got hammered and he was drinking Vodka with Roman Matousek's brother underneath in the workshops. We were out there doing the bikes, but after about an hour Kelly was just rat-assed. Rick Miller had a rent-a-car, and myself, Shawn and Rick jumped in the car to go back to the hotel, but we ended up doing four laps round the track. It was a front-wheel drive car, and Rick was driving with Shawn working the handbrake and I was in the back, and we were getting it sideways and sliding it. By 7 o'clock Kelly had passed out in the van. So we took him back to the hotel and we had dinner, but he missed it all.

He did really poorly in his first race because he was still hung-over and I remember John Scott asking him if he wanted to sit it out and put me in. But he wanted to have one more chance, and he ended up winning every race after that and pretty much won the meeting for us. That was vintage Kelly Moran really – he was awesome.

Billy made his first appearance in heat 11 as a replacement for the struggling Rick Miller. There was no shortage of encouragement as he threw his leg over his 500cc Godden speedway machine. USA skipper Shawn Moran was on hand to pass on any last-minute advice as he slipped his right wrist through the loop of his automatic cut-out cable, and then leaned down to turn on his fuel taps. His Bieffe crash helmet obscured his face from view, and only those who were close by could see the steely glare from his eyes that were in shadow behind a clear Perspex tear-off lens and his JT goggles.

This was Billy's first ride in a World Team Cup Championship, and his feelings were a mixture of excitement, determination and anxiety. He was excited to be given the opportunity to further his country's cause, and he was determined not to let his team-mates – who were heroes to the young Californian – down. But he was nervous as well; there was a big crowd inside the stadium, he was facing top-class opposition and the track had already attracted criticism from the more experienced riders because it was so slick – which meant that making a good start was very important.

Billy pulled on his handlebars, and he was pushed out of the pits and his engine roared into life. He coasted onto the track and into a tense atmosphere, as the scores were delicately balanced at England 19, Denmark 20, USA 18, and the hosts Czechoslovakia 9. Team manager John Scott gambled on putting the inexperienced Hamill in as a replacement for the struggling Miller, in an attempt to strengthen and maintain their challenge which had been established through some hard riding by the Moran brothers and Sam Ermolenko.

Clad in white leathers, Hamill arrived in grid three on the starting gate and began to dig at the shale surface with his boot in order to remove all the loose material and improve his chances of getting maximum grip from the start. His opponents were also carrying out similar preparations, but as the starting marshal signalled for the riders to take up their starting positions, Denmark's Hans Nielsen turned away on the pretence that he needed to clear his vision. This was largely a game of psychology that was prevalent at the start of most of the four-lap races during World Championship events such as this one. This exercise was predominately a piece of gamesmanship, and it was part of a rider's strategy of unsettling his rivals because at this level any sort of an advantage was a bonus.

Nielsen had already won three World Championships and was starting on the prime inside berth. Pardubice was a huge track as it was used to accommodate races with six riders for the prestigious Czech Golden Helmet. Therefore, the inside gates were seen as having a distinct advantage because starting from the outside meant that the rider simply had to have a good start to make up the extra yardage. In this race it was England's Marvyn Cox who was on the outside gate, with Billy alongside him in three, and the Czech reserve Zdenek Kalina in grid two between the Dane and the American. Nielsen's delaying tactics only added to the tension.

With all four riders lined up, the starting marshal stood to attention with all the precision and grace of a military officer, which was the signal for the referee – who was perched high up in the stands over-looking a panoramic view of the oval track – that all the riders were ready and he could, at his own discretion, release the tapes to begin the race. As the four bikes screamed in unison under the restrained protest of their high revs in anticipation of the tapes being released, the riders' heads collectively focused on the starting mechanism.

Billy's anticipation and excitement combined to focus his mind on the task ahead of him. From a standing clutch start he had shifted his weight to the front of the bike by crouching over the handlebars, because once he released that clutch lever the power of the bike would encourage the front wheel to paw the air. It was important that it didn't do this because he needed a good clean start to be on terms with the fast-starting Nielsen at the first bend.

Nielsen made the start but Hamill tucked in behind and scored 2 vital points. He then entered a fierce heat 15 where he was involved in a physical tussle with England's Simon Wigg.

I got a good gate from the inside of Wiggy but we clashed as we headed toward the first bend and then as we hit the first turn he hit me with a lot more force. But I stood my ground and there were a lot of elbows flying. He paid the price for that and finished last, but I was annoyed with myself because I should have won that race and beaten the Czech rider Zdenek Tesar, but he passed me and I was pissed off that I let that one slip.

Billy ran a last in his final outing, but the more experienced riders took control. Kelly Moran won his last race which meant that Sam Ermolenko just had to finish second to clinch America's first World Team Cup for eight years – which to the delight of the American camp he did. Hamill finished with 4 valuable points, and his presence in the side announced that the kids from California had arrived to put the Stars and Stripes back on top again.

That was an awesome experience, not only to travel with these guys who were seasoned veterans by this time in their careers, but I was just a kid and going to see a different country. The track certainly looked big at the time, big and flat, but it looked easy to ride.

Whenever the American team get together there is always a lot of cama-raderie and spirit and everybody chips in and helps one another, and I had plenty of help from everyone. All that was a big learning experience for me and I was inquisitive and I wanted to know. I was pitted alongside Shawn and Kelly and we were helping each other out and it was great.

I remember I went back to America and I went to the AMA awards to receive my gold medal and it was nice to be sitting in the same room as road racers like Kevin Schwantz and Wayne Rainey and the rest of them. I think at that point my family were proud of me. And I remember getting together at Christmas and having a big old party to celebrate my success in England.

Billy had finished the season with an FIM gold medal and a points average of 6.73 for Cradley. When you consider that it was his first season in Britain, that was an impressive figure. He had learned and achieved a lot and aimed to build on that for 1991 but, although he won the Premiership with Cradley, it hadn't been a good year for the Midlands club.

In fact it would be true to say that the discovery of Hamill was one of the few bright spots during a difficult season. Simon Cross was ruled out for most of 1991, but Heathens team manager Colin Pratt was determined to look to the future.

'We are starting to look towards bright new prospects like Billy and Greg. They are our future,' he said.

Pratt's faith in Billy and Greg would not be misplaced. In 1991 Jan O. Pedersen again led the team, but it was the two Americans and the young Dane Gert Handberg who were expected to come up with the goods – and they didn't disappoint.

The World Championship began in March for the Americans because the stadium at Long Beach was due to close by the time the traditional staging date in June came along. The loss of Long Beach and a track that was considered to be one of the best in the world was a big blow to Speedway in America.

They had the American Final in March and Tom Cirello of Cirello Racing had organised this sponsorship for me through Godden. They sent me this motor for the American Final and it came straight from the factory so I wasn't sure how it would be. Sometimes when they came straight from the factory like that they aren't as good without Eddie Bull doing some tuning on them.

But I didn't really have anything as good as that so I put it in. I just couldn't make a start on it to save my life, but it was a rocket ship – it was so fast that I was going round the outside of everyone in almost every race. I qualified using that engine and it was so quick. I scored 10 points and they had increased the number of qualifying spots from four to five and I made it in fifth place.

I came to England with it and I think I did 10-12 meetings on it before I had it serviced and that was way too long for an engine really, but it was so fast. But when I got it back it just didn't feel the same and it wasn't as quick. Then I had another one from Eddie Bull and that one was even better and that was the one that I used in Rovno for the World Championship Semi-Final. If there were any questions then Don Godden was there to be asked, but we took the engines and did what we had to do. I never had a falling out with Don or anything. I guess I kept my distance because I was riding the bikes, and that was my job.

I never had a problem with Don and they sponsored me with a couple of engines. Eddie Bull tuned them and they were good engines. Don was an intimidating kind of guy, and I heard all the stories about the Shawn Moran deal that was pretty public – but I had never had a problem with him. I heard all about how he could be; that he could be very forceful with his opinions and beliefs, and he was. He was not afraid to voice his opinion and he was outspoken and opinionated. But Eddie did all the tuning and servicing, so I didn't really need that much help from him.

Billy started off his second season in Britain in splendid form. The Godden engines certainly seemed to suit his style of riding at that time, and he established himself as a heat leader for Cradley. However, if his commitment and will to win was never in question during a race, it was his speed from the gate that was restricting his scores. Later he would come to realise that he needed to sharpen up his starting technique if he wanted to achieve his goals.

It was no surprise that he returned in 1991 and showed considerable improvement. At the end of 1990 he was returning some very impressive scores, but more importantly he had established a team behind him that would make all the difference in 1991.

His tuner was Eddie Bull, who had worked his mechanical magic over machines ridden by Cradley's World Champions Penhall and Gundersen, and that experience was just what Billy needed to maintain his climb up the international ladder. His mechanic was Morgan Hughes, who was the son of Joe Hughes, who ran a very successful speedway accessories business. Although Morgan was younger than

Billy, he had been around speedway racing for most of his life. With Godden engines beneath him, Hamill was able to race to regular double-figure scores.

Sometimes the second season in Britain can be the hardest for foreign riders, as there is more pressure on them to continue their progress. Mostly a new rider is unknown in Britain when he arrives, so if he has a good night then that's excellent, but if he has a bad night it's put down to a lack of experience. But during their second spell, their team expects them to deliver the goods and build on the first year, as they have been to most of the tracks and should know what to expect.

Gary Hicks was a good example of this. He made a brilliant start to his British career in 1989 with Belle Vue, but in 1990 he suffered a nightmare season with King's Lynn when it was hoped that he would play a heat leader's role. His season was plagued by injuries and his talent was lost to the international scene as he never raced for a British club again. Former Finland international Veijo Toureniemi was another rider who lit up the track at Eastbourne during a difficult year in 1980, but when he signed for Swindon in 1981 he couldn't put a wheel right and was sacked.

For the Bullet, however, there were no such problems and he continued with his progression. Through Erik Gundersen, he also signed to ride in the Swedish Elite League for Smederna (Eskilstuna) – whom he has stayed with throughout his career in Sweden.

I haven't ridden for anyone else in Sweden. Erik Gundersen set it up for me because he endorsed me. They rang me and asked if I would like to do a deal. So I signed for them. I've had a great relationship with them and they've always respected me and that's probably why I've stayed there all this time. A lot of the top riders like Shawn Moran, Kelvin Tatum, Hans Nielsen and all those sorts of guys were riding in Sweden and also Poland. Smederna gets the biggest crowds now on a regular basis. When I first started riding for them a crowd of 600 people was a good crowd, now we're getting 4,000 – so we're doing something right. It's a small town and at the time it was a new experience.

Sweden and Poland were opening their doors to foreign riders, and it wouldn't be long before Billy would be joining those riders and others like them by racing in three leagues during one season. This was the beginning of the nomadic speedway rider whose existence was a punishing schedule that consisted of race, airport, flight, sleep, airport, race, and so on. There was no time for pleasantries during the height of the season, and the best place to catch a word with one of them was at airport lounges. It meant early morning starts and late nights, and such a routine could only work with a good back-up team.

Luckily I learned to sleep well early on in my career and that was valuable because I spend anything from three to five nights a week away from my home. It's not easy and its hard being away from my family — especially when I had to spend three days in Poland for a rescheduled meeting after a rain-off.

The days of earning good money by just concentrating on racing in Britain and on the Continent at the weekends had long since passed into the dusty history of British Speedway. Now a rider had to ride in at least two leagues to earn enough money to earn a decent living and have enough left over to fund his racing programme.

For Billy to be able to take advantage of this he had to overcome his dislike of flying. He once told *Speedway Star* that if God had meant us to fly he would have given us wings.

My bad experiences on aeroplanes have given me more faith in the aircraft itself. I remember during one flight we did everything except go upside down, and I'm more comfortable now than I have ever been — but I wouldn't say I was that comfortable with it.

I remember Greg and I were flying into Gdansk and the plane was being violently blown around. It was getting worse and worse, the whole aircraft was shaking and shuddering and doing all sorts. Greg was making out like it was no big deal and saying that it was like a roller coaster ride at Disneyland or what-ever, but I was shit-scared. Basically he was talking out of his ass and I guess it was his way of dealing with it, but his comments weren't helping me and I told him to shut up!

I'm a very nervous passenger, but I am better now than I was. I had to deal with it if I wanted to pursue my racing career and I've overcome that fear and learnt to cope with it. It's part of my job — a necessary evil I think you would call it.

The 1991 World Final was set be staged at the Ullevi Stadium in Gothenburg, Sweden. In preparation for the final, Billy took advantage of an invitation to ride in an international open meeting at the track. But he aggravated his knee and was sidelined for a couple of weeks.

I caught my leg in a rut and at the same time the rear chain came off. It threw me and I twisted the knee the wrong way. I pulled out of the meeting, but not because of that but because I injured my ribs on the handlebars and I was having problems breathing.

Later in the night and the following morning, the knee got worse and I couldn't even walk on it. I saw a Swedish specialist who poked around the knee and told me that I needed surgery. My mind was in turmoil because it would have meant that I would certainly have been out of the World Championship.

When I got back to England I saw Terry Pinfold and they put me on machines and did some tests on my flexibility and the strength of the knee. They put the results into a graph form. The results weren't too bad and I was told to build up the muscles around the knee with swimming and resistance exercises. It wasn't a new injury as it was the same knee that I had problems with in 1990.

The local derby clashes between Cradley and Wolverhampton used to be some of the most volatile and competitive meetings in the country. As well as racing against each other in the league and cup fixtures, they also staged the Dudley-Wolves Challenge Trophy which was no less competitive. Whenever local pride was at stake, there was never any quarter given during these cut-throat encounters.

On 29 July the Heathens arrived at Wolverhampton for a league match. Led by Sam Ermolenko, who was riding high at the top of the league averages, Wolves were in tremendous form and were also top of the league table and chasing their first League Championship. Meanwhile Cradley were also getting into gear and were lying in second place.

There was even more at stake than just local pride. A victory for Cradley would really strike a hammer blow in their challenge for honours, while a defeat at the hands of the old enemy would be a setback for Wolves who were tightening their grip at the top. The best crowd of the season packed into Wolves' Monmore Green Stadium to witness the marauding Heathens do battle with a rampant Wolves team.

From the opening heat it was clear that the Wolverhampton riders were in no mood to let anything slip. Greg Hancock was the only heat winner for the Heathens during the first nine races. But the Wolves' riders were racing with all the aggression that is associated with that beast and was sending the Heathens, one by one, into the dust.

First of all, reserves Scott Smith and Mark Robinson hit the deck, and then Sam Ermolenko forced Hancock to shut off when he left him with no room and he had to bail out too. But then the Heathens riders were really rattled when their number one, Pedersen, was taken to hospital with a broken nose and concussion after he was shunted into the fence.

The stadium was very tense and the atmosphere explosive when Scott Smith was taken away on a stretcher. Sam Ermolenko fell while he was in pursuit of Gert Handberg and then Billy saw off a hard challenge from Sam's brother Charlie to bring Cradley within 5 points of the lead. Sam and Graham Jones restored a 7-point advantage in the next race, but the loss of Pedersen and Smith was too much for a battered and bruised Cradley side – a fact that did not go unnoticed by a fired-up Hamill.

My whole team were just being taken out left, right and centre by the Wolves team: Jan O., Scott Smith, Alan Graheme, there were only three riders in the Cradley team left. Sam was on the top of his game then. It was always going to be him and Ronnie Correy, and me and Greg in the last heat – the four Americans.

I was off gate four, Sam was off gate three, and then there was Greg and Ronnie. Sam just took me wide on the first bend and he just kept taking me and taking me. I was ahead of him but I just couldn't get enough speed to go around him, so he basically passed me. But as he went by, I grabbed his push bar and held onto it! He was in the lead and I was in second just holding onto him. He was looking round wondering what the hell was happening because he could feel that something, or someone, was holding him back, but he was towing me and my bike. He wasn't hanging about and I was almost getting ripped off my bike. The only thing I could compare it to was waterskiing. I remember thinking, 'I must keep my elbow bent', so that I wouldn't get yanked off the bike. Just as we were going into turn three I let go because I had to turn my bike. Well, he just picked up 20mph in the wrong spot and crashed into the fence. Needless to say he wasn't very happy!

I was pissed off with what had happened to my team-mates, and there I was almost in the fence and having to back off and I thought, 'Screw it' and grabbed

Sam's push bar. It wasn't premeditated or anything like that, it was just an opportunity and I remember thinking, 'What the hell am I doing?'

The referee never saw it because I was on the outside on the back straight so I didn't get excluded. The Wolves' fans saw it and I had pint glasses thrown at me, pens, boards, you name it, it was thrown at me. They never liked me much anyway because there was such a rivalry, and it was the beginning of a bad relationship! But it's always been like that, going back and forth, and it's been good for the sport. That rivalry has spilled over into the Coventry v. Wolves clashes now – a little bit – but not to the same degree. It was an illegal move, but if you don't get caught you're not cheating! Just kidding! They were just taking us out and Sam was involved in those incidents – it was ridiculous.

Christina recalled that this episode made the press, and Billy's mother telephoned and was upset that her son would do something like that. But speedway racing is an adrenalin-fuelled sport and sometimes, especially in the heat and the emotion of a local derby, sportsmen can do things that they are not proud of once the event is over.

At the beginning of the season Billy still lived with the Gundersens until they moved back to Denmark. The Danish legend continued to keep in touch through the telephone or the fax machine and his support was vital to the American.

Billy and Christina moved into a small thatched cottage but it wasn't quite the dream lifestyle that they hoped for.

The following year she came over and stayed with me in a little thatched cottage I rented. I thought it was great for about a month and then I started to get pissed off with it. I was too young and I wasn't ready for that and we went our separate ways – this was in July 1991. We broke up, but we kept in contact.

Billy had an opportunity to ride as reserve for America in the World Pairs Semi-Final at Pocking, but along with his fellow riders Jan O. Pedersen and Finland's Olli Tyrvainen, he was unable to take his place in the line-up because of a delay en route. They arrived ninety minutes after the statutory signing-in time and all three were excluded from riding. Hamill's absence could have made a big difference, as Sam Ermolenko was strangely off-form and the USA was eliminated.

Billy was also selected for his first appearance in the American Test team that faced England in a three-match Test series. By this time the series had lost some of the appeal that it had enjoyed during the eighties, but it was no less competitive. Unfortunately the Americans were hit by injuries and other problems and they lost the series 3-0. But Billy finished as top scorer and also top of the averages. With Ermolenko, Rick Miller and the Moran Brothers all unable to ride for one reason or another, it gave America's emerging stars an opportunity to shine – and they did so at both Swindon and Wolverhampton where their defeats were less than 10 points.

As the reigning World Champions, the USA were expected to do a lot better in the World Team Cup Final, but in Denmark's own backyard at Vojens they had to settle for bronze in a meeting that saw Billy score 9 points for his team.

The World Championship road resumed at Bradford for the Overseas Final and this time Billy overcame his nerves and qualified easily to finish in third place with 12 points – losing a run-off to Ermolenko for second while England's Kelvin Tatum lifted the trophy with 13 points.

For 1991 the traditional semi-final stages of the Intercontinental and Continental Finals were scrapped in favour of two semi-finals. Previously, the English, Americans and Scandinavians would ride in the Intercontinental Final, while the Eastern Bloc riders would appear in the Continental. Now they were all mixed up together and the thirty-two qualifiers for the semis would be drawn to ride at two venues: Abensberg in Germany, or Rovno in Russia. Needless to say, most of the qualifiers wanted Abensberg. However, Billy was drawn at Rovno – and of the four Americans that had qualified for the semis, he was the only one who was heading for Russia. A lone American in Russia in 1991 was not a pleasant thought.

I got booed big time by the crowd because America and Russia were not friends at that point and there was a lot of animosity. I had problems just getting my visa to get over there. Just going across the border in Poland was unbelievable. There was a 17-mile-long line of people trying to get in and get out, and it would take a couple of days for these people. We had an escort so that we didn't have to wait in this line and we all had to stay together. There was myself, Per Jonsson, Henka Gustafsson, Jimmy Nilsen, Mitch Shirra, and everybody had to meet near the border and we got a police escort to get across, but it still took us about a couple of hours.

I'll never forget it because there was a pit, like a hole in the ground, that we had to drive over so that they could check underneath the vehicles to make sure there wasn't anyone hiding underneath, or drugs, or whatever else they thought that we might be trying to smuggle across the border. This guy got it totally wrong and they were trying to pull his car out of there, and I remember wondering how they were going to do it. Once we got through all the checks we travelled through these villages and there were chickens running around on the side of the roads. It was very backward and a real eye-opener to see how the Russian people lived.

Each rider was assigned with an interpreter, which was basically a minder to keep an eye on what you were doing which was the Russian way – Communism was still coming through at that time. I had a lady translator and I couldn't even go to the bathroom without her knowing – it was ridiculous. We couldn't drink the water because you would get ill, and a couple of the guys did. Rob Woffinden came over with us and he boiled the water and had it in a pot noodle, but he was still ill even though he boiled the water. We had brought 15-20 gallons of water with us in the van, all our own food and a little stove. Morgan Hughes came with me and we met in Warsaw because I had been racing in Sweden and we just loaded up the van with all this. It was bizarre. I wouldn't eat anything other than my own food.

Furthermore, Rovno was only approximately 150 miles away from Chernobyl where they had that nuclear disaster. I remember my Mom saying to me, 'Don't eat any of the food', because she was worried about radiation. We traded with the locals and I brought over Levis jeans which was the kind of stuff that they didn't have. The government bought all their machinery and equipment, and we traded stuff like goggles and engines, and I traded a helmet for seven carburettors – they wanted anything that we had. They weren't bothered because the government would give them more equipment, but they just wanted the equipment that we had because we were the rich Western riders.

I also remember giving bubblegum to little kids and they were freaking out because they had never had bubblegum before. I thought that was bad that a ten-year-old kid had never had bubblegum because we take that for granted. There were armed guards at the track and if the kids got too close to the fence near the pits, they would just put the fear of God into them by chasing them off with a submachine gun. They were pointing these guns at these children and I thought it was disgusting. You could see how scared they were. It was pretty weird and they peeled Per Jonsson's stickers off his van.

After I was booed on the parade I felt as though I was in a hostile environment. With what I knew from growing up and hearing about Russia I was taught that they were the enemy – so there was hostility towards me. But I didn't let it get to me because I was there to do a job and get to my first World Final.

Billy produced a robust performance to qualify comfortably for his first World Final. A crowd of 20,000 people packed into the stadium as temperatures soared to 28 degrees – which was the hottest day in the Ukrainian city for eight years. After losing his first race to Roman Matousek, he smashed the Rovno track record by more than four seconds! He scored 12 points and won the meeting, which included a victory over the reigning World Champion Per Jonsson. It was the biggest win of his career to date, and it set him up nicely for his first World Final appearance.

In the end they were cheering for me because I won the semi-final. Everybody was very welcoming, but it was intimidating. The worst thing was the translators because they went everywhere and it was annoying. So we would try and ditch them by saying we were going to do one thing, but instead we would do something else just to get them away from us for a while. It was just to create some breathing space really. All the time we were there we always felt like we were being watched – even at the hotel. It didn't seem that they placed much value on life, and sometimes it feels that way in Poland too.

The track was heavy and deep, and a bit rutty. There was a huge crowd there and on parade they gave all the riders bread. It wasn't a loaf of bread as such, but like a brown bread that had just come out of the oven. I remember thinking, 'This is weird. Why the hell are they giving us bread?' But after the meeting, we had eaten all our food and I was so hungry that I ate the bread and it was the best bread that I had ever tasted. I don't know if it was because I was so hungry but it really was nice and Morgan and I ate the whole thing.

We were there just seven days before they overthrew their President, Mikhail Gorbachev. They got rid of us in a hurry, and I wonder how much of it was planned. As soon as the meeting was over we had a police escort to get us straight to the border, and we had to leave our roubles because we weren't allowed to take any of it out of the country. I remember they were saying to us after the racing, 'Come on, you guys have got to go', and it was a mad rush at their own request really. It took two to three hours to get across the border, and they searched all the vans with dogs.

The semi-final was completed in time for a military coup that saw the end of Mikhail Gorbachev's presidency, a period known as the Glasnost era. For a brief time it looked as though the military leaders would reinstall the Communist Party and reinstate the old ways. Tanks rolled toward Parliament, but Boris Yeltsin and the Russian people stood firm against the military.

The old Soviet Empire was finished before the year was out and eventually Yeltsin took over as the new President of Russia. The Western riders who raced at Rovno will never know how close they came to being involved in a major international incident. They say sport and politics should never mix and while they came close on that occasion, the sport's own bizarre politics came to the fore to ruin Billy's debut World Final in Sweden.

SVEMO [the Swedish Speedway Federation] *were flexing their muscles to try and give their riders an advantage. I had been through tech inspection at the American Final, the Overseas Final and the semi-final in Russia, but here I was at the World Final with the same bike and it failed the tech inspection because my muffler was too loud. It wasn't that you had to have an FIM muffler, you just had to reach a certain decibel level and keep it at a certain rpm to see how loud it was. Nobody's bike was passing the test, and I didn't know any better because all I knew was that my bike hadn't passed tech inspection. It was half an hour before my first World Final and my bike wasn't through tech inspection and, basically, I wasn't riding at that point.*

Some riders were putting wire brushes in the muffler just to kill the noise, and there was no way that they were going to race with a wire brush in their exhaust. They were doing ridiculous things and trying every trick in the book, but I didn't have a clue about that because it was my first World Final and I was inexperienced. I couldn't understand how I could fail inspection when I had passed all the other World Championship inspections. How could it be different?

To get my bike to pass I had to buy a Tolba muffler from a vintage bike that was on display, and it cost me around £100 — and mufflers used to cost about £50 in those days. I had a King make of silencer and they wouldn't let it pass, so I had to buy a Swedish muffler. I put it on my bike and it upset the whole set-up straight away. It was the biggest slug out there and it was all because of dirty politics. That's what I thought at the time and I still think that to this day. Luckily they have changed that rule.

You used to go to some countries — Sweden and Denmark in particular — that were known back then for being hard for machine examination. But now they have a standard inspection that everyone has to conform to. But the Swedes and the Danes used to put their interpretation of the rules into practice at that time and they could give their riders an advantage — which was ridiculous really. I had won the semi-final in Russia, I had beaten the reigning World Champion to win the Semi and I thought that I was going to be World Champion that year — I felt that I was ready for it. But my bike was so slow that I hit the tapes in one race because I knew it wasn't happening, so I was doing what I could just to try and get a few points. It was a horrible experience and I was very disappointed and I felt cheated by the organisation.

My Mom had come over to see me ride in my first World Final, and I felt that I was a contender because I was regularly beating the other riders that were in that final. So I was very pissed off about the whole thing. I just couldn't understand how it was that I had been to all these countries and my bike was fine. But when it came to the World Final it wasn't good enough. How could that happen? And everybody accepted it, they just seemed to shrug their shoulders and say that was how it was in Sweden and Denmark. At that point in time it was unfair. I didn't get any support and I asked the Swedish officials how could this happen, but the answer was: 'This is how it is in Sweden.' Basically you had to outsmart them by cheating with wire brushes and whatever else you could get your hands on. Now it's standardised and you run an FIM homologated muffler and you don't have to have a noise test as long as you have this muffler which is much better. I was very disappointed — it was all bullshit.

Billy's Cradley team-mate, Jan O. Pedersen of Denmark, won his first World Championship with an emphatic 15-point maximum. Tony Rickardsson finished second in his debut World Final and Hans Nielsen was third.

A disappointed Hamill finished down in twelfth place with 6 points that included the exclusion for the aforementioned starting offence. His first experience of the sport's biggest stage was blighted by speedway politics and inconsistency. But for the chaos that was inspired by bungling officials, he may well have made it onto the rostrum.

Nonetheless, 1991 had been a good year for the young American, but there was still a lot to learn and experience. Making a World Final was a major achievement, but there was still more to do if he wanted to be considered as among the world's best riders. It seems hard to believe, but as he packed away his leathers and prepared himself for a winter of sunshine in California, he had still to register a maximum in an official fixture in the British League.

However, it wasn't speedway racing that occupied his mind as he flew home – instead it was a certain brunette with a magnetic personality.

My Mom called me and told me that Christina had a boyfriend and I got jealous – and it pissed me off! So I made sure I called her and kept in contact during the remainder of the speedway season in Britain. When I went back home in the off-season we got back together.

Five

BETWEEN THE HAMMER AND THE ANVIL

It's hard to point the finger at where it all went wrong. I don't accept second best too well at all. There are a number of things in the background that were holding me back and I need to get back to basics.

Billy Hamill (1994)

Cradley Heath was determined to have an injury-free and successful season in 1992. They seemed to have all the ingredients: the reigning World Champion in Jan O. Pedersen, Simon Cross had returned on an artificially low average from his back injury, and they also had three brilliant prospects in Hamill, Hancock and Gert Handberg. Furthermore, with Scott Smith and Mark Robinson at reserve, it wasn't surprising that the Heathens were pre-season favourites to ride off into the sunset with most of the silverware.

The last time they won the league was in 1983, and they hadn't won the Knockout Cup since 1989 – a competition that they almost made their own during the eighties. Billy Hamill had settled in very well at Cradley. His style of racing and his passion for the sport seemed to register favourably with the Black Country fans and the feeling was mutual.

Coming from California it was such an experience because the people were different, the stadium was different and we were different. I think it was a very intimidating place to come to for the opposition because they had to drive in and out of the same gate that the supporters would come through. It would also be intimidating for the home riders too if you didn't have a good meeting. The noise that used to come out of the main grandstand was unbelievable. We had some characters like Simon Cross who, in my eyes, was one of the biggest char-acters in the sport even though he had fallen by the wayside a little. He never really recovered from the back injury he sustained in 1990. We were a good bunch of guys and the Cradley public were totally unique and they were Black Country people. They never wanted to go to Wolverhampton and they were hardcore; they lived it and they were doing every lap with you.

Because of the ties with Bruce and Bobby at Cradley there was some affec-tion for Cradley, and they had affection for Americans too because of their previ-ous associations. We fitted in quite well and we made a lot of friends. It was such a unique place in the way that the people were and it's still the same today. At least once a year, I try to visit the local pub that's situated near to where the stadium used to be and it's still the same. They lived for speedway and these people didn't have anything, and they used to save up all week to go and see the racing every Saturday – that was their entertainment. It was such a passion for them: sometimes that would stir good emotions and sometimes it would stir bad emotions.

I'll never forget the time when Wayne Garrett got into a fight with Neil Collins. I have it on video and if you don't look at the fight but you look at the crowd, you can see three or four girls who must be about thirteen or fourteen, and they're punching every punch that Bodge is punching, and they're punch-ing with him. The place was hard, but I fitted in quite nicely into that atmos-phere because the people were so real and so genuine. When I flipped over backwards I was the biggest asshole around, but the good outweighed the bad.

The track was pretty intimidating at times and it was narrow – especially going into turn three. We definitely had a home-track advantage, more so than somewhere like Coventry which is pretty fair for all. You would do a couple of races and as the track became slicker you would adjust your ignition, gearing and your wheelbase accordingly to make the bike hook up a little bit more. After intermission they would work on the track and, as a result, it could be grippier than when you first started. If you didn't pay attention then it could catch you out. On one occasion I didn't pay attention and in the first race after the interval I ended up riding the fence because I couldn't turn the bike. I went back into the pits and complained to Colin Pratt about it, but basically it was my fault. The track was getting slicker and slicker, so the guy had gone out there with the tractor and ripped it up. Prattie didn't say anything about it, he just assumed I knew. So I paid for it because of my carelessness.

Cradley has a special place in my heart, and because it was my first club in Europe, all my experiences that I had came from my time with Cradley. It's a credit to the people – the supporters – that Cradley Heath Speedway is still talked about. They have kept the name alive and if you go to Cardiff you'll still see a Heathens flag or two, even though the place has been closed since 1996.

'It was just bare bones,' recalled Christina. 'There was nothing fancy about Cradley at all. All the other places had nice bars and roofs over the toilets, but Cradley didn't even have a roof over the toilet! It was home and they liked it that way. If it had been fixed up it wouldn't have been Cradley – there was no place like Cradley at all.

'I remember Billy's mom going into the toilet – which was a portable loo – and there was all this graffiti on the wall about Billy like "Billy is God", and she was so excited that she took pictures of it all. But she didn't want me to see it because the girls were writing all this stuff about him on the wall.'

The rivalry between Cradley and Wolves was like no other local derby in the country. A Cradley-Wolves encounter would generate an atmosphere of such intensity that not only was it menacing, but it bubbled throughout the match like a kettle that was ready to boil over at any minute. Legend has it that Erik Gundersen once walked out onto the centre green and addressed the crowd over the radio microphone to calm it down. Only for the little Dane to then turn to the Heathens' supporters on his way back to the pits, and with his fists clenched and his arms raised he shouted at them: 'Come on!'

'I don't think there was anything like the rivalry between Cradley and Wolverhampton,' Christina stated. 'The supporters down on the terraces would shout "Kill them!" And they meant it! I used to sit there and think, "Oh my God, they can't mean it", but they did!'

That was the passion that the Cradley people had. The Wolves speedway team supported their football team, while Cradley probably supported West Bromwich Albion, so that came into it as well – I think it spilled over. It was already hot when I came over. I remember my first meeting against Wolves and I thought that it was really scary – brutal even. I remember wondering what the hell was going on and wondering why it was like that – it was frightening. It wasn't a meeting that you looked forward to, it was a meeting you wanted to get over with just so that you could get out in one piece.

Now it's Coventry-Wolverhampton but it's not nearly as bad. They don't have the bitter rivalry that we used to get between Wolves and Cradley. I remember when Sam Ermolenko was the reigning World Champion and he came to Dudley Wood and just slid off when he was in the lead, and the crowd just went ballistic – they were so happy! That's wrong really, but they were brutal.

When Swindon came to Cradley, Crossi took out Brian Karger big time, he just fenced him and the Robins fans went crazy. That got pretty tense because we had to race against them at their track in the evening. In those days we used to race against them on a bank holiday Monday morning and then we'd go to their place for the return in the evening. On the way there we got cut up by the Swindon Supporters' Club bus and they started throwing bottles and beer cans at us. So we retaliated with what we could and it was on! At Swindon we had to have a police escort to get out of the place after the meeting!

In 1992 Billy had a lot more responsibility and, on reflection, he admitted that he had taken on too much. However, Christina came over to England with him and they lived in a house in Clifton Campville. As an interior designer she didn't find the décor to her taste at all, but it was home for the British season and they made the most of it.

Times were hard as Billy was still only twenty-one and along with his then girlfriend they were both just learning the ropes. Interest rates on mortgages at this time were very high in Britain, and this put the squeeze on their finances. Furthermore, another recession had hit Britain's economy and, if it was at all possible, speedway racing in England was struggling even more.

Nonetheless, Billy continued registering double-figure scores both at home and away. On 25 April 1992, he scored his first full maximum as he swept to an unbeaten 15 points as the Heathens brushed aside Poole in the Knockout Cup 54-36. Cradley had made a promising start to the season, but the injury jinx struck again when Jan O. Pedersen – who was also celebrating his testimonial year – suffered a serious back injury that eventually brought the curtain down on his career. Incidentally, Pedersen was the third Cradley rider in four years to suffer spinal injuries – a very unpleasant record, but one that illustrated just how unlucky the club was.

Attention then turned to the American duo of Hamill and Hancock. Both had been riding well, but now Colin Pratt was beginning to look toward them for help to fill the gap left by Pedersen. Fortunately, as an ex-rider himself, Pratt was all too aware of the pressures and expectations that the riders were faced with and he was able to guide his young riders through the early stages of their careers and beyond.

He's helped me in every aspect of speedway. His biggest strength is his adminis-trative skills. If he says he's going to do it, then he does it. He's as straight as a die. That's why we've had such a good relationship and that's why I have so much respect for him.

There was controversy over the way the AMA determined the quali-fiers for the Overseas Final. The American Final was scheduled for Ventura, but it was scrapped due to costs and they decided to seed Sam Ermolenko, Hamill, Ronnie Correy, Rick Miller and reigning US National Champion, Mike Faria. The AMA seeded Faria ahead of the very worthy claims from both Greg Hancock and Bobby Ott.

Nonetheless, Billy was defeated by Faria in his first race at the Overseas Final and then finished last in his second outing. Another second place in the last race before the interval put him on 4 points and facing an uphill task to qualify. But then disaster struck in his third race in heat 13 which was anything but lucky for the Californian. While chasing Gary Havelock, his bike suddenly lurched skyward and he was sent flying into the air and fell heavily – just inches in front of the pursuing Martin Dugard and Jason Lyons. Dugard and Lyons did remarkably well to avoid the fallen American, but his World Championship hopes were over.

I can't really remember much about the crash. I was chasing Gary Havelock and I was going to make an attempt to pass him when I locked up and just lost it. I was told that it was pretty spectacular. I broke my left wrist and dislocated my shoulder.

The year before I had been second in the Overseas Final, and here I was in Coventry and I was trying way too hard. I was racing that much harder to make up for the fact that I didn't have the funds available to re-invest in my equipment like I wanted to. I was under a lot of pressure from a financial standpoint, and I couldn't sleep from the worry. That crash came at just the wrong time really because I couldn't ride for six weeks.

'We had no money and Billy had bought this house where everything was painted Orange and Avocado Green – it was horrible,' Christina recalled. 'We were on our own, we had nothing. We would go out once a week, and then he broke his collarbone and a wrist at the same time and we had no money at all. He rented the movie *Days of Thunder* because he was so bored. He then decided to get tips from the movie so that he could win the video game. We missed home a lot then, it was really hard – times were tough.'

The next three years were not the easiest for Billy. He had to take stock and evaluate his career on several occasions as he strived to be competitive and make some money. He would draw on his own strength of character and family values – especially the influence of his grandfather. Gay Hamill believes that Keith Stucki has had a big effect on her son's outlook and approach to life – probably more than he realises.

Having spent some time in his company I realised that his grandfather's strength and upbringing has had a bearing on him. Keith is a self-made man and his strong spirit has rubbed off on his grandson. However, Christina's constant support helped them both come through this difficult period and, but for each other, it seems that they could well have packed their bags and returned to the USA for good.

Billy did not ride for Smederna in Sweden that year, but he did make his first appearance in the Polish League for Rybnik. Racing in Poland is a very different experience and, aside from the dubious politics, the financial rewards can make it worthwhile.

Although I have many good friends in Poland, like Jacek and Thomas, it is very corrupt. I wouldn't say that it is all corrupt, but there is more in Poland than what I have been exposed to elsewhere — especially with people trying to buy races for a lot of money. I don't know how often it goes on because a lot of riders won't take to it. But the opportunity is there for a rider to throw a race and get paid for doing so. But I can assure you that the foreign riders are totally against such a thing.

When I first went over there the reaction I received was very positive. Because they didn't have the opportunities, they always wanted to buy everything we had. And they would give you whatever you wanted, but they're not like that now.

At first it was a lot easier to get double-figure scores because of our superior equipment and, if you didn't, well, you were a piece of shit really. That was typical of Poland because that's what they expected. The Polish League is fun, but the rest that goes with it is not fun. The language barrier is there and sometimes that's a blessing when it comes down to the politics which plays a large role in the sport, as it enables me to keep all that at arm's length. Their way of thinking is different to my way of thinking or the rest of Western Europe. Corruption and scandal is almost a part of life for them — it's almost as if they have to rip someone off. If you don't, you're not trying.

One of the scariest things that I have experienced is the riders' parades over there. They throw stuff at the opposing riders like stones, rocks and fireworks and firecrackers. I remember at Gorzow one time, we were on parade and I was riding for the club with Piotr Swist, and someone threw one of those firecrackers and it hit Piotr on the head and his hair caught fire! But he didn't have a clue, and I was stood behind him patting his head trying to put the flames out and he looked around at me and asked:

'What are you doing?'

'Your hair's on fire!'

And he had a bald patch on the back of his head!

Another time we had won a race — a last-heat decider — and the crowd invaded the track and blockaded me. I was picked up and thrown into the air for the bumps. There were so many people, about a hundred or so, and my steel shoe just whacked someone as they were throwing me up into the air, and it caught one guy and just split his forehead. At the time I felt it make contact, so I tried to keep my leg up after that. This guy had a really bad cut from my shoe, but he was drunk and bleeding everywhere. They took him into the first aid room which was next to the pits, and I saw him and I realised that it was my steel shoe that had hit him – his face was just mangled. But he was so happy that I had won the last-heat decider he just wanted my autograph – I'm sure he wasn't happy the next day.

Despite the financial hardships, there was some success on the track. Billy had been selected to ride for the USA in the World Team Cup Final at Kumla in Sweden – his team-mates were Sam Ermolenko, Greg Hancock, Bobby Ott and Ronnie Correy. They faced the holders Denmark, England and the hosts Sweden. By heat 4, England had established a lead but some of the riders were complaining about the heavy state of the circuit. Billy finished last in his first race when he found that he was fighting the surface instead of the opposition. The Scandinavians complained and after a crash that involved Ermolenko and Gert Handberg, the track staff got to work on the surface.

The Danes never recovered from their poor start and the change of track conditions certainly didn't do the English any favours. Nonetheless, England, Sweden and America produced an epic struggle which was one of the best Team Championships for many years.

The Bullet produced a dashing outside pass on Gary Havelock to win his first race of the afternoon. He was then locked in a thrilling battle with Martin Dugard in heat 13, but Dugard managed to dive down the inside of race leader John Jorgensen. By the time the American had slipped past the Dane, Dugard had established an unassailable lead.

With three races to go, the Americans held a 3-point lead. Hamill stretched their lead further with another all-action effort that saw him blast around the outside of Havelock again in heat 18, and Sweden's Tony Rickardsson followed the Cradley Heath rider but couldn't mount a serious challenge. This race win meant that Sam Ermolenko needed second to regain the title for America from his last race in heat 19, which he did in style by coming from the back – and the celebrations began.

Bert Harkins reported in *Speedway Star* that their celebrations were 'long and loud'. The whole US team paid tribute to John Cook who rode for Kumla in the Swedish Elite League at the time, and his advice was instrumental in helping his fellow countrymen overcome the changeable conditions and pull off a memorable victory.

Cradley again suffered a season that was blighted by injury and they did well to avoid the lower reaches of the league table. But the sport was struggling against financial difficulties and before the season was over there was talk of a rigid new pay structure to cut costs – Billy's future in the British League was in doubt.

The first two years I thought that I was making money, but then it took me another three years to pay off my bills from my first two years. I wasn't managing myself properly, and at the end of the day I wasn't earning what I was spending. I wasn't spending money on social things and cars and that, it all went back into speedway.

The costs were a lot higher in Britain than they were in US, because not only were you riding on bigger tracks but you would only get your engine re-builds done in California two or three times a year at the most. You only needed two engines at home, and you would usually only ride one a year. But over here you had to have a re-build every 10 meetings – and now it's every five – just to remain competitive.

1992 was a terrible year and when I quit the British shores at the end of 1992 I was just swamped with bills and responsibilities. I couldn't buy new bikes because I was still paying the bills from 1991. Morgan Hughes was my mechanic and if something had a scratch I would replace it with a new one. That was pretty ridiculous, but that was the way Erik showed me. I was living beyond my means, and it took me 1992 and 1993 to square up.

When 1993 came along and they introduced the new pay scales, I couldn't believe it. There I was in debt and they wanted to cut my money! There was no way I could ride for Cradley with the terms they were offering. I was trying to come up in the sport and I thought it was ridiculous. It was about a 25% pay cut, and I was still trying to get myself out of debt and there was no way I could afford to do it. I was homesick too, and I missed my friends. When I went home I could see things around me changing and I didn't like the fact that I couldn't be there to experience and see it. I remembered what a great year I had at home in 1989, so I decided that I could go home, race and enjoy myself without the pressures that I had in Britain in 1992. I tried to turn a negative into a positive. I had a contract in Denmark because I replaced Jan O. for Fjelsted in 1992. We won the league – which is the only time I had won a League Championship – and we had Jacob Olsen, Ronni Pedersen, Morten Andersen, John Jorgensen, and I enjoyed it – Jacob was a great team-mate. I enjoyed myself and it was the highlight of 1992.

I didn't have KK with me saying do this or do that, there was no one to talk to apart from Christina and she was learning as well. During those two years we were eating the cheapest stuff we could find: potatoes, eggs, etc. because we were in debt – we were two young kids in debt. We virtually lived on egg drop soup.

It was hard for both of us, but she was making whatever she could to make ends meet. And she gave me total support. When I look back at those two years of my life, I was a wreck. I had those two good years when I was progressing then all of sudden… I was frustrated with myself because I still wanted to do it, but I didn't know how to do it, that was the hard part. I had no one there to guide me. Before I had KK, but now nobody knew and there was no support. And Morgan was still learning too and he was seventeen years old when he first started working for me. So he broke his teeth with me and I think Joe Hughes was petrified, because here was his baby boy with this crazy American guy and he thought that I would lead him astray. He wasn't sure about me because Morgan was a pretty sheltered and timid kid at the time.

I had met Jesper Klausen who used to be a mechanic for Hans Nielsen during 1988. Eddie Bull was doing my engines and also Greg's, and there was a bit of rivalry there. I just felt that Greg was favoured a little more and I didn't think that Eddie and I were connecting as well as we had been. I was getting okay stuff, but I didn't feel that we were working well together. I decided that I needed someone who would give me 100% if I was going to win the World Championship and I felt that Jesper would do that so he did all my engines.

I wouldn't have continued in Europe if I didn't think I could be World Champion. There was no point in being over there when, during those years, I wanted to be at home. In my heart I wanted to be home during 1992. I didn't like the lifestyle, I wanted to be back in California with my family and friends, but that was the sacrifice I had to make. I don't feel like that anymore because I've grown and I've got used to it. At that point in time I didn't feel that way. The reality of it was that I still had the drive, otherwise I would have packed up and gone home, because Europe was and, still is, the place to be if you want to be World Speedway Champion. It was the only thing that kept me going through those tough years.

Colin Pratt was disappointed that he couldn't arrange a deal for his young American as he had hoped that Billy and Greg would form the spearhead for Cradley now that Jan O. Pedersen was ruled out through injury. Just to further compound Hamill's problems, he crashed in Denmark and broke his collarbone during his first meeting for Fjelstad.

However, Billy was seeded to the Overseas Final at Coventry. This time the AMA chose the five riders that had won the 1992 World Team Cup as America's representatives. He scored a steady 9 points to qualify for the semi-final.

Meanwhile Pratt held discussions with Billy and in June he made a return to the British League after the team manager had managed to acquire some sponsorship to secure his return. His homecoming steadied the ship, but once again injuries were disrupting their campaign. And Billy would be no different.

Shortly before his World Championship Semi-Final at Lonigo in Italy, Billy cracked a bone in his wrist. Undeterred, he travelled to Lonigo to take his place in the line-up, but discovered that the support that the doctors had given him was too cumbersome for racing – so he replaced it with duct tape!

On a track that was so slick that gating was of paramount importance, he qualified easily with 13 points and faced Hans Nielsen in a run-off for first place. For some peculiar reason the starting marshal and the referee wouldn't let him start from gate four – even though England's Andy Smith had done so in an earlier run-off to determine the last qualifying spot. Nielsen made a super start and won the race, but Billy was just happy that he was through to his first World Final since 1991.

The 1993 World Final was scheduled to be the last of the one-off World Finals, as it was planned that a Grand Prix system would be introduced in 1994. Therefore, there was an extra incentive for the riders as the top ten would automatically be seeded into the GP.

Held at Pocking, Germany, Billy was frustrated by his performance and scored 7 points. He had done enough to make sure of his place in the GP, but he failed to win a race in a meeting that was won in controversial circumstances by Sam Ermolenko.

I remember that I was slow and I was frustrated because of it. I remember seeing Chris Louis come from behind and thinking that I could ride better than him: 'Why can't I do that?' That's what I felt. Sam was kicking ass – he was on it that day. I was pleased for him and he was at that stage in his career when I remember reading that if he didn't win the World Final he would have been the greatest rider never to win it. I was happy for him and he worked hard to come back from his broken leg and stuff.

It was pretty intense because we were all going for the top ten. Jesper Klausen was doing my engines and, at that point, he was pretty much a no name as far as speedway was concerned. But I just wanted someone who was going to give me 100%. If he gave me 100% then I would give him 100% and we would be successful. So he sponsored me with some GM engines. He was a single dad with two twin girls, and he had been racing sidecars and he injured himself but still wanted to go racing.

Sledge, Rod Saunders, was my mechanic and he was a good time type of guy and one of the funniest characters I have ever met in my life. We drove from Denmark to Germany for the World Final. We were going down the Autobahn in a red transit and we had the Tom Petty song 'Running down the dream' on the stereo. Sledge was in the back seat and we're sitting in the front, and he's wearing these sheepskin boots, shorts and a fisherman's hat and has one foot up on the dash and he's singing along: 'Running down the dream'. It was a classic image!

My Mom had flown over and we had this guy from Raz Video with us, Howie, and he had this video camera. We were in a gas station cleaning our bike, and Howie emerged, and said: 'Hey brother how are you doing?'

'Howie? What the hell are you doing up here in the Bavarian Alps near Pocking?'

'Well I heard that a speedway race was going on and I decided to come over and see my mom.'

He ended up jumping in the van and coming back to England with us.

We travelled thinking that Denmark was next to Germany, but it took us hours because of the traffic jams and what have you. Christina was with us too. We couldn't get in the hotel, and my Mom was with us and we had two vans and Kim Konradsen was in the other van because he used to help us out. We had to drive down to Munich Airport to pick up Jesper and we didn't get there until 2 or 3 in the morning. So it was decided that they should just go and pick him up because they were due to pick him up at 6 a.m.

We slept in the van in the parking lot, and we had a little bed in the back. When we woke up we were starving hungry. There were cornfields all round, and I suggested we should get some corn to tide us over until we got some proper food. So that's what we did, but it was the most revolting corn I've ever had! I was trying to convince Christina that it was all right, but it wasn't ripe and it was horrible really. We didn't get much sleep at all and it was hard work trying to organise it all with my Mom and Jesper.

'That was my birthday weekend too, and Kathrin Sorber remembered and got me a big ginger cake with "Happy Birthday" on it, and that was all I had apart from a loaf of bread on the way home,' said Christina. 'That was a long trip. We were on our way home, and we were in Belgium and we were lost. We were driving around Brussels and doing circles for hours, and Billy and I were asleep. Finally, Sledge stopped the van and woke up Billy: "Billy where are we?" And Billy replied: "I don't know, follow your instincts – you'll work it out." And Sledge said: "I've been following my instincts for an hour!" Finally he asked a lady and we got out of there.'

Another story about Sledge is in 1993. I was in Reading and it was the end of the season, and he was in the van smoking a joint. He had a Pepsi bottle that he made a pipe out of and he was taking a couple of hits before the racing started. Bob Radford, the journalist, wanted to interview me for a preview, and he asked if we could jump in the van and do it. And I said yeah. Well the van just reeked of pot! And Bob's coughing, sniffing and going, 'Okay, well Billy erm,' cough, cough, sniff, sniff. But he never said a word – but I know he knew. I was sitting there and I couldn't believe that Sledge had done this and there I was trying to do a World Final preview! That was the night when my front axle fell out. It worked its way out on one side of the fork leg, and it put me on my ass. It could have been nasty. I was in the middle of the turn, in the lead, and those three guys behind had to miss me.

Another occasion we were due at King's Lynn, and from my house you take the A47 and we were so late that we were just blasting our way there. Jim Lawrence, who is now a referee, was a policeman back then and unbeknown to us he watched us go speeding by but he didn't stop us.

On the way back, Sledge had been smoking and he had already passed out so I was driving. You could smell it and the bottle was right there on the dash. All of a sudden I saw a blue light behind me and I was getting pulled over by the police! Once again the van just stank of pot and I was already thinking, 'Don't give them your real name, give them a fake name', even though I had 'Billy Hamill' written all along the side of the van! We hid the bottle and just sat there wondering and panicking as I watched the cop walk up to my window and say: 'Hey Billy how are you doing?' It was Jim Lawrence and it totally threw me.

'I saw you whizzing all the way up there and figured you were in a hurry so I didn't stop you.' He stopped me because he just wanted to know the result!

He was the guest of honour at a Coventry dinner and he told that story but he never mentioned the smell so whether he detected it or not, I don't know.

While the World Championship was another disappointment, Billy picked up another gold medal – his third in four years – when America retained the World Team Cup in a tense battle against Denmark. Billy scored 10 points as Ermolenko again scooped the gold with a memorable victory over Nielsen. To enforce their status as World Champions, America defeated England 3-0 in the Test series and Billy scored double figures in each meeting for an average of 10.99. But it was the World Individual title that Hamill so badly wanted – and it wasn't happening.

There were no such problems with regard to his contract with Cradley for 1994 and he happily signed for his fifth season when he came over to ride in the indoor ice meeting at Telford. He rode steadily on an unfamiliar surface and helped the Rest of the World team to a victory over an England Select.

This news was a welcome antidote to the one that the promoting partnership of Derek Pugh and his wife Nora had leased out the speedway rights to local businessmen Les Pottinger and Mike Gardner. Happily Colin Pratt was set to continue at Dudley Wood, but although this seemed innocent at the time, with the benefit of hindsight it was the first sign of a storm cloud gathering on the horizon of Cradley Heath Speedway.

A massive crowd gathered for the opening night as the Heathens defeated old rivals Wolves 49-47. It was a good start for the new regime – but it didn't last. The Heathens completed a depressing run of six successive defeats and the injury jinx struck yet again.

When Arena Essex came to Dudley Wood, their number one, Kelvin Tatum, took both Billy and Morten Andersen wide and they collided and smashed into the safety fence. It was reported that it took fifteen minutes to extract the Heathens duo from the fence, and both of them were ruled out with injury. Billy damaged ligaments in his knee again, while Andersen aggravated an arm injury he had already sustained a week earlier at Ipswich. At the time Hamill described it as 'the biggest, baddest impact I've ever felt in my life! The fence was coming and I thought, "I gotta get off the bike".' It would be another troubled season for the club, and also a less than happy one for Hamill.

Following the Knockout Cup clash with Ipswich in which Andersen had sustained his arm injury, a bad atmosphere developed between the two teams when the Witches rode in the fixture under protest because Jeremy Doncaster was prevented from riding. The Heathens knocked the Witches out of the cup, but Ipswich made an unsuccessful attempt to get the tie rerun. When Cradley returned to Foxhall Heath for a league match, the atmosphere was electric and controversy was sure to follow – and Billy would be in the thick of it all.

Sledge was still my mechanic in 1994 and Mitch Shirra used to come over and burn one with him in the garage. I would never say anything to anybody because I knew he had already been in trouble once for failing a drugs test. So there was no problem and he was a friend.

We were racing at Ipswich and after the race we were on the cool-off lap and I pulled up alongside Shirra to shake hands, but he just whacked me! This was early on, and we were on at each other all night. It was a really tense meeting and it went to a last-heat decider and I was in it with Greg against Shirra and Doncaster.

All night Ipswich were complaining that I was moving at the start-line. In the last race I was in gate two or three, and then the green light came on and I was under power. But the starting marshal walked in between us while the light was on, grabbed my front wheel and pulled me up to the tape when I was under power! I just pulled back and wondered what the hell was happening. It was such a dangerous thing to do because if the tapes had gone up it would have ripped his hand off, and I would have probably crashed too. So there was a long delay while I made my feelings known and Shirra was just talking shit. I was tired of him keep going on but I was scared of this guy because I had heard all the stories about him from Rick Miller and Kelly and Shawn, so I knew he was a bad ass – although he was a little guy, don't let the size fool you.

I thought that if something was going to kick off I'd better get the first punch in, and don't stop because I knew that I would get a kicking. They got a 5-1 over us and we drew.

At Ipswich, the way the changing rooms are situated, the Ipswich riders have to walk through the visitors changing rooms to get to theirs. Well Shirra walked through and when he got to me he just smiled and laughed and said: 'Wanker.'

I looked at him and replied: 'Ha, ha, dickhead.' But he kept on walking around laughing and I was sat there thinking and getting so mad, that I just took my steel shoe off to use as a weapon and walked into the other changing room and said: 'Come on let's go!' I was so mad but Chris Louis broke it up and told me to forget about it and not to be silly, but I was pretty angry and said: 'Hey, he wants to go, let's fucking go.' I wasn't going to fight fair because I knew that he wouldn't fight fair either. But eventually Chris calmed it down. It was the big old Maely shoe, and he was just baiting me all night. I worked too hard and too much so I wasn't taking any shit from anyone.

I remember racing him after that and he was still spending time with Sledge but he didn't come over the house anymore because he wasn't welcome. I was doing okay at the end of 1994 and I intimidated him when he came to Cradley; he was afraid to race me. I couldn't wait because I wanted to have this guy because I had no respect for him at that point in my career, and I just thought he was an idiot. You could say that it was all gamesmanship but no way, because he made it personal. At Cradley he didn't even get close to me. I was paired up with Morten Andersen and when Ipswich came to Cradley earlier in the season, Shirra broke Morten's nose! He had a ratchet and he was spinning it around while he was telling him not do something and he hit him on the nose! He quit not long after the altercation I had with him at Ipswich because he went up to the referee's tower and dragged him down by his ear and he was suspended.

Ever since Billy had arrived in the British League he had always been a popular choice as a guest. The guest law is a controversial rule that enables a rider from one team to replace another rider from another team of a similar average. During one such engagement, Billy's popularity at Coventry took a nose dive following a heated exchange on the track.

I was racing for Cradley and I had the night off, but Malcolm Simmons called me and asked me if I could guest for King's Lynn at Coventry. Joe Screen was guesting for them, and in one race Coventry's Paul Bentley just took everyone into the fence. Afterwards I just said to him: 'Watch what you're doing.'

I was on the inside of him and he just grabbed my helmet and just gassed his bike and pulled me along by my helmet! I was just getting my head ripped off my shoulders and I had to gas my bike just to keep up with my head! He had a hold of me and I was stuck. I had to keep the throttle open otherwise I would have lost my head as he had a hold of the front of my helmet. So I just jumped off my bike and straight onto him and we had a big old scrap. After we done tumbling down the track, we just sat there pummelling each other. He's a big guy and I'm not a good fighter and he kicked my ass. Paul Ackroyd, the ref, he called us in afterwards and he fined us: Paul £250 because he provoked it and me £150.

After the meeting Christina made her way to the pits to find security guards and dogs around the van. At first she thought that it must have been a problem with Sledge before she realised that they were there to protect Billy's property after the controversial incident with Bentley.

Hopes of a Grand Prix-style World Championship in 1994 were delayed and a one-off World Final was scheduled for Vojens, Denmark. Billy qualified from the American Final in second place behind Hancock, and just scraped through from the Overseas Final with a sensational last race win over Craig Boyce. But it would be heartbreak again at the World Championship Semi-Final in Prague.

Billy lost a run-off to Greg Hancock for the final qualifying place after he had scored 8 points. A tapes exclusion in heat 5 cost him his third World Final appearance which meant that he went to the final as reserve.

The most frustrating thing for me was losing the run-off to Greg Hancock at the semi-final. There were three of us going for it: Greg won it, I was second and Tomas Topinka got third. I was so mad at myself because I lost; but not only did I lose but I lost to Greg. He was my rival and we were always being compared because we came over together. I was so annoyed and so angry with myself that I just drove all night with no sleep and hardly talked all the way back home. Christina was with me and she was trying to console me but I just said, 'Leave me alone.' I hardly talked the whole way because I was very upset to lose. It put a little thing in my head that I would never let that happen again, and that is probably why I have always rode Prague well after that.

I remember thinking that I was putting a hell of a lot into this on the technical side of things, and Jesper and I were working very closely together. I had everything I wanted but I didn't have the power – I didn't have the right engines. As much as I was putting into it, it wasn't good enough. As much as Jesper was putting into it, it wasn't good enough. He was putting 110% into it and so was I. But it was more frustration because what could I do next? I was doing everything I could, physically and mentally.

There was no consolation of a World Team Cup gold medal this time, as the Championship was revamped to resemble a Pairs Championship and Sweden were the victors. More frustratingly, Billy could only watch from the pits at Vojens as Greg was one ride away from winning the title. Furthermore, Poland's Tomasz Gollob was forced to withdraw because of concussion and Hamill rode in one race and finished third. Tony Rickardsson won a three-man run-off to become the last rider to win a one-off World Final. But for Billy it was time for a serious rethink after what had been a year that had promised much, but delivered little.

At the end of 1994 I had an engine from Neil Evitts and it was like a rocket ship. I just went 'Wow!' And Craiger [Craig Cummings] began helping me in the pits. I asked him if he would help me out, but he wasn't too interested to begin with. So I basically coerced him because he needed the money and I knew he could help me. I paid him some money to be there with me. When I was on Neil Evitts' engine I felt like a different rider, so I knew I had to do something.

As much as Jesper was trying with what he was doing, it wasn't good enough. It was working for me because I knew he was giving me 100% and I couldn't ask for any more, and that was what I was looking for. I thought that was it, but at the end of the day, if you don't have the engines underneath you then you're going to struggle. It wasn't from a lack of effort. I didn't really want to leave, and I felt that, morally, it was wrong. I asked Craiger to come and work for me because I felt that his knowledge would help. I think Jesper was pretty much burnt out on it by then and he was raising his kids, but there were no hard feelings. I feel bad for what the guy put into it and he deserved to be there, but I think he must have known that it wasn't quite working.

So after I rode one of Neil's engines I said to Craiger that I was going to get him to do my bikes. But he told me not to do it, and he was dead set against it. He suggested that I should go to Carl Blomfeldt instead. He had worked with Ronnie Correy and he set the fastest time in practise for the 1993 World Final when he was reserve. I felt that Carl would only give me so much. But Craiger did an Australian tour with him, so they had built up a relationship and trusted each other and he convinced me to go with Carl.

His improved form at the end of the season had helped Cradley reach the Knockout Cup Final, but they lost to Eastbourne. The club's injuries meant that the side finished near the foot of the table.

But the change of mechanical personnel was not the only thing that he would have to alter to make some serious progress again. Interestingly, in its end-of-season review of Cradley, *Speedway Star* wrote of Hamill: 'Not as sharp from the gate as some of his rivals, but comes from the back with relative ease time and time again. His season was a bit up and down, largely through a string of mechanical deficiencies and those engine gremlins didn't help his confidence.'

Six

SPEED KING

Billy will go for it to the very last chequered flag. He'll never give up, which is the best quality that anyone who wants to race can have.

Craig Cummings (Team Co-ordinator and Chief Mechanic)

I never focused on my gating when I was in America because I didn't need to. At home, if I didn't make the start I was able to pass the other riders. It wasn't until I came over to England that I had to think about my starting. Even then it wasn't until '94-'95 that I made a really conscious effort to improve my gating. Because I was racing with guys like Jan O. Pedersen and Simon Cross, who were not good starters and were winning races from the back, I looked at what they were doing and did the same thing.

I tried to make good gates, but I never put a lot of thought into it until the end of 1994 when I realised that I had to make better starts if I was going to be a World Champion. I am a big fan of racers and watching guys coming through from the back, so it was normal for me and I'm also a racer like that. Therefore, I had to put a hell of a lot of thought and focus into making good starts.

Unlike someone like Greg, who can make consistently good gates, I'm more of a natural racer so I've got to focus to make a good start. I had to figure out what was going to work for me as far as my concentration went. I have to put a lot of focus and energy into just making a good start. I can't think about the race. I can't think, 'Oh, if I don't make the start I'll do this', I can't be like that. I've got to totally convince myself that I am going to be there.

I always try to look into the first turn and say to myself that I am going to own that first turn, that's my patch and that's where I'm going. I try to point my bike to where I want to be and believe I'm going to be there first and ahead of the other riders. I have to visualise it and focus, and totally convince myself. I also try to influence myself in another way: that my left hand is my brain. The reflexes and the thought processes that go to your brain make the left hand your brain. And you also have to study the referees and know what he's like on the button – because they're all different. Some are consistent and some aren't – you just try to read things.

Every little advantage, every little detail, even a miniscule thing makes all the difference to me, and that's how I improved and honed my starting skills. Even to this day, if I don't do what I always do that works for me – I miss the start. I don't think that Greg has to put that much effort into it, but perhaps he has to put more effort into being a racer – while I'm the opposite.

Britain had made more changes to the league structure and had amalgamated the First Division with the Second Division to form one huge league that they called the Premier League. It was a new era and everyone was optimistic, although the new lay-down engines were banned from use in the league. Cradley kept faith with their American duo and they were joined by Simon Cross, Morten Andersen, Scott Smith, Jonathan Forsgren and John Wilson.

Swedish businessman Sven Heiding joined the club as a director after another winter of uncertainty about the team's future. Pugh had issued a statement saying that speedway was not viable at the stadium and that all its equipment and assets were up for sale. Eventually, after many weeks of negotiations, the club managed to reach an agreement for another season at Dudley Wood.

Right: Billy, aged three, gets his first taste of horsepower under the watchful eye of his granddad Keith Stucki. (Photo: Hamill Family Archive)

Left: 'At an early age I would just jump on my bike and go.' – BMX racing at age five. (Photo: Hamill Family Archive)

Below left: At fourteen years of age, Billy was already displaying his patriotism. (Photo: Hamill Family Archive)

Below right: 'It was a surprise that he wanted to go into motorcycle racing, he was very keen to get started in it and I have supported him ever since.' – Gay Hamill keeps a check on her son's progress at Maely's ranch in 1984, while a thoughtful Billy looks on. (Photo: Hamill Family Archive)

Billy leads Bart Bast and Mike Faria in 1986 on the basic stock Jawa supplied by Bill and Opal Collins of Fast Old Man. (Photo: Hamill Family Archive)

Above left: 'It was impressive, the whole thing impressed me', – posing for the cameras at Cradley Heath in 1988. (Photo: Mike Patrick)

Above right: 'I had no idea who Peter Craven was, I didn't realise how prestigious an event it was.' – 1990 Peter Craven Memorial Champion. (Photo: Eddie Garvey)

Above left: 'I rode awful; I was out of my depth and I wasn't ready.' Disappointment at the 1990 Overseas Final as Greg Hancock (left) commiserates with his colleague. (Photo: Mike Patrick)

Above right: USA, 1990 World Team Champions: From left to right, back row: Billy, John Scott (team manager), Rick Miller and Shawn Moran. Front: Sam Ermolenko (left) and Kelly Moran. (Photo: Alex Alexander)

Left: Gay Hamill and Billy with his cousin, John Lee Yoho, at the 1990 American Final at Long Beach, California. (Photo: Hamill Family Archive)

Leading the way at Bradford in the 1991 Overseas Final. (Photo: Mike Patrick)

Team manager
Colin Pratt
(centre) leads the
discussion with
his Heathens
riders Jan O.
Pedersen (left),
Greg Hancock
and Billy in
1991. (Photo:
Mike Patrick)

Right: In his workshop in the early 1990s. (Photo: Eddie Garvey)

Below: Inside Brian Karger and Andy Graheme at Arena Essex in 1993. (Photo: unknown source)

Above: Billy and Christina in the pits at Pocking shortly before the 1993 World Final. Note Christina's appropriate 'Harvest Days' t-shirt. (Photo: Hamill Family Archive)

Left: Winning his third World Team Cup trophy in four years at Coventry in 1993. (Photo: Eddie Garvey)

'Cradley has a special place in my heart, the fans lived it and they were doing every lap with you.' – Billy and his Cradley team-mates and supporters celebrate their Four-Team Championship victory at Peterborough in 1995. (Photo: Mike Patrick)

'All the hard work was starting to pay off, I had got over that hump and rode myself out of a rut.' – The 1995 Austrian Grand Prix, Billy celebrates his first GP win flanked by runner-up Tony Rickardsson (left) and Hans Nielsen. (Photo: Mike Patrick)

'There was always a shield put up by both of us because we could never become good friends because we were competing against each other.' – Greg Hancock (left) and Billy putting on a show at Sheffield. (Photo: Ken Carpenter)

I had worked that hard for all those years and it came down to just one race.' – Billy leads Greg Hancock during the final race that clinched the 1996 World Championship in Vojens, Denmark. (Photo: Mike Patrick)

A kiss for the champion: Christina and Billy celebrate his World Championship success. (Photo: Mike Patrick)

Opposite, below left: Billy relaxes between races at the 1996 British Grand Prix, as his mechanics get to work on his bike. (Photo: Mike Patrick)

Opposite, below right: With Erik Gundersen, who did so much to help Billy during his early years in Europe. (Photo: Mike Patrick)

'He had a smile on him that was as wide as the Grand Canyon' – 1996 World Champion. (Photo: Mike Patrick)

'I had a lot of pressure from being the World number one, but a lot of it came from me because I wanted to do it again.' Defending his World title in 1997. (Photo: Mike Patrick)

'It's tough when you face any top rider, it's gonna be a battle and you're gonna be trading paint.' – Inside Tomasz Gollob at the 1997 Swedish Grand Prix. (Photo: Mike Patrick)

'I was so angry that I just grabbed a handful of throttle, popped the clutch and T-boned him.' – Billy and Gollob have a heated exchange in the pits during the 1998 German Grand Prix at Pocking. (Photo: Mike Patrick)

Left, above and below: 'At first I didn't know what I had done, but my legs went into convulsions or something and I knew it was serious. I had never felt anything like it, and I had no control over it. My legs were twitching and I couldn't breathe.' – The crash during the 1998 Polish Grand Prix at Bydgoszcz. (Photos: Mike Patrick)

Below: Displaying the new distinctive fairing at Coventry's press day in 2000. (Photo: Mike Patrick)

'He was right back in the World Championship and he was a contender again.' – Billy celebrates his victory in the 2000 Czech GP in a year when he finished runner-up in the World Championship. (Photo: Mike Patrick)

Team Roberts Speedway team 2001. From left to right: Chuck Askland, Craig Cummings, Billy, Mick Sheppard and Kenny Roberts. (Photo: Mike Patrick)

In action during the 2001 Grand Prix series. (Photo: John Hipkiss)

On his way to his last Grand Prix victory, Billy leads Jason Crump during the 2001 Czech Grand Prix in Prague. (Photo: Mike Patrick)

Despite a painful back injury, Billy holds on as he leads Tony Rickardsson during the European Grand Prix at Bydgoszcz, Poland, in 2002. (Photo: Mike Patrick)

Above: Well done son: Gordon Hamill congratulates his son after he wins his third US National Championship in 2002. (Photo: Hamill Family Archive)

Left: The Hamill family: Billy and Christina with their two children Kurtis and Margi. (Photo: Hamill Family Archive)

During the winter Billy and Christina were married on 3 December 1994, at Christina's local church in Monrovia and they too were looking forward to better fortunes in 1995. However being an international speedway rider doesn't meet with everyone's approval, as Billy discovered when he moved into a house in a small village near Tamworth.

I had a lot of trouble when I first moved into the village and I had complaints and fights with the neighbours. On one occasion we were riding at Cradley on the Saturday evening, and then we were riding at 11 o'clock the following morning at Eastbourne. We had to wash our bikes and stuff after the meeting at Cradley, so we were out there at midnight washing the bikes off with a pressure washer. One of the neighbours came over and he was not happy and saying stuff like: 'What the hell do you think you're doing? Who the hell do you think you are?'

And I replied: 'Hey I'm really sorry, but I gotta race tomorrow and I gotta wash the bike. I'm only going to be about ten minutes.'

But he called the council about me. He wrote a letter to them, and the council came over to see me and discuss his complaint. My neighbour had contacted them about my pressure washer. They came out with a decibel meter to measure the noise and to see if it was causing noise pollution. But the result was that a lawn mower was louder than this – so that was okay.

I built my garage at the back but it wasn't a permanent fixture. It said that you don't have to have planning permission if it's not a permanent building. It's on a pad and its removable – it's not bolted or framed to the ground. I had a builder and he told me not to worry about it and that I would be all right.

After the pressure washer complaint, he then complained about my garage. I saw the letter and he described it as a 'monstrosity, a big garage and an eyesore to the village'. Chris Manchester was living with me at the time and when we saw him, or he was around, we used to say stuff like: 'Oh this is a monstrosity!' We basically used to egg him on and take the piss out of him. They hated us, but our attitude was if they wanted to mess with us, then come on, we could play hardball. This guy then complained that I was running the American Speedway team from my home in Clifton Campville. I've been here so long now, and I've never had any problems from my immediate neighbours but it's always the others.

I understand the village culture and the cliqueness, but I never had a clue back then. I'm not interested in all that. It's all bullshit as far as I'm concerned.

I think some of the problems were because I was an American and here was this kid, a professional motorcyclist, so I believe there was a bit of prejudice and jealousy too. I still don't take part in their cliqueness, and I've never fallen into that.

I had a lot of grief from him for about two years. I had a hell of a time with them all. I guess it was because we were driving diesel vans and our hours were late because of the nature of my business. We were up to one or two o'clock in the morning, and we would have parties now and again. We were just young kids and we didn't know any better — it was more ignorance than anything. We didn't realise that we were disturbing anybody and some of the hassle I got was warranted, but some of it was ridiculous too.

I've also experienced the same sort of thing in California when we moved back two years ago. It was summertime and I was home for a week and I decided to have a barbecue. We had a big party and my grandfather came down to San Diego, and I invited all my family and friends. I guess it was around forty people and we were loud and it lasted a couple of days! In California, as I live in a community, you have a Home Owners' Association, so there are certain rules like you have to keep your yard tidy and all this sort of thing to maintain the value of the property in the area and so forth. Every month you have to pay your Home Owners' Association fees and you get the use of a community swimming pool, sauna and the gym, which are benefits that are included in the fees.

So if your neighbour has a problem with you, he doesn't tell you, they write a letter to the Association. Then the Association gets in contact with you and say that they have received a complaint. Well, they complained. My grandfather had his truck there, it was a truck with a camper on the back and it was parked at the front for a couple of days. And the rule that I supposedly broke was that I wasn't allowed to have a motorhome parked in the driveway for more than twenty-four hours, or something ridiculous like that. But basically it was because we had a party and we were loud and we kept everyone up!

With Craig Cummings now operating as his mechanic and Carl Blomfeldt doing his engines, Billy Hamill was on the pace almost immediately when the tapes went up on the new season. He was a different rider: fast, enthusiastic and winning most of his races. Cummings' organisational skills came in very useful for Billy as he admits that, by nature, he is not an organised person at all.

He began 1995 with 16 at Ipswich, 13 at home in the return, and then, on 8 April, he scored his first paid maximum against Peterborough since 1992. A paid 17 followed at Eastbourne and then another full maximum at home to Reading was followed by 11 against Coventry for an average well in excess of 10 points. But during a bank holiday Monday clash against Swindon, Hamill's enthusiastic exploits seemingly earned the wrath of Colin Pratt.

Cradley required a 5-1 from the last race to snatch a draw. Their American duo of Hamill and Hancock swept into the lead and seemed to be heading for a match-saving 5-1. Billy held a commanding lead and he looked back to see his team-mate in second. As they entered the final lap the celebrations began, but Greg made a slight mistake on the first bend and Swindon's Peter Nahlin was suddenly upon Hancock's back wheel. As they swooped into the third bend, Greg was on the outside and Nahlin was hugging the inside.

Billy was blissfully unaware of the tight duel going on behind him. As he exited the final bend and speeded toward the chequered flag, he pulled a celebratory wheelie. However, he looped and bit the dust! Meanwhile, Hancock and Nahlin were beginning their race to the finish line when Hamill was sliding along the fence line and drifting across the track! Suddenly Hancock had to shut off and change direction to avoid running over his fallen team-mate, while Nahlin was able to sneak in and take second and clinch a last-gasp victory for Swindon – even though he too had to shut off to avoid Hamill's machine.

The supporters couldn't believe it; the Heathens fans were stunned, while the Robins fans were ecstatic. Colin Pratt was also far from happy as the incident had cost them the match, and he issued a statement saying: 'No More Wheelies'. Billy later discovered that the statement was a result of some 'over-excited journalism'.

In 1995 the Speedway Grand Prix got underway at last. The first round was scheduled for Wroclaw, Poland, and the organisers took the eighteen finalists from the 1994 World Final as their competitors. The two reserves from that final, Billy and Sweden's Peter Karlsson, began the first GP at reserve. But the first reserve – Hamill – would then replace the lowest-scoring rider from the first round in the second GP.

Just as he was getting used to watching from the sidelines, Tommy Knudsen crashed and sustained concussion and was unable to continue. Hamill made his Grand Prix debut in heat 9 finishing third behind Hans Nielsen and Tomasz Gollob. Karlsson replaced Knudsen in his next scheduled outing, but then Billy had another chance in heat 19 and defeated Chris Louis, Craig Boyce and Mark Loram.

After sixteen heats were completed, the top four scorers entered the A-final where the Grand Prix winner would be decided; fifth, sixth, seventh and eighth entered the B-final; ninth, tenth, eleventh and twelfth the C-final, and the last four the D-final. As he had 4 points, Billy had qualified for the D-final and finished third behind Jan Staechmann and Andy Smith for 4 unexpected Grand Prix points.

The second Grand Prix at Weiner Neustadt in Austria indicated that the Bullet had really turned the corner. All but a handful of riders were using the lay-down engines in the GP, which allowed the riders to not only be faster because of their lower centre of gravity, but also made the bike more stable in the corners. Billy was still recovering from his financial constraints and could only afford to use the traditional upright engines. This wasn't a problem in Britain because lay-downs were banned from British racing – although in 1996 even Britain couldn't hold back the tide of technological change. Therefore, as a result, many believed that Hamill was at a distinct disadvantage.

Nonetheless, the in-form American, who was at the top of the Premier League averages, scored 10 points to meet Tony Rickardsson, Hans Nielsen and Mark Loram in the A-final.

I had the third choice of starting gates in the final. Tony picked one and Hans two which I pretty much expected, but I didn't know whether to go off three or four. I gambled on four because I thought that they would be going for each other and I was hoping to get a good run around the outside.

I made the gate with them – I was a little behind – but I got that run around the outside and had a really good line. Tony was in the lead and he was concentrating on fighting off Hans and I just came around the outside when he didn't expect it. I remember thinking, 'Be smooth, don't make a mistake here buddy'.

It was unbelievable. That was when all the hard work was starting pay to off and things were starting to come around. I had got over that hump and rode myself out of a rut. I was grateful that I didn't feel the same way as I had been feeling over the past three years – and I thought, 'Man this feels good!'

I was one of the few riders that were still on an upright engine. In fact I think I was the only rider still using an upright in the World Championships. I knew what I was riding and they were good and comfortable. Everybody was having problems with carburettors on the lay-downs but I knew exactly what I had. I am the only rider to have won a Grand Prix on an upright engine. Carl tuned the engine and he was fairly easy to work with at that point and he seemed to know what I needed.

*Craiger's mechanical knowledge and his attention to detail on the mainte-
nance side of things made a big difference. I had seen what he had done for
Ronnie Correy and other riders, and he was very good. He was driving a truck,
and he had just bought a house so he wasn't about to go into an unsecured
mechanical job full time or anything. I just took him on as a person to oversee
things and advise us, as a Race Co-ordinator, as I called him. He could oversee
these things for me and tell the mechanics what needed to be done and I could
concentrate on my racing. He was a great mechanic, but I wouldn't say he was a
great engine tuner. Craiger's not the type of person you would have a laugh
with, he's quite serious and pensive. But we got along because he's a straight
person – I had the whole package now.*

He certainly did have the 'whole package', as his form was nothing
short of brilliant throughout the season. Later it was revealed that he
completed the season with three upright GM's – the third arrived late
in the season – and he maintained his position in the Grand Prix series.
So impressive were his performances that some experts were wondering how close he would have been if he had not started the series from
reserve.

Christina was pregnant during the 1995 season and she was experiencing some problems. It was an important Grand Prix meeting in
Sweden for her husband so she kept her problems to herself.

'I was really sick, and I had to be hospitalised, but I couldn't tell Billy
because I wanted him to have a good meeting,' she said. 'I was in the
hospital all day to find out what was going on and they needed to do
more tests, so they told me I needed to stay overnight. I told them that
I needed to go back to the hotel and get some things. So I had my
Mom and Dad run me by the track and my Dad was going to stay,
while my cousin and my Mom were going to drive me back to the
hospital. I went in to say goodbye to Billy, but he didn't know that I
wasn't watching the meeting. In those days, after a GP they kept them
back until 11 p.m. and no one at the hospital spoke English at all. He
came to the hospital and he was so mad at me and said: "How could
you not tell me?"'

*Craiger came along and said: 'I've got to tell you something, your wife's in the
hospital.' 'What?' It was really dramatic and I was scared. It turned out that she
was experiencing some blood pressure problems.*

Christina gave birth to their first child, Margaret (Margi) Alise, weighed in at 6lbs 5oz, at 11 a.m. on 15 September. Billy was a dad for the first time and in a magazine interview the proud father said that he would be spending the winter at home learning to be a father and would not succumb to the temptations of racing in Australia.

He finished third in the German Grand Prix at Abensberg and finished the competition with 80 points and in fifth place – thus ensuring his place in the 1996 series as the top eight were automatically seeded. Hans Nielsen had won his fourth World title, but in Hamill it seemed that the Grand Prix had discovered a new star.

Billy also finished the season at the top of the Premier League averages with an impressive 10.86 figure. He made his first appearance in the Premier League Riders' Championship at Swindon and finished second in the final to Bradford's Gary Havelock. Following an uncharacteristic last place in his first race, he had battled his way through the qualifying races and the race-off. In the final, he wheelied his way past Martin Dugard, but he just couldn't catch Havelock and he finished second – to date this is his best performance in the British League Riders' Championships that have been held in Britain.

He also made up for his mistake during the Cradley v. Swindon match, by winning the last race of the Premier League Fours Championship at Peterborough that clinched the title. Cradley, the hosts Peterborough and Bradford entered the final race on 18 points apiece. Billy rolled out onto the track to face Mick Poole, Gary Havelock and Leigh Adams of Arena Essex in a pressure-race environment. Whoever won the race would clinch the Championship for their team. After 28 heats of racing it all came down to the last race.

Billy made a dream start from the inside grid, and although Poole chased hard there was no denying the American who secured the club's first major trophy since their Premiership win in 1990. Suddenly, under the warm pleasant sunshine of an August afternoon at the East of England Showground in East Anglia, the injury worries and the uncertainty surrounding their beloved Dudley Wood Stadium all seemed a million light years away as the Heathens fans, riders and management celebrated a deserved victory – it was their day in the sun.

It was a great feeling to win. It was a pressure race but after winning the Austrian Grand Prix my confidence was high. Everyone played their part and it was a great team effort.

'If Billy felt any nerves, he didn't show them,' said Sven Heiding. 'He absolutely flew off gate one and with the track getting slick, there was no way that Poole was going to pass him. It was a superb result for our supporters and a great day for speedway. Billy had far and away his best season in the sport and he was the difference between what we did and what we could have achieved. He was so consistent and gained bags of confidence by doing so well in the Grand Prix.'

In fact, Billy only once failed to score double figures during the season for Cradley, and in August he was only beaten on one occasion by an opposing rider in five matches. He had experienced a wonderful season, but the best was yet to come.

No sooner had the dust settled on the 1995 season when the train of despair and heartbreak came rolling into the station and unloaded misery on Cradley. All season they had been riding with the knowledge that they could be homeless in 1996, but even when the inevitable news was confirmed in November, it was still extremely hard for everyone associated with the club to take. Never again would the roar of methanol-burning speedway bikes be heard at the Dudley Wood Stadium. The stadium was set to be sold off for housing, so the only solution to keep the club alive was to move to another site.

I remember sitting in those supporters' club meetings with the rest of the team and saying: 'The fight has only just begun.' We had the support of the local borough council, but it was the county council who wanted to get rid of it. There was no other form of entertainment around that area. There were no football teams; speedway was it and because it was so important to them they were not going to take it lying down and that's a credit to them. There are still people printing t-shirts and coffee mugs with the old Heathen body colours on them, and there is still a passion there for it. That logo has almost become a fashion statement in that area and also within the British Speedway community itself.

The Cradley team, as it was, moved into the Loomer Road Stadium at Stoke, where they were known as the Cradley & Stoke Heathens. It would be the last hurrah for the exiled club, as the promotion suffered heavy losses and couldn't continue. Apart from a few meetings as a nomadic Conference side, Cradley Heath pretty much died when they closed the doors on Dudley Wood – although the fight continues to revive the Heathens club.

Billy and Greg moved to Stoke with the rest of the team, but while all this uncertainty was surrounding their British League careers, the US duo were putting in place a new concept that would help them in their quest to become World Speedway Champions.

Sam Ermolenko had an idea to form a team with Carl Blomfeldt. I remember having a meeting with Sam and Greg and he wanted to form a Grand Prix team and it was his original idea, but nothing ever materialised – so Greg and I took it and ran with it. We knew that Sam was more into it for himself and it wasn't going to be a 50/50 deal. I knew that, and Greg knew it too. Greg and I understood that we could do this after we realised that nothing had occurred with Sam. His idea was what other motor sports had already done in Grand Prix motorcycle racing and Formula One. It would be fair to say that he called us and proposed it and it was ambitious – so we just took it and ran.

Troy Lee actually suggested the idea to approach Exide because they were Greg's sponsor. He said that they were a big company and he thought that even if we had to ride in the GP for nothing for a year it would be worth it, just to get their backing. He told us to approach them and if nothing materialised then we hadn't really lost anything. So we did. I never got a nickel that year from them – not even after I had won the World Championship. But I did the following year and the year after that, I got a hell of a lot of money at that time and it was by far the biggest sponsorship in the sport.

Greg was already sponsored by them, and we had a man called Jeff Davies who helped us put a package together to present to Exide. He did a lot of work for us and basically put it together, while Nigel Harry of the Windmill Village Hotel gave us a meeting room. Jeff did a big presentation with Greg and I to add to it and we showed them what we wanted to do and what we wanted to achieve. Jeff used a flip chart to illustrate the advantages and benefits to the company.

Greg had two girls who were running his fan club for him at the time, and they went to Cradley, Wolverhampton and probably Coventry and they did some market research. The information we got from them we used to formulate graphs and pie charts for our presentation to Exide. The kind of question was the percentage of men that went to speedway, the percentage of children, the

*percentage of women and the percentage of families. We knew that they would
have the demographics of their customers, so we had to show them that speedway and batteries could go hand in hand. We convinced them that we were the
right people to promote their product and if they didn't they were foolish. The
kind of money we were asking for was peanuts for a company like them – it was
less than $100,000. In those days for road racing, a modest budget was $3.5
million, so our budget was miniscule in comparison.*

*Tony Summers was the man that we presented it to and he was associated
with Greg Hancock. I basically agreed to ride for nothing for that first year, I
don't know what sort of deal Greg received because he was already associated
with them and I wasn't – it was his sponsor. The following year we could go
back and say to them look what we've done. Speedway let us down, the sport
wasn't really ready for it and we were way ahead of our time. The sport didn't
grasp the concept at all, and there was no marketing there. They didn't see the
potential that there was for corporate companies to be involved with the Grand
Prix. And, to be honest, I still don't think speedway is ready for that even now.
If it was, then others would be doing it. They were only interested in having
someone like Exide as a series, or a meeting sponsor – there was no forward
thinking.*

*There were no obstacles put in our way, and Ole Olsen ran the GPs single-
handed and it was his toy and his pet project. There was only a certain amount
of support, and they made sure that we were pitted together, but we didn't really
get enough support to make it really happen. What we were hoping was that if
we could show that it was successful, all the other major companies like Kodak
would also want to be involved. But no one ever took it and ran – it never
happened.*

Nonetheless, the new sponsorship arrangement meant that Billy and
Greg would have a budget available to them so that they could have a
real strike at the World Championship. After such a successful year in
1995 Billy felt that he could do well and with a good back-up team
that also included Trent Bucholz and Glyn Bower alongside him in the
pits, he was hoping to build on 1995 and continue his climb up the
ladder.

However, finishing top of the averages and being one of the emerging world stars doesn't allow for any preferential treatment from your
rivals. It just means that they are even more determined to beat you,
and even question your tactics when they are not successful in lower-

ing your colours. This was illustrated during an early season encounter with Ipswich.

It was a wet rainy night, it was the last lap and I came underneath Jeremy Doncaster. He had to go wide, and on the outside it was slop. I pushed him wide to get by him and get on the line, but I never touched him. But unbeknown to me at the time, he had fallen off. It was a good clean move as far as I was concerned. I had passed him fair and square and I didn't know he had fallen off. I respected Doncaster but he was from a different era from mine – he was more of Shawn and Kelly's time.

When I went by on the slowdown lap, he was yelling and screaming at me as I passed by. I was so positive that I didn't do anything wrong, but he was still yelling at me and giving me the finger so I turned to him and said: 'I never touched you.'

Straightaway he was in my face, and then he headbutted me with his visor – he stuck the visor right in between the jaw part of my helmet and goggles and struck my nose. I just unloaded and I got some punches in the best way I could in the area above the jaw part of his helmet. It was a full-scale brawl, but I think I spooked him and he was scared of me.

It was because the track was wet that he fell off, he wouldn't have fallen otherwise. We apologised to each other and we never had a problem after that. He thought he was right and I thought I was right. And I remember Chris Louis came up to me and said: 'Hey, what are you doing to the old man? Come on, leave him alone.'

Apart from that little incident, Billy had begun the new season pretty much as he had left off – an 18-point maximum at London promised much for the future as the British Grand Prix was due to be held there later in the season. It was a strange experience racing as Cradley at Stoke, not only because of the unfamiliar surroundings, but also because for the first time since he had arrived in England Colin Pratt was not the team manager. The managerial reins had been passed over to former Heathen Jan O. Pedersen. But because of the way it was structured, the riders found that Pedersen didn't see to all the riders' needs like his predecessor.

The Golden Hammer was staged for what would be the final time, and Hamill became the last winner of Cradley's top individual meeting. He still has the trophy at his home and came across it during one of our meetings for the preparation of this book.

Billy arrived at the first Grand Prix at Wroclaw's Olympic Stadium resplendent in his new Team Exide leathers and in a confident frame of mind. Craig Cummings revealed that they had six new lay-down GM engines, two of which were dedicated to the GPs, two for the British League and one each for the Polish and Swedish Leagues.

But there was plenty of controversy over the use of tyres in the series. The FIM tried to introduce a solid block tyre for all competitors in the Grand Prix and any World Championship meetings. However, the Grand Prix Riders' Association refused to let the riders participate in the series as it was felt that insufficient testing had been carried out. Initial reports were that the tyres were unpredictable and dangerous.

I tried the solid blocks and they were crap. Ole Olsen tried everything to force it on us. Steve Brandon ran the Association for us and he was the General Secretary, but Sam Ermolenko and Hans Nielsen were the key riders behind it. Steve was an unbelievable representative and worked tirelessly. He butted heads and made a lot of enemies. But he believed in what he was saying by represent-ing the riders, and we believed what we believed.

I crashed when I used them in Italy and there is a book with a picture of me doing a wheelie on the front, but I was actually falling off while using those solid block tyres. They weren't a speedway tyre as far as I was concerned. When you slide a bike into a corner doing 90mph you get used to a certain feeling because your bike's designed for that feel; then all of sudden when you don't have that feeling it's a big change. There was no research and development done before they tried to force them on us, and perhaps they could have been adapted, but you don't force that on riders even with a limited amount of testing in the winter.

I believe that it was all to do with money. Hans Nielsen and Ole always had a thing for each other, but when Hans and Sam got out of the GP that's when everything went wrong. Hans didn't mind going against the grain, and he was very honest and a what-you-see-is-what-you-get type of guy — that is why I always had the utmost respect for him as a man and a rider.

I probably had a bad impression of Hans when I first came over. I was always hearing about how he was a tight ass and he was always out for himself, but really it was because he was successful and he was winning. I don't think he had a lot of friends, but then he wasn't racing to make friends. He didn't mix with the boys, he didn't drink and he didn't party like a lot of those guys did at the time — that wasn't Hans. My experiences with him were that he was blunt and honest, and I respected him because of that more than a competitor. He proved that to me because, initially, I didn't have that impression.

The tyre dispute would last all season, although the riders did compromise and agreed to test them during the first practise session. But the reaction was always the same: dangerous.

Nonetheless 26,000 fans attended the first GP of the season in Wroclaw. Billy scored 11 points and qualified for the A-final where he met the Scandinavian trio of Tommy Knudsen, Hans Nielsen and Tony Rickardsson. From gate three he finished fourth behind the winner, Knudsen, Rickardsson and Nielsen. Although disappointed not to make the rostrum, it was a hard-earned fourth place as his team were experiencing a few mechanical gremlins on a track that Billy admitted wasn't one of his favourites.

The second Grand Prix took place at Lonigo in Italy. Under the baking hot sun, the racing was fast and furious. No one was giving an inch, and this environment suited the never-say-die racing of Hamill. The changeable track conditions didn't help matters, but Billy was riding hard and defending his position with some determined first turns. He finished the qualifying races as joint top-scorer with Knudsen on 13 points. It was the same quartet that lined up at the start line for the A-final in the first GP.

This time Billy was starting from the inside gate, but his race for glory was blocked by Nielsen who firmly slammed the door shut and took off into the lead. The American relentlessly pursued him, but he was unable to find a way past and finished second.

After two rounds, Nielsen was leading the Championship with 43 points, while Billy was placed fourth with 36 points – 2 adrift of Rickardsson and 5 points behind Knudsen. With two A-final appearances behind him and four rounds to go, he was aiming high and on target.

However, his assault on the World Championship took a major setback at the German Grand Prix, when a bout of flu combined with some difficult conditions saw the American score just 5 points in the qualifying races. He found himself in the unfamiliar territory of the C-final where he faced Jason Crump, Leigh Adams and Mark Loram. He made his one and only good start of the evening and won the race, while his rivals fought over the minor placings.

Nielsen won his second GP and extended his lead at the top. Billy had managed to move up into third in the Championship standings, but he was now 23 points behind leader Nielsen with just three rounds remaining. Hamill wasn't giving up and he unwittingly displayed some foresight when he told journalists after the meeting: 'It's disappointing for us to see Hans so far ahead, but I'm sure there are a lot of dramatic moments left in the series.' What followed was one of the most exciting showdowns in the history of the World Individual Speedway Championship.

The Hamill team arrived for the Swedish Grand Prix at Linkopping with no doubt as to what was required to close the gap at the top. A team effort was needed from everyone in the Bullet camp if there was any chance of snatching the title away from Nielsen – starting in Sweden.

By heat 12 Billy had scored 7 points with Nielsen on a subdued 5. In his first outing the American laid down his marker when he finished second behind Rickardsson but ahead of Nielsen. However, heat 15 would go down as a legendary race which illustrated the desire and passion that Billy had burning inside him to win the 1996 World Championship – it would be one of the defining moments of the 1996 series.

Ever since he threw a leg over a speedway bike as a junior, his style had been dictated by his will to win. In the early days it wasn't pretty, but as he gained more experience his style became more polished. However, his enthusiasm and determination had not smoothed over the rough edges and he was hard, but fair. He was quite comfortable standing his ground, as Simon Wigg discovered in the 1990 World Team Cup Final when he tried to intimidate the then inexperienced Hamill during a first bend clash. The result was a last for Wigg, and a crucial second for the young American.

Billy took an early lead in heat 15 at Linkopping, but some unexpected grip yanked the American's front wheel skyward and he nearly struck the safety fence. His opponents swept past him with Ermolenko in the lead, and Joe Screen and Jason Crump believing they had seen the last of Billy 'the Bullet' Hamill. Sensing that an all-important A-final appearance was slipping away, he got his head down and aggressively gave chase. Swiftly he passed Crump, but no sooner had he dealt with him when he ran into Screen, but both managed to stay upright to continue the battle.

He resembled a rodeo rider as his machine bucked like a horse as he picked up unexpected grip in places, but his skill and control was such that his granddad would have been proud. He set about taking second from Screen as Crump continued to threaten him for third. But there was no denying Hamill when he was in that frame of mind and he switched to the outside and passed Screen for second. It was too late to mount a serious challenge on Ermolenko but he was still heading for the A-final.

'It was an unbelievable race – fantastic,' recalled Craig Cummings. 'It proved the racer that he is.'

Every situation is different. If you see a hole you just go for it, but if you know you're faster than a rider then you just set him up – and sometimes that can take you a lap. You might set up your pass a lap later. But usually when you're in third, you're pretty much looking for a gap from the start and you're riding on instinct.

I'm a very instinctive racer, but most of the good racers are. Some of the guys are more calculated than others, but I race on my instincts. I may sometimes do it from the seat of my pants and most of the American riders have that style. But you've got to rely on your brain, experience and wits. Just like you study referees you study riders, so that you know what their strengths and weaknesses are and you know that going in. For example Nicki Pedersen is a rider who will not leave you an inch.

But anytime that you come up against the top riders in the world you know that if you get on the outside of them you have to be ahead of them, otherwise you're not going to be ahead of them. I've had battles with all of them. When I first came over to England, Neil Evitts and Jeremy Doncaster were two riders who it was said that you shouldn't get on the outside of because they would just squeeze you. Once I came up against Evitts and I was faster than him, but I couldn't go under him I could only go around him. And because of what I had been told about him, I wondered what I should do? So I went for it; I was scared as I went for the outside but I got around him. I never really had any problem with either one of them, but they had that reputation.

The previous race had seen Nielsen finish in last place which meant that an A-final appearance for the Dane was almost out of the question. Hamill booked his place with a race win over Sweden's Henka Gustafsson, who was on great form that night. They would meet Greg

Hancock and Tomasz Gollob in the A-final, but with Nielsen in the C-final it was a great opportunity to even things up – this would be Hamill's high but Nielsen's low.

There were ignition problems on Billy's number one bike, so he had to wheel out his second machine for the choosing of starting gates while his crew worked on his first-choice bike. As he bumped off to ride his way round to the start line, his crew met him at the pit gate with his repaired first bike and he jumped on that one for the start of the race.

He lifted coming out of the third gate and was in last place with the Swedish crowd cheering on Gustafsson. The talented Swede was all set to win his first GP, as Hamill passed his Team Exide colleague Hancock for third. But Hancock fell and the race was stopped. Greg was excluded from the rerun and the three remaining riders had to do it again. This time Hamill made a clean start and took command of the race on the first corner and was away for his first GP victory of the season.

However, as Hamill celebrated with a series of wheelies, there were many who believed that Hancock had fallen off deliberately to allow his fellow countryman another chance. Some of the fans had invaded the track and as Billy came round the third and fourth bends, one disgruntled Swedish fan attempted to kick the American. Fortunately no contact was made as he swerved to avoid him.

England's Gary Havelock, who was a guest on *Sky Sports* live TV coverage, said: 'In my opinion Greg dropped it in the A-final. I have no doubts in my mind because world-class riders do not slide off coming into the bend. After seeing a couple of replays it had become quite clear that Greg helped his team-mate. Henka was never going to be caught until Greg came down. It doesn't take a lot of working out to know what the game plan in Greg's mind was. We'll never know the real truth, there's no way in a million years that they would openly say what the game plan was.'

I knew it was total BS. I wouldn't do it for him and he wouldn't do it for me. It was stupid and I knew that because we were so competitive. The last thing Greg wanted was for me to be World Champion before he was. But just because we were team-mates – in Exide as well – they made a big thing about it.

If you look at the video you can see that he just falls off. There was a big hole and he just went in too hot and hit the hole and he got thrown. Anybody who has half a clue about speedway can see that he just fell off. I remember confronting Havvy [Gary Havelock] about the situation afterwards, and he said that he had to say something because Sky wanted him to do that. And Havvy being Havvy was right in there because he thrives on controversy, and he said that he knew that it didn't really happen.

I didn't like it because you're telling people a lie, and it was taking the credibility away from my win. I had been racing in Poland and Sweden before I got back to Britain, and I couldn't believe the fuss that was going on about it. It wasn't 'Hamill wins GP' it was 'Greg lays it down so that Billy can win' and 'Exide: Team Orders'. It was totally ridiculous from my point of view because I knew that nothing could be further from the truth. I was so pissed off that people could think that, I had to go to the gym and work it off. I even cracked a joke about it because it was so silly.

Hans Nielsen won the C-final, but Billy's win had put him into second place with 70 points while the Dane had 77. Tony Rickardsson was still in the hunt in third with 68 points, but Nielsen's off-night had evened things out.

There was much interest in the British Grand Prix at London's Waterden Road Stadium – the home of the old Hackney team – and it was another night of tight racing. The sport's press may have viewed the evening's action as a Nielsen *v.* Hamill battle, but for some riders it was a tussle to avoid the Grand Prix Challenge at the end of the season. One of which was Australia's Jason Crump who produced one of his best performances of the series to finish on 10 points and qualify for the A-final. But it was Nielsen who led the qualifying scores with 12, followed by Hancock on 11.

Billy won the opening race, but despite putting in 200% effort he never won another heat! He struggled with his set-up all evening, which was illustrated in his second race when he spent virtually the whole of the back straight of the opening lap trying to get his front wheel on the track. He held a brief lead in his fourth outing, but he couldn't do anything about Craig Boyce who blasted by for a win. Nielsen defeated Billy in heat 18, but 'the Bullet' grabbed a vital second from Sam Ermolenko on the back straight.

With one race to go, it all depended on the last qualifying heat. If Peter Karlsson got a second or better, then Billy was in the B-final. It couldn't have worked out better. Karlsson, who had looked fast all night, was a little overeager at the start line and he nudged the tapes and was excluded. The Hamill camp celebrated as he was in the A-final, and he admitted that he cheered when PK was excluded. It was an instantaneous reaction that didn't go down too well with some of his rivals, but he didn't care as he was in the final and that was all that mattered.

The final race produced four pulsating laps. Crump passed Nielsen on the outside for the lead, and Billy came hard up on the inside on turns three and four. But he had gone in too hot and he had to pull a 'full-locker' to avoid crashing and was relegated to fourth. Hancock tried to lunge down the inside of Nielsen, but the Dane slammed the door shut. It was a harsh move, but this was the kind of racing that one expects in a World Championship and Hamill took advantage of the situation and grabbed third from Greg.

After the A-final, Crumpie had won it, Hans got second and I got third. We were getting ready to go out for the presentation and I asked Hans, 'What's the score spread now?' I couldn't work it out, but I knew he knew and he told me the scores and added: 'It's between you and me now baby!' I had won in Sweden, but he won the C-final and got ninth. I got ninth in Germany which was my worst. I didn't really think about the World Championship, I just wanted to win a Grand Prix. When I won in 1995 I wanted to win another one. I totally stepped away from the World Championship because, mentally, it would ruin me.

Nielsen held a 9-point lead over Hamill going into the final GP at Vojens in Denmark – it would be a memorable showdown. Writing in *Speedway Star*, Gary Havelock said of the decider, 'Although Hans is "going home", his World title luck has always deserted him in his native land and with Billy shadowing his every move, it could go right down to the wire.'

Nielsen, dubbed 'The Professor', knew exactly what the situation was as he said on the eve of the final: 'I know that if Billy wins the meeting I have got to get third in the A-final. If I come fourth and he wins then we would have to have a run-off – something I prefer to avoid.'

The final Grand Prix was a tense affair for Hamill and Nielsen, but there was also a clutch of riders who were eager to score as many points as possible to automatically qualify for the series in 1997 and avoid having to race in the dreaded challenge at the end of the season. This meant that there was a lot at stake for everyone. But Nielsen could at least count on the support from the large crowd at Vojens.

He was in Denmark and it was a similar situation to 2003 with Crumpie – he had everything to lose. I had nothing to lose and everything to gain – it was almost comparable. It was his home Grand Prix, everyone was there to see Hans Nielsen win the World Championship and he had a 9-point advantage and everyone was convinced that he wasn't going to lose 9 points in his home Grand Prix.

We were in the changing rooms before the meeting, and I started stretching and warming up, which was my normal routine before the meetings. It sort of bothered him because he got dressed, walked out and then came back in and laid down to show that he was so relaxed – but it was eating him up. There was something about him and I knew that the pressure was getting to him. He was trying to intimidate me and show me that he was so cool, so relaxed and he was 'The Professor' – but he wasn't. I could see it, and he showed me that he had a weakness and he wasn't as strong as he thought he was.

I was in the first race and he was in the third. I knew that if I won my first heat it would put pressure on him. So when I went out and won my first race, I threw the gauntlet down right there. He got third and I just stacked the pressure against him, so that was what motivated me to win these races because I could see that I was stacking pressure on him and he was collapsing. I was taking advantage of that and I was on my game. It all started in that changing room because he gave me the confidence because it was the first time I had seen a weakness.

After he ran a third, I knew that if I won my next race that would put the pressure on him even more and that was my motivation. Heat 12 was a big race because I remember that Tommy Knudsen was on my inside, and he was off gate one and I was off gate two. Well gate two wasn't really working that well but I trapped on him and I thought, 'I'm doing good'. I was pretty confident when I met Nielsen and I didn't know where he was in relation to the scores.

Hamill sensed that this was his time to shine. Everything that he had worked hard for since his first ride at Maely's ranch was coming down to this one September day in 1996. This was what it had all been about, and he knew it. It all seemed like a dream when he was a youngster in

Duarte, but the dream was there and the spoils of glory were sparkling on the centre green.

A reported crowd of 17,000 saw Billy win race after race as Nielsen crumpled under the pressure that the American was putting on the four-times World Champion. They met in heat 16 and the announcer had the crowd chanting 'Nielsen, Nielsen, Nielsen!' But Hamill made a superb start from the outside gate and went into the lead, with the Dane tucked into second. But Sweden's Henka Gustafsson got the run on the outside and was followed by Rickardsson and suddenly Nielsen was relegated to last – and that's where he finished.

Nielsen won his final programmed ride, but then the tactics and calculators came into play. There were all sorts of conversations and debates carrying on in the pits before heat 20 – the last of the qualifying races and Billy's final ride where he faced Sam Ermolenko, Mark Loram and Piotr Protasiewicz.

'Basically Hans had to miss out on the A-final for Billy to be able to win the World Championship,' recalled Cummings. 'Prior to his last race we had a look at the programme and it was quite apparent that if Billy was to finish third or worse, Sam and Mark Loram would make the A-final and that would eliminate Hans from the A-final. Greg was already in the A-final and Billy was too, having won his first four races. I spoke to a life-long friend of mine, Norrie Allen, and asked if he would mention to Mark the situation that Billy was in – that he had to win the A-final – just so that he was aware of it. I mentioned it to Sam and I mentioned it to Greg, and they said that they were all aware of the situation and what would happen, would happen.'

I was just racing, and Craiger came up to me and said: 'You gotta let Sam and Loram beat you, but you've got to get third, not fourth, and then Nielsen would be in the B-final.' This was just before I was about to bump off, and it was like: 'I gotta get third? How do I do this?' I was on a roll at that point. To be honest that's what we had to do to make sure that Nielsen was in the B-final – he was vulnerable. 'Let Ermolenko and Loram beat you, it doesn't matter what order, just let them beat you', Craiger told me.

As the tapes went up on the all-important heat 20, Billy made the start but one could see that it was a tactical race. Loram had to get around Ermolenko to win the race, but Hamill, although clearly faster, was content to hold back Protasiewicz. It was done: Hamill was in the A-final and Nielsen wasn't.

'I knew I had to win the B-final and the Billy would have to win the A-final,' said Nielsen. He made a swift start from the outside to keep the pressure on the American and he won the B-final. Hamill was watching from the pits with his crew.

I remember watching Hans in the B-final and I remember thinking that I could be World Champion if I won my next race. Well I became so nervous that I couldn't breathe, I simply could not inhale air. I had to take a step back from that and say to myself, 'You shouldn't be thinking about that Billy. You should be thinking about the rut you're going to start in, the gear you're bike is going to have on, how much revs, where your hand's going to be on the clutch.' I just had to think about the basics and the details and totally step away. If I started thinking about the fact that I could be World Champion I would have lost it right there. I had to totally step away from that, which I did, and mentally I didn't even think about it.

At that time we used to walk out on the track before the final to choose our gate positions, and I think you could see that I was just thinking about my strategy. I was thinking about the basic necessities of 'I'm going to start in this rut and line up here and ride this line'. I knew, because it had just happened a minute ago, I honestly couldn't inhale, I was so into it. If you can imagine, I had worked that hard for all those years and it just came down to one race. I often wonder if it will ever come down to that again when the World Championship is decided in the very last race of the last GP – I hope it does.

He took the outside gate, which was the starting position that Nielsen had taken to win the B-final. His opponents were his long-time rival, Greg Hancock – who was eager to secure third and a bronze medal – fellow American Sam Ermolenko and Mark Loram. The last two riders were desperate for points to qualify for an automatic Grand Prix place in the 1997 series. There was a lot to race for.

But as the tapes rose, Billy Hamill exploded from the outside gate and swept across his rivals and took command on the first bend. He sped away into glory and let his rivals settle their own battles behind him. Loram took second, his Team Exide partner Hancock was third and did enough to secure third overall in the Championship, while Sam was fourth.

I was on my game. I was that confident that I picked gate four and I knew that I could make it from there. That was where I wanted to be and I knew the rut I wanted to be in. Every time I go back to Vojens I look at that rut, because it's still there, and it's a certain spot in gate four that helped me win the World Championship. I was so focussed that it didn't really dawn on me that I had won the World Championship. I was so relaxed, so calm and so cool.

I had just won the World Championship and yet I did a couple of wheelies. I don't even know how I did them because my legs were shaking. How I had the balls to do that after such an emotional thing had happened to me I don't really know, but I was still having fun. When I crossed the line and punched the air with my right hand I pulled the kill switch out and I had to put it back in! You should never do that but it was just the emotion and the reaction of what I had just done. It was a dream that I had realised and I didn't sleep for two days after that.

When Jacob Olsen interviewed me after the race, I remembered watching the Super Bowl one time and they were interviewing the top players and they asked one of them what they were going to do now they had won the Super Bowl? And one of them replied: 'I'm going to Disneyland.' So when Jacob came up to me and said:

'You've just won the 1996 World Championship, what are going to do next?'

I replied: 'I'm going to Disneyland!'

It just happened that he said it like that, and that reply popped into my head. It was a totally spontaneous reaction. It was pretty amazing. I would have been quite happy with second because I had a good season. I don't think anyone gave me much chance because I was in Nielsen's backyard. I remember when they were talking about the 2003 Championship and everyone was saying that there was no way that Crumpie was going to lose it. And I didn't think so because on the parade you could see that the nerves were just eating him up. I think Jason lost it, I don't think Nicki won it.

'Just before we were walking up to the starting gate from the pit gate, Sam said to me, "Tell Billy he's going to have to race me for it", and that's what I did,' recalled Craiger. 'There was no way that Sam was going to beat Billy on that day anyway. I've never seen Billy before or since in the frame of mind that he was in that day. Unfortunately, the focus that he had for that meeting he has never been able to achieve since then. He certainly had more than one World Championship in him; he was certainly good enough as a rider to win the title again.

'It's a very strange feeling winning the World Championship with somebody, because all my life as a speedway mechanic I always wanted to win the World Championship. I came close with Shawn Moran, and I won a lot of major domestic competitions like the US Nationals with Bobby, the Overseas and Intercontinental Finals with Shawn, and I won a few Grand Prixs with Billy, so you'd think that winning the World Championship is going to be something that is really, really special. But it's actually like a relief when you win it, it's like the Holy Grail. So it's more of a relief than euphoria winning it. And that night in Vojens we were so emotionally and physically drained we just went to bed!'

It had been an amazing night of speedway history – what a climax. I have never seen a rider look so pleased and happy after winning the World title. He had a smile on him that was as wide as the Grand Canyon itself. It was the realisation of a child's dream, and it showed – he kissed the *Sky Sports* TV interviewer Julian Ryder on the cheek! His family was there to see him make his dream come true, and Christina and his daughter Margi were also in attendance for his big night. Just to make the night completely perfect there was even a Californian state flag flying in celebration.

He was so focussed that while he was on the rostrum he still felt as though he had to go out and make another start. Was he World Champion? Could it be true? It was true. Nielsen was gracious and sporting in defeat and, although obviously disappointed, he congratulated the American. But typical of his night, while he was stood on the rostrum he couldn't even open the bottle of champagne for the celebrations! A new era had begun.

There was a press tent and right after the meeting there was me, my wife, Trent Bucholz, Craiger, Krusty and Paul Willits of EBE Motor Factors, and we just had a beer tap. We just sat there drinking beers. When we left that stadium there wasn't a soul left! We were the last ones to leave, and then we went back to the hotel and had a big party there. I got to bed at 3-4 in the morning but I just couldn't sleep because I was so excited. When I got back to England the phone never stopped ringing with people congratulating me and I was still pumped up with it all. I was just doing press things from that moment on, and by the time I got to the Elite League Riders' Championship I didn't want to race. I was not into it at all and it was very difficult to concentrate after winning that and I only scored 3 points.

We took the World Championship trophy and sat it in the bar at Cradley, or Stoke as it was, and just had a beer with everyone. Greg had got third too and we just savoured the moment because we were living the dream.

We had a huge party in America. My Mom put on a party in the old Clown Town where we used to go when I was a kid. Now it's called 'Club 101', and we rented it out and hired a band and invited 300-400 people. Different people from throughout my career got up and gave a speech, people like KK, and it was brilliant. We had a couple of fights which you have at all good parties because it's part of a country and western style. My grandfather said to me: 'You've established yourself in your sport now – congratulations son.' There was no more said. I'm able to talk to my grandfather and my father about our different professions because they are comparable on a competition level.

Billy was the fourth American to win the World Championship, and he was invited to the AMA Awards dinner where he was also nominated as pro-athlete of the year – which went to motocross star, Jeremy McGrath. He was the only American motorcycle World Individual Champion that year, so you would expect his country's federation to make it a memorable occasion and they didn't disappoint. Drawing from all their knowledge of speedway and their usual attention to detail, Billy's wife Christina remembered it well.

'Billy had just won the World Championship and he was the first American to win the Championship since Sam – and this was a big deal,' she said. 'So we were all there in Las Vegas, my whole family, and we were all sat at this table and then the big announcement came: "Ladies and gentleman, the new World Speedway Champion, Billy Hamill!"'

'And there was a picture of Hans Nielsen on the wall! They didn't even have a picture of Billy, it was a Danish rider! And I was so mad, and he never said a word. He didn't even say something like: "Oh don't I look like the guy behind me?" I was so upset that our own federation didn't even know what he looked like. If it was Greg I could have accepted it more, but they had Hans Nielsen, the man he defeated to win the World Championship and he was Danish. That was bad. And he never said a word, he never told the AMA or anything.'

Cradley & Stoke finished fifth in the Premier League, but it wasn't financially viable to continue racing at Loomer Road. The Heathens management were unable to return to Dudley Wood or find a suitable site to build their own venue. All the riders were made available for transfer, and for the first time since 1990 Billy and Greg would not be riding in the same team – Hancock had signed for Coventry.

Hamill would have no problems finding a new British club as the reigning World Champion and he had finished at the top of the Premier League averages for the second successive season. He signed for Belle Vue where he found himself in a team that resembled Little America. His team-mates were Sam Ermolenko, Chris Manchester, Charlie Venagas – who were all Americans – and Jason Lyons and Nathan Murray. It was a strong-looking team, and they were expected to do well in another re-structuring of the league. Belle Vue were one of the glamour clubs of British Speedway, but since their forced move from the famous track at Hyde Road to the Greyhound Stadium at Kirkmanshulme Lane, the magic of the Aces had already begun to disappear by the time Billy had joined them.

The Premier League had been scrapped and was replaced by a three league structure – the Elite, Premier and Amateur Leagues. There was no promotion or relegation and it is this format – the Conference has now replaced the Amateur League – that is in place at the time of writing.

During the winter Blomfeldt & Associates was also dissolved, and Carl Blomfeldt was planning to leave speedway and go home to Canada. Blomfeldt & Associates had become a well-known brand in speedway racing, having successfully worked on engines for many international riders. It was Blomfeldt's tuning that had powered Hamill to World Championship glory, so Craiger and Billy were keen to keep him in their team.

Carl and Sam Ermolenko split up for whatever reason and Carl was going to go back to Canada. My way of thinking was that I had just won the World Championship with Carl and now I was going to have to change engine tuners. He was obviously an asset to my racing programme, and I wanted to keep him to try and retain the Championship. He suggested to Craiger and myself that we open a business and, if we were prepared to fund it, he would come and work for us and then I would have Carl Blomfeldt doing my engines. That's how Bullet Enterprises came about, and Craiger was going to work alongside him because he was interested in that aspect. It cost us around £20,000 to start the business and the idea was that it would fund itself by doing other riders' engines.

Sam and Carl Blomfeldt had a big falling out and I was kind of piggy in the middle. And then Sam and I were team-mates and he wasn't very happy with me, but I didn't do anything. Carl was doing a lot of riders' engines, not just mine. I was hiring him to do my engines like Peter and Mikael Karlsson were, and Carl and Sam had a business agreement. I had won the World Championship riding engines he had worked on so I wanted to keep him onboard. It was business, and I had nothing against Sam and I didn't do anything directly to him.

As the reigning World Champion, Hamill discovered that there were responsibilities that went with the crown. He was the figurehead for the sport, and there were more media and press engagements than ever before. He appeared on BBC TV's *A Question of Sport* programme and also made an appearance as a guest on Sky Sports coverage of the booming World Superbike Championship. And, of course, Exide also made as much use as possible from having the World Champion promoting their product.

I wanted my natural rewards and it was everything I hoped it would be. I got paid from Exide and it was very rewarding. It's difficult for Americans to reap the rewards compared with the English, Danish or the Swedes because they were at home. But we were 5,000 miles away from home and you can only attract so much attention. I knew that was the reality.

I remember the World Superbike programme was the Carl Fogarty show. It was based around Foggy because Sky was British, and it was a bit ridiculous because there were other riders out there other than Foggy. The presenter was Keith Huewen. I had met Troy Corser in 1996, who went on to win the Championship in Spain later that year. As a sport, all we had to do was emulate what they were doing – the writing was on the wall.

I also did the Motorcycle Show at the NEC and that was cool. We were on TV and we were riding at the head of a parade of 200 bikers. Although we never really saw eye-to-eye, Tony Summers was very clever with his marketing plan and he opened up a lot of doors for speedway in general. We did things like that and the sport gained some notoriety and it benefited from the exposure it got.

During the winter I did a two-day desert bike ride from Los Angeles to Las Vegas. It was 500 miles and I was riding a Honda XR650 and we were just hauling butt across the desert and it was a really cool experience. It came about through one of my sponsors and they told me they had a bike ready. I had a really good time but it was so tiring because we were riding nine hours a day. We went from LA to Bairstow and slept in a hotel there, then on to Las Vegas. Some of the terrain was unbelievable and the towns we went through were full-on Western towns and they still had the rail in the front of the saloons to tie your horse up! I didn't think there were still towns around like that, I was really amazed. This time, however, they were littered with motorcycles.

It was 80% dirt and 20% road, so in order for me to be able to complete the course I needed a road licence to go on the road. And you're supposed to have a California motorcycle licence. Well I never had a motorcycle licence because luckily I knew the organiser. And he said: 'Oh you'll be all right.' But one day I decided to take the test to get a licence. I went in to do the written test and I failed! I failed it twice and I just passed it the third time – I didn't study for it or anything. They were multiple choice answers of A, B, C or D. You would think that it would be common sense but it's not, you have to do what the instruction manual tells you – I couldn't believe it. I got my permit, and then I had to take the riding test. It seemed too much of an effort, and I remember thinking about the publicity: 'World Speedway Champion fails test.'

I always had road bikes because that was the way I used to get to and from school. So I had some experience. This was in 1992, and I felt so vulnerable on this bike, and the traffic was a lot worse than when I was a kid. I thought that it was too dangerous because you are basically battling cars.

We saw a really bad motorcycle accident and it put my kids off riding a motorcycle on the road. I was sat in the passenger seat and Christina was driving. We saw a guy get hit by a car doing about 70mph, and it happened right in front of us. Our kids were in the back with our nephew. We slammed on the brakes to avoid hitting him, but his bike was still going – ghost riding. He was just wearing a t-shirt and jeans, and he had fallen off the side. He ended up coming to rest right in front of us, so naturally I jumped out to help him.

He was trying to get up and I told him to just lay there. Someone had already called the ambulance, so I just sat there with him and my kids were sat in the car wondering what their dad was doing in the middle of the freeway with this guy who had fallen off his motorcycle and was covered in blood. I stayed with him for a good ten-fifteen minutes and he was badly busted up. You can imagine that was a long time for a guy who had a broken wrist, and two broken legs. He was wearing a half-face helmet so his face was cut badly. It spooked my kids and they don't want to get on a bike on the street after they saw that. That was hairy for them, and hairy for me too because when I see blood I can pass out. His leg was broken and there was a lot of blood. I can't believe I did what I did, it was only because he landed right in front of us and I was the only one there – I had to help because he had two broken legs and he was trying to get up.

'He cannot deal with it,' said Christina. 'I look after the kids in that way because he cannot deal with the sight of blood, and I look after him too. If it was the other way around we would have split up because he just cannot deal with it. Kurtis had to have stitches in his chin after a fall and the doctor said, "Can you please ask your husband to go and sit down because if he doesn't, he is going to pass out on us."'

I raced better in '97 than I did in 1996. I had a lot of pressure from being the World number one, and a lot of it came from me because I wanted to do it again. And I wanted to be a good World Champion. I had to be on the top of my game, and if you did get beat then they would rub your face in it. As World Champion you were not allowed to get beat. I remember Garry Stead beat me at Bradford one time and it was the biggest moment in his career. Being the defending World Champion motivated me. I was training very hard during the off-season and I had a personal trainer and every spare moment I had I spent it in the gym. I was training five days a week and I was on a good diet. I just elevated myself because I knew I had to stay up there.

One of the things that mainstream motorcycle racing did that Billy and his team tried to bring in was the merchandising. In both MotoGP and World Superbike everything is licensed and trademarked. But in speedway racing this is not the case. A prospective souvenir seller can purchase an exclusive licence from one of the promoters and sell the club's merchandise at the track. But a rider receives no money from the sale of his image from the seller or the club.

Therefore, Billy had 'official' merchandise commissioned for sale such as t-shirts, stickers, pens, posters and photographs. This enabled him to market himself and reap some of the financial rewards and plough some of the funds back into his racing programme. However, this did not please some of the souvenir vendors who believed that they had the sole rights to sell his image at the various venues and didn't want to purchase a licence to do so. John Jones, the Belle Vue souvenir vendor, was aggressive towards Billy and his team over the situation, even to the point that he told Hamill on his return to the venue as a Coventry rider that he had to hand over his Belle Vue Aces race jacket from 1997 because he had the souvenir rights! It was yet another indication of the fact that speedway racing still wasn't ready for a marketing campaign on a full commercial scale that is commonplace in other forms of motorcycle racing.

Billy's form for the Aces was second to none as he soared at the top of the league's averages, but the club was underperforming as a team. After spending his entire British career within the family atmosphere of Cradley, a season racing for John Perrin at Belle Vue was an eye-opener.

I found John Perrin very difficult to work with as a team manager. I had to keep my distance if I wanted to be a Belle Vue rider. The team spirit wasn't that good and I just used to go there and do my job.

He was very vocal with his criticism. He used to get so pissed off that halfway through the meeting he would get in his car and drive off! He would be gone and we wouldn't have a team manager. There was no one to tell us who was in the nominated race or anything. It was like, what should we do? There was no-one there to do it. We used to have to make those decisions ourselves and as Sam was captain a lot of it came down to him. It was ridiculous but that's the way Perrin was.

I had to keep my distance otherwise there would be a lot of confrontations. All that starts at the top and to a certain extent John Perrin creates that negative atmosphere.

Surely the Aces management couldn't have found any cause for grumbles from Hamill's performances as he was an out and out number one for the team. Only once did he fail to score double figures at Swindon, and even then his score was 9 plus 1 bonus point for finishing in a scoring position behind his team-mate – therefore he was paid for 10 points.

In his second meeting for the club he scorched to a 15-point maximum and in 40 matches he only scored less than 12 points on nine occasions. Even bringing in Paul Smith and Paul Thorp couldn't turn the club's fortunes around and they finished in sixth place out of ten clubs and were trophy-less. A situation that frustrated the Aces manager, as Hamill recalled:

I had a great year when I rode for them and finished at the top of the averages. At the end of the season we went to the dinner and dance: I had my wife and daughter with me and Craiger had his wife with him. And the presenter asked Perrin about the season and he replied: 'Oh it was fucking crap!'

All he did was slag off every individual rider, and I remember that I was very close to getting up and walking out. This was at the beginning, before the event had really got underway. He was so negative and it was a very negative environment. I didn't feel that I deserved to be slagged off after I had finished top of the averages and won a hell of a lot of races for Belle Vue. I made up my mind right then that I wasn't going to ride for Belle Vue again.

His defence of the World crown began at Prague in the Czech Republic, when in his first race he was surprisingly beaten by Poland's Slawomir Drabik. And then he finished third in his next race behind Henrik Gustafsson and Hans Nielsen – not a good start.

I was leading the second race when it was restarted and I ended up third in the rerun. It started to look bleaker and bleaker, but I kept my head up and going into my third ride I knew I had to win it. I had the outside gate and made the start over Tomasz Gollob and Piotr Protasiewicz and I was leading when it was stopped again! I was getting cheesed off, but I couldn't let it get to me.

I went to bump off for the rerun when Craiger stopped me and said that we had a flat tyre. So with the riders on a two-minute time allowance to get to the tapes I had to jump onto my second bike. Fortunately it was okay and I won the race and from then on I was all right and qualified for the A-final with Greg, Gollob and Drabik.

When the tapes went up I was last, but I just rode around the fence, but I was going so fast that by the time I got to turn three I had to slow up! I had lost my momentum and there was no way I could catch Greg and I was second – which was a good start.

In the second GP in Sweden I had problems with my first bike and my second wasn't right for the track. From that moment on we were chasing our tails but I hadn't given up hope of retaining my title.

Hamill was 13 points adrift of the Championship leader Greg Hancock going into the unfamiliar venue of Landshut in Germany for the third GP. The wet weather forced the postponement of the original staging date of Saturday and it was rescheduled for the next day. Billy made up for the Swedish disappointment by qualifying for the A-final. But in a typically tight and tough final, Hancock's foot peg punctured his rear tyre and he was out of the race. Hans Nielsen won the meeting and he sneaked into second place overall and relegated Hamill to third. Greg was looking comfortable at the top of the standings with a 14-point cushion over Nielsen.

The Bullet was doing his racing the hard way – coming from the back. And his tactics in the British GP at Bradford did not please the crowd who jeered the American after a ruthless ride against Nielsen. He collided with the Dane on the back straight and Nielsen retired from the race. Earlier in the evening he had also been involved in another tight tussle with Gustafsson and the Swede bailed out – he had recently returned from a broken leg and he was unable to make the rerun.

It was a controversial situation with Hans but it was a manoeuvre that I learned from him! It's not something I would practise every day but it was a technique, a calculated move. He had done it to me many times and it was payback! It was a fierce move but we were in the World Championship.

I had a coming together with Mark Loram too. I think we both had the same thing in mind and we collided big time and did well to save it. I got second to Brian Andersen and I felt that if I could keep plugging away I was still in with a chance.

Hamill was equal second with Andersen on 68 points. Hancock's lead had been reduced to 7 points because he was riding borrowed equipment after the van that was carrying his bikes and equipment caught fire en route to the track. The Championship race was on.

In a controversial Grand Prix at Wroclaw that saw the meeting delayed for nearly two hours to allow the track staff to work on the terrible surface, the 35,000 crowd witnessed Hancock stretch his lead at the top with his second GP victory of the season. Despite a fall, Hamill finished second in the A-final but he was now 12 points behind and he said: 'If I cannot win, that looks unlikely now, then there is nobody I'd rather see taking over than Greg.' And then, prophetically as it would turn out, he criticised the Polish safety fences: 'They should take a long look at their safety fences. There are a lot of injuries that are caused by the fences and they should see what they do in Sweden.'

Greg's fourth place in the final GP at Vojens clinched the title and Hamill took the silver medal position. He fought to the end, but his poor performance in Sweden proved too much of a handicap.

Greg and I had a respectable rivalry. Greg is a totally different character to what I am. He would spend a lot of time to manipulate situations in his favour. I'm a competitor on the track, and then when it's over I want to relax and have a beer and have a drink with my friends. Greg's not like that, he works on his racing on and off the track.

We had the Penhall and Schwartz type of relationship. We weren't best buddies before we came to England and, apart from a few, we never shared the same friends before we came to England. We lived together, we helped each other, we rode together, but on top of all that we raced against each other too. There was always a shield put up by both of us because we could never become good friends because we were competing against each other.

I remember getting pissed off because Greg would compete off the track. It would hurt and I couldn't believe he would do that because he was a good guy. I didn't compete off the track, but he would do things off the track to manipulate the situation and back me into a corner. Overall I think it helped me and made me more determined.

He wanted to be World Champion, and he was the blue-eyed boy of American Speedway while I was rough and raw. So how could I win a World Championship and him not? I think it was the fear of not being World Champion that drove Greg in 1997. Both our World Championships were two different situations. I only had the pressure I put on myself, while Greg had a lot of expectation because of the Penhall connection, and because I won it first it motivated him. We bounced off each other. It wasn't that we weren't getting along, we had so many people involved in our racing programmes over the years and they were competitive too. My guys wanted me to win, and his guys wanted him to win. There was a lot of rivalry between the mechanics, and even our wives really. I honestly think that I was pretty fair and genuine off the track, while behind the scenes Greg was doing things to go in his favour – good or bad, that wasn't me. I'm saying it's wrong and I'm not saying it's right, but that's the way it was.

Hamill finished the season at the top of the averages for the third successive year – there is no reward for finishing as the top rider. England faced the USA in a one-off Test match in memory of the US team manager John Scott, who died in 1997. Hamill scored 14 points – dropping his only point to Chris Louis – but the Yanks lost 49-47.

Five days later Hancock and Hamill teamed up again in another memorial meeting, the Tom Johnson Memorial Trophy. Wolverhampton staged a match against the old Cradley team as it seemed possible that a new site had been found for their Black Country rivals. The gate receipts were to be put back into the fund that was trying to revive the Heathens.

A huge crowd gathered to watch these two old rivals do battle once again, but Wolves were the winners 49-41 – despite an 18-point maximum from Hancock and 10 points from the Bullet. Even two maximum heat wins from the American duo couldn't save the Heathens, but it was hoped that the hammer that was displayed on their race jackets wouldn't be lost to the sport for ever.

Unfortunately all the optimism was unfounded as sadly Cradley did not come to the tapes in 1998. Hamill left Belle Vue and once again teamed up with Hancock at Coventry and formed a potent spearhead that also included Brian Andersen as a third heat leader. A new period with the Coventry Bees was about to begin.

Exide also became involved with Coventry Speedway and they also staged a training school at Sheffield where their two American stars passed on some valuable tips to the novices. Billy has always taken much pleasure and satisfaction from helping the youngsters and took part in the Interspan Training Schools at the end of the British season.

I helped Matt Becker out with helmets and stuff like that and he was called the 'Pellet' because of my involvement with him. I particularly like working with the kids because they are the future of the sport. I don't talk down to them; I try to get on a level with them.

Some of the drills I did at training schools I actually incorporate into my schools now. I think the best thing about the schools is that early on in their riding career they don't pick up bad habits, they learn the right technique and the right way to do it and you don't have to correct it later. I think that's most beneficial. Just learning how to do things the right way is half the battle. It was with me, and I think that applies to a lot of the kids who don't have dads that used to ride speedway. That's where it was extremely important to me. Just learning drills and exercises, it was a case of just being shown and then it was up to you how much you wanted to practise and learn this or that. Once you know that, then at least you know you are on the right track. Speedway is such a unique motorcycle [sport] that the technique is totally different.

Hamill happily renewed his relationship with Colin Pratt, who was the team manager at Coventry, and with another former Heathen in the side in the shape of David Walsh; there was more than just a hint of a Black Country influence about the team. But there were changes made to Billy's own personal team.

Craiger and Carl are both strong-willed characters, and they both wanted to do the same thing and they were butting heads. I was piggy in the middle of all this, and Carl threw up his hands and said that he couldn't continue. I think he solicited Tony Rickardsson at the German Grand Prix in 1997. He wasn't happy with the situation because he wasn't happy with Craiger's attitude. Not only was it not a good atmosphere, it was having an effect on my racing and I found that negativity very distracting.

Craiger basically convinced me that he could do the same job that Carl used to do and run the business, so I put my faith in that. I don't honestly feel that either Craiger nor I really got out of it what we put into it – especially for the amount of effort that we put in. We both put our heart and soul into it for many years and we really didn't get anywhere – and I still feel that way.

Billy made a disappointing start to his career for Coventry when he broke a bone in his foot after a collision with Mikael Karlsson during a challenge match against Wolverhampton. He was then in the wars again in a horrific spill against his old club Belle Vue when he crashed with Jason Lyons and sustained a broken toe, a gashed chin, concussion and a wrist injury.

After two weeks on the sidelines, he returned to score a stunning 21-point maximum against Swindon and then followed that up with a paid maximum against Eastbourne. Three more six-ride maximums followed in the weeks ahead and he was sitting at the top of the Bees averages. It looked as though he was capable of regaining the World title and, racing for Coventry, he was as close to feeling at home in Britain as he could possibly get.

Seven

DANGER IN THE DUST

I saw the crash on the video in the pits then ran out to see if he was okay. You could see that he was in a lot of pain and couldn't breathe. You don't like to see that happen to anybody, but when it's one of your closest buddies, it's even worse.

Greg Hancock (Coventry, Exide and US team-mate, 1998)

'Go hard or go home' was the phrase that Hamill used to describe the kind of racing that the new racing system had brought into the Grand Prix. It was a knockout format that was similar to the one they used in the USA but on a larger scale. Basically, if a rider finished third or fourth twice, then he was eliminated from the rest of the meeting.

The old A, B, C and D finals were scrapped in favour of a Grand and Consolation Final. The field was also increased to twenty-four riders and split into two qualifying groups, the pre-main and the main event. Then the top eight from the main event would progress to two semi-finals where the top two from each would qualify for a winner-takes-all final. The latter was where the eight seeded riders would start, and the top eight from each Grand Prix would start in the main event at the next GP.

Greg Hancock, the defending champion, openly admitted that he didn't like the new format. However, it was brought in to spice up the competition and it didn't disappoint. Virtually overnight the racing took on a new level of previously unparalleled intensity. Daring was often replaced by desperation, and aggression was frequently overshadowed by attack!

The first GP took place in Prague and Tony Rickardsson won his first Grand Prix in an incident-packed meeting. Billy took second place after rounding Tomasz Gollob on the opening lap. It was a good start to the series and if the format was designed for TV – as it was suggested – then they were going to get both the pictures and excitement they wanted.

The second round in Pocking was a watershed meeting for Hamill and the series. The racing was action packed, dramatic and brutal – on and off the track. In an electric atmosphere Hamill and the spectacular Pole, Gollob, had a disagreement on the track that spilled over into the pits.

I remember that my engine wasn't working all that well. I wasn't as fast as everyone else. I was basically riding out of my skin, that's why that GP changed me. I shouldn't have been third; I should have been ninth or tenth.

I had passed Gollob earlier on, and although he was faster than me I was on the racing line so he couldn't get around me. After the race he gave me the finger, so I just said, 'Fuck you, dickhead', and he roared off. When he got into the pits, Craiger approached him and said, 'What's your problem?' Gollob kept pumping the clutch at Craiger; he was revving the bike and popping the clutch at him. When I came in and saw this, I was so angry that I just grabbed a handful of throttle, popped the clutch and T-boned him. I got off my bike and said: 'Come on, let's go.'

He was basically threatening Craiger. And then Mick Sheppard jumped down from the crowd and kidney-punched Gollob! I didn't know who this guy was and I thought, 'Great!' Gollob didn't know who he was either and he's like: 'Who's hitting me?' And I thought I gotta have this guy on my team! So Mick joined my team! He's been with me ever since and he's been very loyal over the years and his boys too – they've all helped me. They do it because they love it and we're very good friends. Mick used to be one of the track staff at Coventry before he hooked up with me and the guy has been a great help. Nothing's too much trouble for him.

I think it's tough when you race any top rider, and it's going to be a battle. Any time when two top riders clash you're gonna be trading paint. I enjoy pushing myself to that level and I enjoy succeeding. I don't think I enjoy it that much at the time because I'm so wrapped up in it, it's not fun but it is rewarding.

I was working with Anton Nischler at the time because Carl had left and I was working hard on my set-up. I had pretty good engines, but they weren't as good as Greg had and we hadn't achieved what we wanted to achieve. I was putting in a lot of effort and a lot of money to get technically competitive, and I wasn't. I didn't feel that I was on a par with top guys like Rickardsson, Nilsen and Gollob – and I rode out of my skin. It just drained me and burnt me out. There I was working, working and working, and not getting what I was putting into it.

I lost a hell of a lot of motivation after that GP. I was burnt out for the whole season. I had nothing left to give because I gave so much in that GP – mentally and physically. I gave it everything I had, physically, mentally and emotionally – there was nothing left, I just couldn't give any more. I had nothing in reserve: I had no motivation, no enthusiasm and I had lost the fight.

The 2003 ELRC was a perfect example of how draining the Grand Prix series is because all the top riders were spent and burnt out. And that system creates that. Probably more emotionally than mentally, but it all goes together.

Tony Rickardsson had won the opening two Grand Prixs back-to-back and Hamill's third place put him in second place in the Championship standings – 12 points behind the Swede. Vojens proved to be a disappointment as he failed to get to the semi-finals for the first time and slipped down the leader board to fourth. Jason Crump won the British round while Billy finished third in the Consolation Final to maintain his fourth place.

But a disappointing night at Linkopping in Sweden saw him slip down the Championship ladder to sixth on 61 points. He was close to eighth place but a reasonable performance in the last round in Poland should have guaranteed his place in the 1999 tournament.

But before the final Grand Prix, he teamed up with Greg and won his fourth World Team Championship.

We were delayed and Sam Ermolenko, who was the reserve, drove out there and he was there waiting and got as much ready for us as he could. We got to the track 5 minutes before the first race. We missed the rider's parade, and we got changed and just had time to put our gear on and then we went out for the first race against the Gollob brothers.

I remember sitting there on the plane at Copenhagen and Greg was stressing, and for some reason I was really relaxed about the whole situation. And I remember saying to him: 'Well, hey, at least we're not going to have any down time! We get there, do our job and get out of there – it'll be great. At least we won't have to sit there and go through all the bullshit.'

And that's what we did: wham, bam, thank you ma'am. We got there, a rainy night, and because we rode together at Cradley, Greg was on the inside and I was on the outside and we just did what we always did. We smoked everyone, great performance, and one of the most enjoyable things I've done and it was nice to do something like that together.

We never even spoke about riding together. It just happened, it was just magic. We never spoke before the race about strategy or tactics – we never did. It was something that happened. It was just mutual respect more than anything. Early on, Greg was a better team rider than I was – I just wanted to win – and he still is. I'm a better team rider now than I was then, because I was brought up to look forward not to look back, so I never really looked for other people. I think it came natural to Greg.

The Polonia Stadium in Bydgoszcz was staging the Polish GP for the first time. It was Tomasz Gollob's home track and a sell-out crowd assembled to provide an atmosphere that was more like an audience for a rock concert than a speedway meeting. This pulsating atmosphere of expectation, excitement and hostility could be felt through the Sky TV screens.

Billy's first race was in heat 3. He needed a good start to the meeting and his opponents were wild card entry Tony Kasper, Henka Gustafsson and Jason Crump. The latter two riders were desperate for points to ensure their places in the 1999 GP – just how desperate would be illustrated to the Bullet in the cruellest of ways. He was about to discover how fragile a speedway rider's career could be.

As the tapes rose, a seemingly-out-of-control Crump moved across and into Hamill's path. At the 30-yard line – a white line that indicates a mark where the riders are expected to maintain their lane to the best of their ability before turning – Crump was already into the side of the American. He careered across the field taking Hamill with him until the Bullet was deposited onto the track and he slid helplessly and heavily into the fence.

Crump was off gate one and I was off two, and the other riders were Kasper and Gustafsson. He effectively took me out and we were going for the top 8. At first I didn't know what I had done, but my legs went into convulsions or something and I knew it was serious. I had never felt anything like it, and I had no control over it. My legs were twitching and I couldn't breathe. I just could not breathe, and I knew what it was like to have the wind knocked out of me from other crashes. I thought my lungs had collapsed or something because I couldn't grasp any air and I knew that I was seriously injured straightaway.

The first thing I remember was that it seemed to take forever for anyone to get to me and help me, probably because I couldn't breathe. They were there but they weren't helping me. I was in a hell of a lot of pain, and I didn't know if I was paralysed but I thought I could be at that point. My legs were going into spasms and I couldn't really control them. I had some feeling but I didn't know how much. They injected me straightaway with something to help me with the pain and to calm me down because I was scared and wound up. I remember seeing Erik [Gundersen] standing at the back of the ambulance and I thought, 'Oh fucking hell, how ironic is this?' He just tried to reassure me by saying: 'You'll be all right.' They put me on this backboard and they were all very careful with me and made sure I was as comfortable as I could be under the circumstances, but the ambulance just stormed off and the bed just went whack into the end of the wall of the ambulance from the sheer acceleration from the vehicle.

Luckily Craiger was inside with me to hold stuff in place and the hospital was only about a kilometre away from the track. But as you came out of the stadium there were all these speed bumps, and a big sweeping right-hand turn, and this guy was driving over them at around 40mph and everything was flying around the ambulance – all the medicines and everything. The siren was wailing and Craiger was shouting at the driver to slow down by saying some-thing like: 'What the fuck are you doing, you fuckin' idiot!' That was an experience in itself.

Meanwhile his wife Christina was at home watching all the drama unfold on the television screen with their daughter Margi and Craig Cummings' wife.

'I was pregnant with Kurtis at the time and it was scary,' she said. 'I assured Margi that papa would be okay. I saw the look on Greg's face when they had a close up of him on the TV and that worried me. Craig called me to let me know what was going on so I knew that he wasn't paralysed and I just wanted him to come home. I spoke to Billy and he was doped up with morphine, but he said he could move his legs. I just wanted him to come home.'

'I kept calling her to let her know what was happening with her husband and that wasn't very pleasant,' admitted Craig. 'But these things have to be done. It was upsetting to see one of your best friends and the guy you work for in so much distress. At the time we weren't really thinking about that, we were thinking about Billy's health. To get hurt in Poland is a pretty scary ordeal at anytime, but to break your back in Poland is even worse. Per Jonsson and Roland Danno have been badly injured there and maybe they didn't have the best of medical treatment at the time.'

Crump wasn't excluded from the rerun. He too had collapsed onto the centre green after the incident with a shoulder injury. According to the reports of the time, he had dislocated his shoulder and at the scene it was put back in. *Sky Sports* presenter Keith Huewen, a former 500cc road racer who was a team-mate of Barry Sheene, couldn't believe that the Australian had recovered sufficiently to race and speculated that he may have been 'shamming'. His fellow Aussie riders suddenly emerged with duct tape and proceeded to tape his injured shoulder over the top of his leathers!

Studio guest Kelvin Tatum, a former World Finalist and World Long Track Champion described the scene as 'silly'. Crump had collided with Hamill almost as soon as the tapes had gone up, and yet here he was, 'taped up' and about to take his place in the rerun while his fallen rival was being injected with morphine to combat the pain.

I suspect that he knew what he was doing. I think that because in my opinion that's the way the guy was and still is. I never held anything against him until after I saw the video of the meeting, and I saw what looked to me to be him faking a shoulder injury. I thought that he put on a big Hollywood act, and decided that he was the biggest piece of shit that I had ever raced against.

When you're involved in these big crashes and someone is injured badly, you should – in my view at least – give them a phone call and see how they are doing. But the guy never attempted once to do anything. So I pretty much lost respect for him altogether and I held a grudge to a certain extent. I've been raised not to hold grudges, and his lack of respect made me treat him with the same level of respect.

In competitive motorcycle racing you're going to have accidents, but there is a line there and I suspect that he crossed that line. He seemed to show it by the antics of 'Oh my shoulder came out of its socket' and all that bullshit.

Later at Peterborough I had beaten him in a race and he came round to shake my hand but I refused. He roared off and made a big thing out of it to the crowd on the home straight, but I wasn't interested. There was a bit of debate about it in the pits after the race, but I had no respect for him at all.

A long time has passed now and I don't have a problem with him as such, but I don't think I shall ever respect him because I think I saw his true colours. People change, but I wouldn't do that and I wouldn't expect it to be done to me. It was way over the top if he did fake that shoulder injury and they were all out there trying to duct tape him back together – give me a break! I don't think you can duct tape someone's shoulder together over the top of his leathers, and then send him out in a 'you can go out there and win now' type of situation. I even sometimes suspect he did a deal with Kasper – who was a wild card entry – to drop some points so he could get in for 1999. Armando Castagna, who is a person who has very strong morals and has high values, allegedly felt the same way. He was friends with Kasper and apparently told him that he wasn't his friend anymore for doing that, and wondered where his morals were to do that while I was laying in a hospital bed. This was going on while I was in the hospital and I only found out about that later. It was the lowest point really.

Once I was in the hospital it was a totally different story – it was brilliant. Per Jonsson had been in there before because that was where he sustained his injuries in 1994. I think it was the same doctor, and he looked at me and said: 'Speedway? Back?' And he just shook his head and said something like 'Oh no', and I was scared.

When I saw the doctor do that I was worried, and I thought I was in big trouble. The worst thing that ever happened was that they fitted a catheter to me

– basically they stuck a tube down my dick! They did this because they didn't know if I could control my bladder or not, so they stuck this tube in me. I just couldn't believe that this was happening to me and I turned to one of the nurses there and said: 'You know shit is supposed to come out of there – not go in!'

It drained my bladder and I didn't have to push or anything. It just drained the liquid that your body produces. But I knew I had feeling at that point because it hurt. At that point I just asked them to give me drugs to control the pain because I couldn't deal with it anymore. Craiger sat there through the whole thing, from the start to finish. He saw all of it.

'I was with him all the time,' recalled Cummings, 'the ambulance ride, the hospital, the X-ray room, the CAT scan, and I was holding him down on the trolley when they were putting the body cast on, it was pretty difficult. He couldn't have got any more intense medical help if he had been in any other country. The doctor that was treating him was absolutely fantastic. He explained every little thing that was going on in English at every stage of the way. He did a really good job for Billy, which was quite surprising when you hear all the horror stories about Polish hospitals. But it probably cut Billy's career short by a couple of years I would say.'

After they discovered what was wrong with me and how they were going to treat it, they had to straddle me to fit this torso cast. What they did was they put my head on one bed and then they had to pull the other bed away to about my knees, so I was suspended between these two beds in mid-air. They wrapped this torso cast around me to help keep my back straight and to heal together properly.

Obviously my body was going to flex because of my weight, so Craiger was holding my legs down as I was farting and gagging and he was right there. We laughed about it afterwards and I would say that he has been with me through thick and thin, even when I was farting in his face and gagging at him. They had me full of morphine at that point and, although I could still feel the pain, I was high and I was having fun with the nurses.

Christina was pregnant with Kurtis and Margi was little, and I talked to them on the phone before I went in for the CAT scan. Margi saw the accident and she was scared because she didn't really understand what was going on and I remember saying to my daughter, 'Don't worry, I'm okay and I'll be home tomorrow.' And that was horrible having to say that to my three-year-old daughter while I was laying there not knowing what was really wrong with me at that point – that was pretty heavy. I remember I said to one of the nurses: 'What's your name darling?'

'Agnes.'

'Well, let me tell me you Agnes, if you take care of me, if we have a daughter I promise I'll call her Agnes.'

I spoke to Christina the next day or whatever on the phone and I said to her, 'If we have a girl we're going to call her Agnes.'

'Oh no we're not,' she replied. But fortunately Kurtis was a boy.

Any country's hospital you go to they give you an experience. After the accident they wrapped me in a cast and they kept me in overnight. I remember that when I finally got back into my bed, and I managed to get as comfortable as I could be, I could hear the final going off – that was how close the hospital was to the track. The windows were open and I could hear the bikes and I could hear the crowd. I thought Tomasz Gollob won because the crowd went nuts, but Tony Rickardsson had clinched the World Championship. And I remember thinking that this sucks! When I was lying in that hospital going through those machines, I didn't want to ride anymore. But I'm talking for about five minutes at the most, but I did wonder why I was doing it.

And then they had to take me up to X-ray because they didn't come out good enough or something. There was this nurse who would give you an injection and just sort of laugh and watch. It always reminded me of that Black Crowes song 'She talks to Angels', and there's a line which says: 'The pain is going to make everything all right.' And this nurse, she had dark circles under her eyes and I think she must have been a druggie or something, because the way she looked at me when she administered the injection, it was like she was saying: 'You like that, huh?' And I was just spinning. It was weird and that was odd.

They took the X-rays and took me back and I eventually went to sleep at around 4 a.m., and it was about 7 a.m. when I woke up. I had a graze on my left arm, and I was sleeping with my arms on top of this torso cast, then all of a sudden I felt this pain on my arm. I knew I had a graze there, and there was this guy sat on the end of my bed rubbing my graze. It was an open wound, and although it wasn't deep or anything it was sore. I said, 'What are you doing?'

And he started talking in Polish.

'I don't know what you're talking about buddy.'

And then two more of his friends came in and they were wearing these white gowns. I was next to a psychiatric ward and these guys were loonies, they were whacko! And they came in and sat on my bed. They had been next door having breakfast or whatever, saw me there and came in and started messing around with me! After about five minutes this doctor came in and told them to get out and leave me alone. Well, that was it; I got on the phone right away to Craiger and told him to get me out of there. The hospital was so mad at me for discharging myself because I was supposed to stay there for a couple of days. I basically got into the back of the van. A mattress was laid out in the back and I got in there and drove to Gdansk Airport from Bydgoszcz while I was just popping pain pills. But I got home.

'It was typical of Billy's character that we took him out of the hospital on Sunday morning and went back to England,' said Craiger. 'It was a bit of an ordeal getting him on and off the plane at Copenhagen and then having to wait for a second flight to Manchester and then having to drive him home from Manchester.'

Hamill had broken L4 and L5 vertebrae in his back and, ironically, as he lay in hospital, Crump only did enough to finish on the same total as the injured American with 62 points. If he had been fit, Billy would have faced Crump in a run-off to determine eighth and ninth places. So Jason Crump had secured his place in the 1999 series almost by default.

'I held it against him [Crump] for quite a long time because I thought what he did was wrong and I still think that,' said Cummings. 'I thought what he did was overly hard riding at the time. I think the right thing to do would have been for him to have at least phoned up and seen if Billy had been okay. Obviously he wasn't, we knew he wasn't, but it's difficult to accept that after somebody has crashed with you and broken your back, they can't be bothered to pick up the phone and wish you the best of luck, or say you're sorry, it was a racing incident, or you didn't mean it, or whatever. That was quite disappointing for me, especially as I had known Jason since he was a little kid.'

'When Billy came home I had to change the bedclothes three or four times because his cast was still wet and hadn't had time to set properly,' recalled his wife. 'I was pregnant so Billy was able to wear my maternity clothes over his torso cast and they were about the only things that would fit.

'Jason had borrowed a boot from Billy because he had an ankle injury, and Billy had this boot specially made for when he hurt his foot. So he had our telephone number so I was disappointed that he didn't at least call to see how he was.'

Hamill says that Crump has never mentioned it to him even when they have been sat next to each other on an aircraft. In *Speedway Star* Crumpie said: 'It was an unfortunate incident with Billy, I don't really know what happened. My bike had a sudden lift to it and for a second I thought I was going to go over the high side or straight on through.'

I saw Terry Pinfold, but he told me that I had to do what they had told me which was to stay in bed. That was horrible because my wife was pregnant and we had a three-year-old daughter, and I had to stay in bed. When I was laid up with my back I was so bored that I got a Play Station and then I built model airplanes for a while. That was good, I enjoyed that. It took about two months to build and two minutes to crash!

'I was pregnant and I was huge,' said Christina. 'I had to stick my stomach under the table to be able to get close enough to do the cutting so that he could put it together.'

On the second day at home, I decided that I was going down the pub and I walked down. Christina said that I couldn't do that because of my injury, but I just said to her: 'You just watch me – I'm doing it.'

And I walked down to the Green Man and had a beer. I didn't say anything and I couldn't sit down so I stood. I didn't say a word until after I had had a pint, and one of them said: 'You look stiff, did you have a crash?'

'Yeah, I've got a broken back.'

'What?'

They still talk about it and say: 'Oh yeah he came in here with a broken back.' But I needed a beer.

I think they said that I had to stay in bed for four weeks. I was in the cast for six weeks and then they put me in a brace for four months and I was strapped up. At the end of December, I was able to take it off. At that point I could take it off to sleep.

Billy's back injury occurred just three weeks before their second baby was due. They had just finished watching the movie *Titanic*, when Christina went into labour.

'I hate that movie, I cannot watch it,' she said. 'I should have been induced but because he had a back injury they wouldn't induce me before he got out of the cast – I was a week overdue.'

Margi had just turned three. Craiger and his wife Carrie watched her, and Craiger loves pizza so I got him some pizza. They came over and probably watched Titantic! *The following morning Kurtis was born.*

When Christina got in the shower I could see blood running down her leg, and I asked her if that was normal. It was just dripping, but she seemed cool. So I told her that I would call her mom and dad, and I had a list of people to call. I fell asleep, but when I woke up there were six messages on the phone and I had not even heard the phone ring. They were all messages from the hospital. I called them straightaway, but they wouldn't tell me what was wrong, only that I had to get over there. So I drove about 100mph to get there. But by then everything was done.

Following the birth of Kurtis, Christina was still bleeding but the doctors didn't seem too concerned despite her worries.

'They didn't believe me, they didn't listen to me,' she recalled, 'it was only when I was passing out that they rushed me down to surgery. All I can remember was hearing Kurtis crying and then all I could think of was calling my husband. Then I had to sign all the papers to say that if anything happened to me I wasn't holding the hospital responsible. I didn't care at that point I just wanted to get well again. It was pretty traumatic.'

If the doctors didn't act when they did it could have been tragic. When she was released she wasn't allowed to do anything but that was difficult with her husband's injured back. Just to make matters worse, Billy discovered that he wasn't in Coventry's plans for 1999 due to a new 40-point team limit imposed by the BSPA (the British Speedway Promoters' Association).

Coventry got the Exide sponsorship through the back door somehow and I don't really know how it came about. Whether it was Tony Summers that approached them or not, I don't know. I never found Tony was trustworthy when it came to business, he was Greg's sponsor and I think he favoured Greg really – which I could understand. We were basically promised that they were going to continue at the same level, but then we got a telephone call at the end of February 1999, basically saying that everything had gone tits up.

It was after I had broken my back so it was a case of it never rains but it pours. I had been loyal to Coventry and Colin Pratt and here I was stuck in this because of my average. Brian Andersen had been at Coventry a long time and it came down to seniority and loyalty, and then Greg had been there before me. It wasn't decided on performance, so it was a little bit of a slap in the face to be honest with you. We decided to move to Sweden as I was still racing for Smederna in the Swedish League.

Sven Heiding, who I had known since my Cradley days and [had] met through Erik Gundersen, helped me to put together a racing programme between racing in Poland and in America with flight details and schedules. He was the vice president of SAS airlines. At this time he had retired from that and was a consultant in the travel industry. He played a vital role in getting me set up in Sweden and helped all of us out. We didn't really know where we were going or what we were doing.

We had a guy, Willie, who was a trucker and he basically took our furniture over there for nothing. Everything else I just loaded up into my Iveco van and it was packed head to toe. When I first loaded it up I had to unload it again because it was so off centre and way overweight. There wasn't any place to sleep or anything. We drove to Dover, got onto the ferry to France and drove all the way up to Denmark, and got onto the ferry to Gothenburg and then down to Eskilstuna. We were living like gypsies.

We looked at half a dozen places but didn't find anything that was suitable. And then Sven called me when we were in England, and he said that he had found something and I told him to just take it if he thought that it would be okay because we were running out of time and we needed some shelter. We were just planning a short-term stay to see how it would go and we've been there ever since.

The 1999 season was a struggle for Billy. Returning from a back injury is not easy, but the FIM and the Grand Prix organisers did recognise his value to the series and gave him a permanent 'wild card'. He eventually got a team place back for Coventry, and also teamed up with Hancock for a GP team but on a much smaller scale. It was the first time that the fairing had been revealed but it hadn't been perfected yet – more about that later.

I tried to change my style of riding after that crash. I always rode at 110%, but that accident definitely left a mark on me, as it should otherwise you're not human. It changed my whole outlook on racing.

My whole idea was to come back and give it 80% in the leagues, and be able to step it up for the Grand Prix – and that would keep me out of trouble. I decided that I should learn to ride by using my senses and I wouldn't get hurt.

I could see riders out there not putting in as much effort as I was and they were still scoring points, guys like Leigh Adams and Crumpie know when to back off when they have to.

But it ruined me – I couldn't race. Because of the way I am, and my whole make up, it wasn't me, it wasn't me at all. It took me the whole year to figure it out. I tried to do it that way, but I couldn't. Why wasn't it working? Because it's not me, I'm not that good in that way. My strength is my aggression, my desire and my want – that's always been my biggest strength. I didn't really realise that until then; I thought I was good enough to do that but I wasn't.

It was a horrible season. I remember that I went to Klaus Lausch, and I basically said: 'Can you give me some engines that will work? If you can't, then I'm gonna quit – I'm not doing this anymore.' And he came up with the goods and I was back. There were a lot of people who were not happy that I had that permanent wild card, which was fair enough, but I thought it was warranted.

At the end of the six-round Grand Prix series, Billy travelled to Lonigo for the Grand Prix Challenge. With the exception of the final round at Vojens when he qualified for the semis for the first time that year, he had struggled throughout the series. He had a point to prove in the challenge meeting, and he was only headed once by Henka Gustafsson as he stormed to a memorable victory.

I was ready, and that's when I'm at my best when I'm backed into a corner like that. So many things had gone against me when I was returning from my back injury, that I felt totally distracted at times. But I was fired up for the Grand Prix Challenge and I won it at Lonigo. I had a point to prove, I was deter-mined to earn my Grand Prix spot and it was one of the best moments of my career – an emotional win. I remember Richard Clark, the editor of Speedway Star, *said to me: 'You're back aren't you.'*

Eight

THE BULLET – RELOADED

I'm happy to be involved with someone like Billy who wants to move his sport forward. I'm interested in motor sport in general and I was impressed by his professionalism.

Kenny Roberts (Team owner of KR Racing)

The Exide sponsorship had fallen by the wayside, so there was no funding for a team. I had won the 1999 US National, and sitting at the next table was Kenny Roberts Senior [triple 500cc World Champion], Kurtis Roberts, Nicky Hayden and the rest of the Hayden family. Kenny Roberts was my all-time hero, but I had never seen the guy in person at that point.

Christina was with me and I told her that I wanted to go over there and introduce myself. But I knew he was a pretty hard character who would say, 'Who the hell are you?' I was intimidated, so I just had a couple of drinks for courage, and went over there and introduced myself. He had been on the red wine too and was having fun, so I went up to him and said:

'Hi I'm Billy Hamill, I have a workshop in England too which is probably half an hour away from yours.'

'Really?'

He was totally cool and he had been a dirt-track racer himself so he took an interest. We sat there for a while discussing each other's work. Then we had some photos taken for the press, and he told me to give him a call, and that was it – no more said really. I was racing during the off-season in David Tapp's series in Australia, but when I got back to Europe I phoned him and asked to speak to Kenny.

'Kenny's not here right now, do you want to speak to Chuck?' came the reply.

I didn't know who Chuck was but I just said, 'Yeah ok'.

He was an American guy and I said: 'Hi Chuck, I'm Billy Hamill and I race speedway, and I met Kenny Roberts Senior at the Las Vegas awards.'

Chuck was totally cool and he told me to come by. Well I was doing a BSPA press launch at Oxford on that Friday and he said: 'Come on by and I'll give you a tour of the shop.'

At this point we had just come out with the fairing for the front of the bike. So we went to the press launch and I called them afterward and Chuck said it was fine to drop by. He was very mellow. So we went to their factory and workshop in Banbury, and it was me, Craiger and Kevin Titman. He gave us a tour of the shop and we showed him the fairing. He knew about the Exide deal and he asked us about it. Exide had financial problems in the end and the company had to file for bankruptcy. He had watched speedway on Sky TV, so he knew who I was. We brought out the bike and showed him the fairing and told him that we were the first people to do this, and that we were trying to bring speedway up.

A guy named Rob, who was a hairstylist and artist, myself, Greg, Bill Hancock, Craiger, there were many people involved in it. The idea was to make a speedway bike look like it belonged in the 21st century and to make it more marketable. Obviously, technically it couldn't be a disadvantage. The hardest part about it was to make sure it didn't hinder the performance of the bike, and that was where Craiger came into it quite a bit. We showed it to Kenny Roberts Racing. That was in 2000 and I had a good season. It sort of built up a relationship between us and Chuck Askland who used to ride dirt-track, and he ran the business at Banbury. We had a lot in common because we were both

*from California and he was a mellow kind of guy, and we both had families
living in Europe.*

'A friend of ours was an artist, Rob Bowers, a sculptor and we
explained to him roughly what we wanted and he came up with some
drawings,' recalled Cummings. 'Then during the winter he and I spent
one day a week in the workshop, and we put a bike together and we
used the bike to make a mould for the first fairing. We made the first
fairing but it wasn't quite what we wanted. We tried different things
like putting the fuel tank in a different place to where we had it and we
wanted to change things around and make it bit more radical, but it
didn't quite work so we had to have a rethink.

'I did a lot of "cut and shut" and we came up with something that
actually worked. Then, when we had it working fairly well we took it
to Team Roberts who helped out with the quality. Their carbon fibre
specialist gave us some help and from the experience he had, he passed
on a few tips to me that helped to improve it and it was really good in
the end. It took a lot of hard work. We had a Mark II model ready for
Billy to use, but when I went to work for Team Roberts he chose not
to use it. The Mark II model has never been seen by anyone apart from
me and it is even more futuristic – something special. But that is something that I will keep to myself for another day.'

The fairing gave Billy Hamill a unique look. Benfield Sports
International (BSI), who hold the marketing rights to the Speedway
Grand Prix, used the bike for some of their press and promotional
work. Its modern and distinctive appearance was just what they were
looking for. Other riders expressed an interest in using the fairing.

'We never really marketed it because we wanted to keep it for
ourselves because it was something different,' said Cummings. 'One or
two of the top riders of the time expressed an interest in running it, but
we kept it for ourselves because we wanted to be different. We stood
out from the crowd and I thought it looked really good and made the
bike look nicer when it was all painted up – especially when it was
compared with the other bikes. I don't think it's any more expensive
when you take into account the price of the mudguards and covers
that you are replacing.'

David Tapp had stolen a march on the FIM in 1994 when he
announced a Grand Prix-style tournament to take place in Australia. At

the time it included the reigning World Champion, Tony Rickardsson, Sam Ermolenko, Simon Wigg and a host of other top riders. The series was called 'The International Masters Series', and its success had done much to improve the image and standing of the sport Down Under.

Billy was invited to take part in the series during the 1999–2000 close season and overall he finished runner-up to the winner Leigh Adams. It was one of the most enjoyable competitions that he had ever been involved with.

It was wild and memorable and I did okay. I didn't win a round, but I've got a trophy somewhere. There was Ronnie Correy, Toni Svab, Rune Holta, Matej Ferjan and I had a mechanic from New Zealand. What I liked about it was that we all had to kind of look out for each other. We all travelled together and we each had a rent-a-car and we paired up with two riders and two mechanics. We went all over the country, and all the bikes were transported in a truck. Although I had already raced against riders like Rune Holta and Matej Ferjan lots of times, I never really knew them apart from passing the time with them in the pits before and during the meeting.

David Tapp had all these foreigners and we were travelling to the same hotels and it created a really good atmosphere – probably one of the best things I had ever done. At that time I had pretty much raced all over the world, but I had never ever been on a tour with so many friends and experienced such cama-raderie. You can imagine with riders, mechanics and the whole crew, there were some good times. We were living in motels, and then we would have a week off. There was a lot of partying and a lot of racing.

Tapp put a hell of a lot into it and a lot of hours. He had a passion for it and he wanted to do it right. And his family would do the tour with us. His name was big in Australia because his father was a well-known commentator so his name was on the line, but he made it happen. We had promotions to do such as radio, video and TV.

For example, he would have a press day and he would pick four riders and we would do wheelies, interviews, and so on, and we were covering a lot of miles. Sometimes we only had just enough time to get there, but at other times we would have a week to get there. It was our responsibility to make sure we were there because we were contracted to do a job, and he had provided the transport to enable us to do that.

When we were in Perth, Johnno [Steve Johnston] was friends with the local Hells Angels, and he had a lot of friends there. He looked after us and organised a barbecue and a boat trip to an island just off the coast. We rented bicycles and terrorised the island on these bicycles and went in the local pub and had a few beers. We went back in the afternoon and went to a local club for Hells Angels or something like that: it was a private club, with beer and strippers and so on. A few of us got in because we knew Johnno and we sat down around this stage, and there were girls dancing around naked to AC/DC or whatever was on at the time – it seemed that AC/DC was on all the time.

We were sitting there and there were two guys who were dressed as bikers but they didn't look right. One of them had something in his hand that was quite small, about the size of a tape recorder or a mobile phone, and it looked as though he was taking pictures. He was doing it very discreetly, and he seemed to be taking pictures of me, or one of Johnno's friends that was with us. But I didn't say anything because I thought that it would cause trouble. Besides, what did I know? I was in a strange place and I was a guest.

Later on that night we went to a house which was a big mansion and it didn't seem that this biker type of guy would live in such a pristine house, but he did and that was cool. We took a taxicab home and we were sitting in the back of the cab, when this car pulled alongside us and started taking photos. He had a 35mm lens and he was just clicking away as we were doing 70mph along the motorway. What the hell it was, I have no idea. I can only put two and two together, but I don't know what the hell was going on so we decided to get out of Perth. We'd stumbled into something, and I have never discovered what it was all about.

We had a New Year's Eve party at Trevor Harding's house in Surfers Paradise, and we had to race the next day, and that was pretty funny. Everyone was hungover apart from Leigh Adams who smoked everybody. I rode on some tracks that I had never ever ridden before and one of them, Lismore, between Sydney and Queensland, was just a big circle – there was no straightaway. When you came across the finish line, if you shut off the gas after you crossed the finish line, then you would nearly hit the fence. So you had to stay on the gas to get round the bend because there was no straight. You had to make your own straightaway otherwise you just went round in circles. And then I raced on some 600 metre tracks that were huge, and that was the closest thing I had ever done to Long Track. There were six riders in a race and there was plenty of room and I loved it. The speed, being able to dice with the other riders because you had so much room to manoeuvre, it was awesome. At that stage in my career I thought that I had pretty much experienced everything, but during that tour I was exposed to some new experiences and I enjoyed it all.

Billy also enjoyed a testimonial meeting at Coventry which was staged on Sunday 20 March 2000. It was an individual event that came down to a winner-takes-all final. Hamill finished second to Denmark's Nicki Pedersen.

Inside the programme Richard Clark of Speedway Star *put a message inside that said: 'Billy… it's been emotional, all the best from* Speedway Star.' *During 1999 we went to London and watched the movie* Lock, Stock and Two Smoking Barrels, *and at the end of the movie Vinnie Jones says: 'It's been emotional.' No one understood that message except me and him, and that was a nice treat.*

Hamill was now the epitome of the modern racer: a modern look, a motor home and a schedule that was punishing. But he was enjoying his racing and was riding well for Coventry. Billy 'the Bullet' Hamill was back in 2000 and began his Grand Prix campaign with a victory in the Czech Republic. He defeated Mark Loram, Chris Louis and Todd Wiltshire in the final and looked a good bet to regain the World title. He came out on top during some exciting clashes with Loram and Gollob. He was a contender again.

However, Sweden proved to be a disappointment for him as he failed to qualify from the main event after another tremendous all-action effort that saw Jimmy Nilsen put the squeeze on the American to such an extent that he tested the credibility of the new air fence and was eliminated. The air fence was introduced by Benfield Sports International and this seemed to give the riders the confidence to race even harder.

Hamill was right back in the World Championship hunt when he finished second to Tony Rickardsson in the Polish Grand Prix at Wroclaw. He borrowed a brace from rival Mark Loram to support his injured shoulder, but this didn't prevent him from producing some very spectacular racing. He was in third place and was just 4 points behind the Championship leaders, Rickardsson and Loram.

With the next round scheduled for Coventry, he seemed poised to make a strong challenge for the Championship lead. Shortly before the GP he scored an 18-point maximum for America in a World Team Cup qualifying round in Landshut, Germany, while for Coventry he warmed up with an 18-point maximum against Wolves and a paid maximum against Oxford.

It had been raining before the meeting, but there was never any real threat to the meeting. Billy was hot favourite to at least reach the final, but he was on his back foot after his first race. He had passed Henka Gustafsson and began lining up Ryan Sullivan for the lead, when suddenly his machine spluttered to a halt. This meant that he would face an eliminator in his next race. Starting from gate three he made a good start but surprisingly tumbled out of the race and severely dented his Championship hopes. He finished the meeting with just 5 points and, although he remained in third overall, Rickardsson and Loram had opened up a lead over the American.

For whatever reason, I slipped off the back of my bike. I made the start but I couldn't turn and I crashed. I didn't know if it was because I had a two-piece leather suit and they sort of slipped down when I let out the clutch, or if the material on my seat wasn't grippy enough. I couldn't believe it, there had to be a reason because stuff like that doesn't just happen. How could a rider of my calibre let that happen? I'm not going to fall off the back of my bike. I didn't know what it was but I knew there was a reason. Any leathers I have, I have different material on the seat of my pants, inside my legs, and I get the grippiest material I can find. And my seats are made of a different material to most riders because of the way my starting style is – I have to be forward on my bike – that's the way I set up my bikes. Obviously I fell off the back somehow – but I never discovered exactly why.

But when I lost that engine before the Danish Grand Prix that's what messed it all up. It was lost in transit and although I got to the semis and finished second in the Consolation Final, the whole weekend was a struggle really because our preparations were messed up. I name all my engines after my dog. I used to have a chocolate lab called Chocolate Mousse. The engine I won the Austrian Grand Prix on was a Mousse. The first engine I received from Klaus Lausch, which was lost in transit, was also called Mousse. And the one that I had as a replacement, which I eventually sold – because it was shit – was also a Mousse.

The engine that was lost was the one I used to win the GP Challenge at Lonigo. I got it the year before and it was the engine that stopped me from retiring. Lausch got me another engine within a week and it was set up exactly the same. It had the same dyno reading and it was set up exactly the same as the old one. But the new one was one of the worst engines I've ever had. And yet it had all the same readings as the other one according to all the graphs. Engines are weird. Lausch couldn't understand it either. It wasn't as if I didn't give it a chance – I did. But I hated it, and I sold it at the end of the year. When I won the last GP, Craiger actually did that engine for me.

The final Grand Prix of the season was staged at Bydgoszcz – the scene of his accident. He still had an outside chance of winning the title, but it was down to Mark Loram to do what was needed to win his first World Championship – which he did despite failing to win a single Grand Prix.

For Billy it was another Grand Prix and any psychological scars that may have been left over from his serious injury at the circuit were put firmly to the back of his mind. He entered the meeting in fourth place in the Championship standings, but by the end of it he had unexpectedly surged to second. He won his second GP of the year at Bydgoszcz with another typically gutsy display.

Deservedly all the plaudits went to Loram who clinched the World title, but Hamill was only 8 points away from taking his second World Championship, and he could feasibly have been taking the step up for gold instead of silver.

'In 2000 he had a fantastic year and nearly won the World Championship,' said Craiger. 'With a bit more luck he would have won it again. It was all there, he wasn't quite the Billy of old, but he was still good enough to nearly win the World Championship.'

I honestly didn't realise that I had done that. I was just thinking about winning the final to get my second Grand Prix win. My team and I had achieved that without a major sponsor which was quite an achievement.

But I would say my injuries played a factor in that. I would say that the experiences of winning a World Championship and then being in a hospital bed in Bydgoszcz, then to get a wild card spot in the GP the following year, going to the GP Challenge, and then winning the first Grand Prix in 2000, it didn't mean that much to me anymore to be World Champion, I just wanted to have fun racing again. I just wanted to get on a good engine and get out there and entertain people, and I wanted to have fun doing what I do. You're going to have success; I know I'm gonna if I'm out there having fun. At that point in time, being World Champion didn't mean as much to me. I had other things in life; I had other ideas and I was moving into a difference phase in my life.

Billy was happy to enjoy his racing after quite a traumatic eighteen months. He was back on form and he helped Coventry to a runner-up spot in the Knockout Cup Final and also a victory in the Craven Shield. He thrilled the Brandon faithful with some memorable races, and he had some thrilling clashes with Mark Loram.

One of which was during a last-heat decider at Poole where Loram found himself in a titanic struggle with the American and had the tyre marks to prove it!

'Greg and Billy are never an easy pair to beat and I missed the gate and was pleased to see Gary [Havelock] in front,' Loram said. 'Unfortunately when I went past them the first time I found myself right behind Gary and I had to slow up. That let Billy back in and I got a burn from his tyre on my arm when he ran me wide.'

Mark's been over with me and did the LA to Vegas race. We were pitted next to each other in the GPs in 1995 and 1996, we raced together in Sweden, and Craiger is Scottish and Norrie [Allen, Mark's Manager/mechanic] is Scottish, so he kind of had the same relationship that I had with Craiger. We've built up a liking and a respect for each other on and off the track.

He came over with Lawrence Hare and we did some dirt-bike riding together in the desert. I showed him the Californian desert, and we had a campfire and had some fun. They watched the Super Bowl with us and the Super Bowl is massive in America. Loram is one of my most respected rivals and I love watching him race. He's probably the hardest rider to keep behind you when you're in front. For four laps it's just all action, but very rarely does he take any unnecessary risks because he's so talented.

Speedway and mainstream motorcycle racing such as MotoGP and Superbikes have grown further and further apart. Not since the early eighties has speedway been able to rub shoulders with its more media-friendly cousins inside motorcycle magazines and daily newspapers. It is a sad fact that bikers, by and large, do not go to watch speedway racing anymore, and one has to wonder about the wisdom of losing such credibility – especially when over 100,000 British fans turned up to watch a World Superbike round at Brands Hatch in 2003.

However, in 2001 it seemed that Billy and his team had finally rebuilt the bridge between road racing and speedway, when, on the eve of the new season, Bullet Enterprises and Kenny Roberts Racing announced a new exciting partnership. At last it seemed that speedway racing was finally moving into a modern era.

Chuck and I hit it off quite well and I built up a friendship with him. I realised that we should hook up and do something, so at the end of 2000 I approached him and he told me to call Kenny and go and see him at his ranch, do some riding and talk some business.

I drove my truck up there and took my motocross and speedway bikes, and Kurtis was there and Kenny Roberts Junior had just won the 500cc Grand Prix World Championship – which is now called MotoGP. We just went out on the mini bikes, the XR100 and they had like a TT track at the ranch, and I played around with those guys and they just kicked my ass and sent me to school. I had a really good time and I learned a lot.

They had a quarter-mile track, like an oval, so we were out there kicking around with a speedway bike and a Flat Track bike. Junior came in with a BMW saloon car – the fastest he could buy at that time. He just came in driving this car and just cranking it around this oval – just rallying it! It was lowered and everything and he was just trashing the car, and I thought, 'What an idiot, this guy doesn't give a shit. This is great!'

Kenny Roberts Senior said that he had ridden a speedway bike with Peter Collins at an event near Exeter years ago, but Kurtis and Junior had never rode a speedway bike before. Well the old man just smoked them, but Junior said that he couldn't ride the speedway bike. He was hot at that time because he was the reigning 500cc World Champion, and he just smoked all of us on the XRs and on the Flat Track bike. It was a really good experience and I stayed there for two days and talked some business.

I told Kenny Snr that our sport was growing and that we had BSI involved; I said that we could get way more airtime and that we could get a minute of slow motion after every race. Basically I gave him no reason whatsoever not to help me. He was game to help, but he didn't know where he was going to get the money from, so he decided to split some from different parts of the organisation. And he did; he went to everybody. They have a motorcycle show every year in Indianapolis and he set up some meetings there for me with Alpinestars, Parts Unlimited, PJ1, and a few others. Alpinestars and Parts Unlimited agreed to come onboard. We were looking for a little bit more from KR Racing, but at the end of the day speedway was only speedway and road racing is their priority. Proton helped and they gave me a car to use, but KR Racing were getting all their funding from Proton so we were in a whole differ-

ent bubble. And again, we're talking miniscule compared with the budget they were getting.

I remember Senior told me that Telefonica Movistar bought Suzuki for $3.5 million when the going rate was $5-8 million, and that pissed him off because it devalued it for everyone else. And I would have been happy for just half of that $3.5 million and I could have run a team and given them just as much exposure and buy the best riders. We were in a different league. I just wanted to elevate the sport I love and do the right thing by it – he was my trump card really. We were hoping they would be able to shed some light on our technical side, which they did to a certain extent but not to what we had hoped they would. I don't think they took us that seriously because we weren't making enough money to make them money. By their own standards we were talking peanuts.

Peanuts or not, it was an important step forward for the sport to be associated with a motorcycle racing legend. It was a first-class link that came at a time when it appeared that speedway was beginning to enjoy more exposure.

'It was more of a partnership than a sponsorship,' said Chuck, 'it was a kind of cross-branding from one form of motor sport to another. It seemed to me that speedway was on the up, as the racing was exciting and it was attracting a lot of interest on TV and we could see a lot of potential there. The way we looked at it was that we were already getting exposure from sixteen MotoGPs a year, and by being involved with speedway it gave us another six weekends of publicity. So we arranged backing for him from Alpinestars, Proton and Parts Unlimited, on the basis that they would be getting exposure to a new audience.

'We developed a speedway frame, which Billy said was the best that he had ever raced on. They tested it at Maely's and the bike also had a carbon-fibre clutch fitted to it. But when Billy dumped the clutch the bike just took off! I remember Craiger calling me and saying that they had wrote it off. But they repaired it and Billy used it in some domestic races, but it was just torpedoing him into the fence – so that was pretty much the end of that chassis!'

The Grand Prix series also took a major step forward when it moved the series into the Millennium Stadium in Cardiff. The future did look bright and Billy was one of the series' stars. With a modern up-to-date image combined with a professional but friendly manner, he was one of the competition's mainstays.

His form for Coventry was, if anything, better than in 2000, but for some reason he couldn't transfer this form into the World Championship. In atrocious weather conditions he crashed out of the opening GP in Berlin, and he failed to make the 'Super Eights' in a memorable meeting in Cardiff where once again he was eliminated on an unpredictable temporary surface. He fared little better at Vojens, but when he arrived at Prague in the Czech Republic he salvaged his GP campaign by snatching a memorable victory by defeating Rickardsson and Crump.

All those guys were going for the World Championship – I wasn't. I was just watching them, and we made some changes before the semi-final and it all clicked into place. It was very satisfying and it felt really great to win a GP again. We had been disappointed with the results up to that point because we were all putting a hell of a lot into it, and it was frustrating. But that night everything just fell into place.

I was really happy to be racing inside the Millennium Stadium, but I can't say that I enjoyed the experience because of my results. I was unhappy with myself and my set-up. Am I happy for my sport? Absolutely! Do I like to see my sport put up in the Millennium Stadium? Yeah, I'm very proud of it.

All those air horns are ridiculous. I don't like it, I like the atmosphere but when you have 30,000 of them pointing at you it's not that cool. It's very loud, but it's an experience. I'm very happy that my sport is showcased in a national arena, and the indoor atmosphere adds to the excitement. Air horns should be banned though. Whatever GP it is, the riders are all wearing ear plugs because it is so loud. But, of course, I like it.

Tony Rickardsson won the Championship that year, and he has elevated the sport in such a way that the guy just spends money to win. He'll pay whatever it takes to win and he'll get the funds from somewhere to do that. We're basically the same age, and he's the only other rider that I have looked at that I thought was more aggressive, and wanted it just as much as me. Any other rider that I have looked at, I've wanted it more and rode harder. But Tony is the only guy that I can say that about.

Billy made the final again in the last round in Poland but failed to make the podium, and finished the Championship in sixth place, his place in the 2002 series guaranteed. However, many will remember an unforgettable race with Greg, Leigh Adams and Tomasz Gollob, when Billy came out on top in a race that has been described as the best in the history of the Grand Prix. All four riders were battling for supremacy for most of the race with Hamill taking control on the final lap.

He was top of Coventry's averages and won the US National Championship for the second time, but he faced another winter of uncertainty when the BSPA decided that the Elite League teams could only field one Grand Prix rider. With Greg Hancock also involved in the series, it was between those two riders for the spot. This time Hamill got the nod to continue racing in Britain and took over as captain, but Greg was frozen out of the British League.

Nonetheless, Billy was in and after announcing another big sponsorship through KR Racing – a big fashion house in the Czech Republic called CWF (Catwalk Fashions) – it seemed that he was set for a good season in the GP.

After 2001 I was quite happy to be a top rider. I didn't want the responsibility of being World Champion and all that goes with it. My attitude was that I just wanted to be a top rider and try and win Grand Prixs. That was how I looked at it. I didn't want speedway to rule my life anymore, I wanted to be myself and have some free time for my family. I was quite happy winning Grand Prixs and just being among the best riders in the world – especially after I had come back from my back injury. I was happy about the whole situation: I had good engines and I was enjoying my racing.

KR Racing got the CWF sponsorship for us and that was supposed to have been a big-budget deal – twice as much as Exide was. I was promised four staged payments from CWF throughout the season. But these payments were not materialising and when I spoke to them about it they promised that it would be the following week. I was promised time and time again, but I never saw a dime.

However, I was spending money based on this agreement and the promises made by them that I would be receiving these payments. It was that bad that we were seriously thinking about pulling out of the Australian Grand Prix because I didn't have any money to spend. By June or July my racing programme had deteriorated because CWF did not honour the agreement: my season was going nowhere fast. 2002 was a hard year for me. It wasn't just the cost, it was the whole thing. Bullet Enterprises had a lot to do with this, even the thing with KR Racing was not going in the direction I wanted it to. I think Craiger had a lot to do with that, not intentionally, everyone's intention was to win races and to strive for that, but we weren't working together like we used to.

Billy wasn't the only one to suffer from the collapse of the CWF sponsorship, as Chuck Askland explained:

'CWF were already involved with a 125cc Grand Prix team and they seemed genuine,' he said. 'The idea was that we would also carry branding on our Grand Prix bikes as well as speedway so they would receive exposure through both forms of motorcycle sport. We were all pretty excited that we had found a backer and we intended to run a two-man team in SGP. We had always planned to do that because that was our way of doing things. In MotoGP we run a two-man team, it's the best way when you are testing and developing and we intended to do the same thing with the speedway team. But although they signed the agreement, they reneged on the deal.

'That was pretty frustrating and it was the first time in twenty years of being involved in motor sport that we had got burnt – it had to happen eventually I guess. Tony Rickardsson put together a two-rider team and Jimmy Nilsen did too so we set the example.'

It was a difficult season at that level for Billy, which was not helped by another back injury which at first was thought to have been caused by a crash with Billy Janniro in a US National Championship round. But the injury had its origins in a match staged earlier in the season.

It was discovered in America but the injury happened at Wolverhampton. I had a crash with Peter Karlsson and he put me into the fence on the first turn during a last-heat decider. I was off gate four and gunning for him and he knew it. I ended up in the fence and it was a hard, heavy crash. I got up and rode in the rerun but got a last. I was very sore, but I was due to ride in Sweden the next day.

I was sitting in Birmingham airport and I had a couple cups of coffee in the lounge, and it was around 9.00 a.m. and my flight was due to leave at 11.00. So I went to the bathroom to take a shit, and I was sat on the shitter and exercising my neck like I normally do, slowly twisting my neck and head from side to side. And then something happened, and it hurt so much it took my breath away for a second or so and I couldn't breathe. I just thought it was one of those things and it would pass. I got up and washed my hands and went back into the lounge.

The Bullet – Reloaded

Andreas Jonsson was in the lounge and I was talking to him, but I was in so much pain that that I couldn't really concentrate. I couldn't really say anything, and then when we were walking together to board the plane, every step I took was agony. It wasn't only my back it was my shoulders – especially my right shoulder – which was killing me. It felt like a pulled muscle so I thought no big deal I would just have to work it out, and after a little massage it would be all right. We got delayed; I was supposed to ride at the Luxo Stars team, but because of the delay I couldn't make the start time and I missed the meeting. I was pretty thankful because I don't think I would have been able to ride, and I never had enough balls to say that I couldn't ride because I didn't want to let my team down. So it was a blessing in disguise that I didn't make it.

I got some massage from a masseuse and I felt a lot better. The Bydgoszcz Grand Prix was just after that, and it hurt me. The pain was in the spot in your back where you can't reach. I was having Craiger pick me up and crack my back and what have you, and I had this spray to numb the pain and I did what I could. I did well in that GP and got to the semis, but I rode my balls off even though my engines were crap and it was a similar situation to the German Grand Prix at Pocking in 1998. I felt the same way. It was 'Here I am again, trying, and I'm getting nowhere', and I was hurting every time I raced. It eased off a bit, but it was still there although it was no big deal.

But then I crashed in America with Billy Janniro and Eddie Castro – it was just a first turn situation. It was really Janniro and I; we hooked up and whenever we rub elbows it usually ends up in tears when we race each other because we're both pretty hardcore. So we locked horns and he hit me and I wheelied straight through the fence. The impact was such that it broke the front wheel rim! I got up, and my bike was ruined and I only had one bike in the US at this time. I borrowed Chris Manchester's bike, rode in the rerun and the final, and my back was so bad that I couldn't even walk to the car and I had to be carried to it!

I was taken straight to the hospital where they told me that I had broken a vertebra, T6, in my back. But it wasn't an injury I sustained that night but an old one. And then I realised that I did it at Wolverhampton so when I was sat on the toilet and cracked my neck that's what was happening. I thought it was a pulled muscle and it didn't have the same effect as my previous back injury which immobilised me. I don't know if it was the adrenalin that was pumping, because you never know, but I didn't feel that bad after the Wolverhampton crash. I felt all right the next morning even though I was sore. If it was that sore that I couldn't get out of bed or whatever, I would have called them and told them that I wasn't going to ride that day. But I didn't feel that bad until I was sat there, and I thought, 'What the hell is this?' And although it eased off, it was always there.

Even now it's still that way and T6 is always troubling me and it's right between the shoulder blades. If I can get a lot of massage and some chiropractic exercises then it's okay. But if I'm travelling and racing a lot and I don't have the time to look after it, then it will catch up with me. A lot of it is to do with a lack of fitness too. With speedway riders, because of the way we ride a bike, you build up a lot of chest muscles, which means that the other muscles are weaker and it causes an imbalance. So what I need to do is training on my back muscles to get them balanced again.

I know before the meeting if I'm going to be struggling that night because it affects my strength. I've had meetings when I've had problems holding onto the bike because my schedule hasn't allowed me the time to look after T6. But what am I gonna do? It's my life!

When I broke T6 I rode in the GP at Gothenburg but I wasn't fit – I could hardly ride. I had Christina and my kids with me, and after the races we had to walk through the bar to go and have dinner. We saw John Postlethwaite and the rest of his crew, and he came over to me and basically told Christina to go and sit down and take the kids because he wanted to talk to her husband.

First of all, I thought, 'Don't tell my wife where to go' – I thought that was rude. He told me: 'Don't worry about it – you don't need to ride here. You'll be in the Grand Prix next year. I'll give you a wild card slot next year. You're guaranteed a slot, don't kill yourself trying to get there next year and get in the top 10.' I remember replying: 'Thanks man, that means a lot.'

And I've brought a lot to the sport, because I was the first to bring in a pit board and a TV monitor into the pits, the fairing and he knew that. But there I was thinking to myself, 'I don't want to be in the Grand Prix'. I wanted to finish inside the top ten so that I could pull out, to prove to everyone that I was one of the top riders in the world and that I didn't need help from the organisers to make that happen.

In an expanded Grand Prix that had now increased to ten rounds that included a round in Australia, Billy wasn't performing well in the series. With the promised finances not appearing from CWF, this put unnecessary pressure on everybody. He crashed out at the Millennium Stadium again and was clearly not happy on the temporary surfaces – obviously these didn't help his back problem.

Struggling with another back injury and strained finances that were restricting the amount of investment he could put back into his racing, he was battling to make sure of his place in the top ten to guarantee his place in the 2003 Grand Prix. After failing to make the semi-finals at the European Grand Prix in Katowice, Poland, Billy travelled to Denmark knowing that he needed a good result – especially if his budget couldn't stretch to the trip to Sydney for the final round.

Nine

PARTING SHOTS

*I am taking things one day at a time at the moment and I
am not looking too far into the future regarding my racing.*

Billy Hamill

Returning to the scene where he memorably clinched his World title,
Billy was in tenth place in the Championship standings as he lined up
for the opening race in Vojens. He won the first race and then finished
second to Tomasz Gollob to make sure of his place in the Main Event.
Racing on a permanent track was making a big difference to him as he
comfortably qualified for the semi-finals where he faced Jason Crump,
Greg Hancock and Rune Holta.

His long-time rival and fellow countryman Hancock lifted and
went wide on the first bend and 'the Bullet' shot into the gap and into

the all-important second place with all the spirit of a Wild West hero. It was his first final appearance of the season and he met Tony Rickardsson, Gollob and Crump in the race to determine the 2002 Danish Grand Prix Champion.

Rickardsson jetted away from the tapes and took the lead and secured his fifth World title, while Crump crashed out and handed the American a rostrum finish which lifted him to ninth position and an almost certain place in the 2003 series.

The final round at Stadium Australia in Sydney produced one of the best temporary surfaces of the year. Hancock won the final GP of the season, but despite winning his second ride, Hamill was eliminated following a fourth place in heat 22. He had finished the season in ninth place with 95 points, but Australia was also the setting for the announcement that the famous Hamill-Cummings partnership was at an end.

He was as frustrated as I was with the situation. We were both putting in more than we were getting out of it. His wife was pregnant with their second child so he was under a lot of pressure. I was funding Bullet Enterprises and I was paying for it out of my own pocket and it was costing me a fortune. I was racing in three leagues to fund it because I was thinking it wouldn't be a problem once the money came through from CWF and it would continue. But things went tits up and I was still expected to pay him [Craiger] and pay my bills, so it was very hard.

'Billy didn't want to be in the business anymore and he didn't want to be in the Grand Prix,' recalled Craiger. 'That left me in an awkward position because I had put the business to one side to concentrate on helping him in 2002 because there were so many Grand Prixs, and it was a year dedicated to him. When he said that and, because of that, things happened and the Roberts four-stroke deal came up where they were looking for engine builders for the new four-stroke project. I asked if they had any jobs going for the wintertime, because when the speedway season came to an end, my work came to an end and I had to find work for the winter. And the man said no, but they had a full-time job if I was interested in doing that.

'I talked to Billy about it out of politeness and my loyalty was to him because before I made any plans of mine I needed to know what his plans were because I didn't want to leave him in the lurch. He basically said: "Well I don't know what I'm doing. I don't know if I'm going to be riding in England because of the way things are in England it changes every year, you never know if you're there or not. In my opinion you should go for it." So I did and I got the job and that was it. We dissolved the business partnership, Billy got a job racing for Coventry and he downsized his racing programme considerably. We were very loyal to each other: we were friends and allies in the speedway world.'

He needed a job for the winter, and Chuck called him when we were in a hotel during one of our racing trips and offered him this job. Craiger told me about it and I told him to take it. He was frustrated and he wasn't happy and I wasn't happy. We were working against each other during our last year because of the circumstances and the pressures that had grown up around us. He needed some security, and I was happy for him. CWF was the whole reason why Bullet Enterprises stayed open because otherwise it would have closed the year before. But their broken promises made the whole situation worse.

Craig Cummings joined KR Racing and began working on the new four-stroke Proton V5 for the MotoGP series – motorcycle racing's Blue Riband event. Although Hamill's average had slipped for Coventry, he won the new-style US National Championship for the third time. Just to prove that he was still the country's top rider, he also won the National title that was staged at Costa Mesa. Costa Mesa was not an AMA-sanctioned track so they staged their own National Championship that was decided in a one-off final.

But Billy's US National Championship commitments had an adverse effect on Coventry's push for the League Championship. They had qualified for the play-offs, but they were drawn against Wolverhampton on a date when their three Americans – Hamill, Janniro and Ryan Fisher – would all be fulfilling their commitments in the US. Despite attempts to get the date changed, Wolves refused and Coventry went to Monmore Green with a weakened team and they were controversially eliminated. It was felt that the situation devalued the whole concept during the first year that the play-off system was in operation to determine the League Champions.

The American meeting had been logged in the fixtures since February and I think it was absurd expecting Coventry to go to Wolverhampton without all three of us. It devalued the competition and made a mockery of it.

Billy was still one of the world's biggest speedway stars, and one of only four World Champions that were still active in the title race. And although it's easy to look back and see that his split from Cummings was the first indication that things were not going very well, it seemed unlikely that he would withdraw from the GP. But in February 2003 he announced that his GP career was over and he was just going to concentrate on racing for Coventry in Britain, Smederna in Sweden, Zielona Gora in Poland and the occasional trip back to California.

Obviously promises were broken and I was in debt. I was riding in three leagues to fund my Grand Prix. I had been riding three/four leagues since 1994, which is 100 plus meetings a year. It's hard not to get burnt out after so many meetings, and you're working your ass off trying to do better and always strive to do better. I wanted to do the Grand Prix, I honestly did, but I wanted to be in it the way I wanted to do them.

To give you an example: Lance Armstrong, who wins the Tour de France every year, he doesn't do every bicycle race every year. Every bicycle race is a build up to the Tour de France. I wanted to be World Champion again. I didn't want to be in it to be a number, and I wasn't prepared to sacrifice myself and I thought: 'Ok I can win here and I can step myself up.' And in order to do that I needed funding. I have the knowledge and I know how to be World Champion. But I didn't want to do three leagues again and the Grand Prix. I wanted to do one and a half leagues and selected meetings to stay race fit. I wanted to spend a lot more time training so when I went to the Grand Prixs I was fired up to win. I was happy to be second and be a top rider, but that's not really me, and I wasn't doing myself justice. I decided that I wasn't going to cheat myself anymore – or my fans. If I was going to do it, I was going to do it right, or not at all. I knew what I had to do to win, and I wanted to win.

All these reasons and aspects combined to form a decision and I wasn't happy with the organisation of the GPs. I wasn't happy with the one-off tracks, and there was no understanding between the riders and the organisers – apart from a couple at the top. There are no GPs in America and it doesn't look like there is going to be in the near future. So you're not a vested interest and you're looked at as just a number, which is business and that's the way it is. I wasn't happy with the communication from the organisation.

The GP Riders' Association was the best thing ever. That was one of the reasons why I got frustrated with the GPs because there was no Association. Sven Heiding worked very hard at it, but he tragically died, and Bo Wirebrand couldn't do it. Ole Olsen, the FIM and BSI wouldn't recognise it, and they basically talked to the top riders of the time like Tony Rickardsson and Tomasz Gollob and told them not to worry about it. No Association was ever formed after that, so that's why the riders are weak and they are riding on these poor tracks. They are kind of biting the hand that feeds them, and it showed when they had to cancel that GP in Gothenburg.

The tragedy about that was they passed it off on SVEMO, and I know, because I was a part of it, that it's not SVEMO it's Benfield – it's their series and they should make it happen. My biggest gripe about it, and what I can't understand, is that I am a huge fan of the air fence; it's the best and most innovative thing that has come into speedway. I wouldn't have broken L4 and 5 in my back if they had the air fence – it wouldn't have happened. They have a dozen guys who go to each and every GP to make sure that the fence is up and running properly – and that's the right way to do it. But they don't do that for these one-off tracks. Putting a track inside a stadium in seven days is a little bit harder than just pumping up the fence. They should have the same team on the tracks but they don't, it depends on the organisers.

Benfield have only done what they said they were going to do. They haven't shown me that they are looking to increase the level. It's ridiculous why corporate teams can't really come into speedway because I feel that they will get more value for money as advertising goes with branding and logos. If you take Proton for example, you don't get Proton on the MotoGP series because they are running at the back of the pack. You only see the top 5, top 10 if you're lucky, you only see them if you watch qualifying or practise. But because it's a mainstream motor sport and you're associated with that, then that's what they sell. Speedway still hasn't stepped up to that. That's why the branding and the amount of airtime on TV would be much better in relation to cost when compared to what they are paying in MotoGP. It's probably not even a third of that cost to run a Speedway GP team.

If those companies came in there would have been others that would want to do it. And it is still like that to this day. You need business people and professionals to do that, and the riders are carrying that GP right now. The riders have stepped everything up and that's why the costs have gone through the roof

– even though the prize money has never changed. But as long as the riders are tolerating it then the organisers will be happy. But the series will never go where it should go, until somebody gets in there and makes it work.

I wanted to slow down as I had been racing in all these leagues and the GP. One of my biggest attributes is my enthusiasm for racing and when I lose that, it shows.

Team Roberts were unable to offer any more support and withdrew from the Speedway Grand Prix to concentrate on developing their new four-stroke bike for the new revolution in MotoGP.

'We lost interest in it because we were getting more and more busy with our four-stroke bike and the temporary tracks didn't help the overall show,' said Chuck. 'The promoters, for whatever reason, didn't seem to recognise the value of having Kenny Roberts involved with speedway racing. The CWF thing was a big blow to all of us. Billy wanted to be World Champion again and we wanted to help him achieve that. It was a fun project and a pleasure to work with Billy and his team; they were all a really good bunch of guys. But it wasn't as successful as we hoped it would be, but I do believe speedway has a lot of potential.'

No longer in the GP, Billy was free from the pressure of that environment and many noticed that he was more relaxed. During 2003 all three of his clubs were involved in a trophy chase. Smederna came very close to winning the Elite League and Coventry were also there. But winning is a serious business in the sport and some will go to any lengths to achieve this – no matter what it takes.

Zielona Gora was facing an important match against Bydgoszcz – Tomasz Gollob's team – and it was important that Hamill was there to ride. But he was in America defending the US National Championship and it seemed highly unlikely that he would be able to make all the necessary flight connections to get there on time. However, they insisted he tried and that he must be there.

I didn't want to do it and I tried to talk them out of it because it was four flights, and the chances of getting a connection for each flight were not good. I had tried to do it before and not made it, but in their eyes I had to do it because they needed me, and I would have been letting my team down to a certain extent if I didn't make it. So I had to try even though it was almost physically impossible. If there was a way I had to try, so I agreed to do it.

They were afraid that I wasn't going to make my connection. Then the plane got delayed four hours in New York. I had been racing the night before so I had no shower and no sleep. I went from Sacramento to Phoenix, Phoenix to New York, New York to Warsaw, and then jumped on a little private plane because I was late. I had to leave my gear bag — it's pretty hard to ride without my knee braces these days and I pretty much have to have them. I was getting calls on my mobile phone to see where I was while I was in the small plane. But we kept getting a beep beep beep on the computer of this small aircraft warning us of another aircraft coming in our direction. This meant that we had to change direction to avoid the other aircraft's flight path. So what was a 40-minute flight took about an hour and 20 minutes.

When we landed I saw this small aircraft doing what looked like figure of eights in the sky. I asked the pilot what this plane was doing but he didn't know and didn't seem too bothered about it. The guy who picked me up in this car didn't have a clue where he was going and I hadn't been to Bydgoszcz in a while — certainly not from that airport.

We finally figured out where we were going and I got there 4 minutes after 6.00 and the race technically started at 6.00. The new rule in Poland that year was that if you're not there at 6 o'clock or 4.00 or whenever the meeting was due to start, you're not allowed to ride. Well, Tomasz Gollob took the referee to where the cars come into the pits and waited. At one minute after 6.00, Gollob must have told the referee that I couldn't ride now. He made sure that I wasn't going to ride and it was an important meeting. I got there at 6.04 and they're on the rider's parade and I ran out there, I wasn't in my leathers or anything, and I was told that there was no way that I could ride! I wasn't out until the third or fourth heat, so I could have rode but I had just been in the air and in airports for twenty-six hours — it was all for nothing.

And then they refused to pay me! I ended up having a fight with the guy in the pits and took his mobile phone off him, and told him that he wouldn't get it back until he paid me. The man who was in charge wouldn't talk to me and they tried to say that it was my fault that the plane was delayed. But delays at airports are a fact of travelling, and you can't do anything about it. You can only make allowances for such delays by giving yourself plenty of time — not like this episode. I didn't want to do it in the first place, but I tried because it was important. Then they left me high and dry in the pits, but luckily Todd Wiltshire and his mechanic Marvyn Cox came to my rescue and helped me to sort out a flight. I had to get back to Warsaw to pick up my gear because I needed it to race in Sweden on Tuesday.

We went back to our hotel and organised a flight and had something to eat. The Gollobs came in for dinner and their translator came over and told me that it was Papa Gollob who was in a plane diverting us. It was Papa Gollob who I saw above doing figure of eights to make sure that I wasn't going to make the meeting on time. And they were so proud of themselves that they had done that, they had to tell me because they thought it was so cool and clever.

Sportsmanship and things like that don't go very far in Poland, and that was a prime example. I enjoy the racing but I can't tolerate all the politics that go with it. This is not the first time something like that has happened and I have been deliberately delayed at customs and that happened in 2003 at Wroclaw. But I don't want to be involved in all that corruption and I don't want to be a part of it. I want to go out there, do my job, get paid and get out of there – and that is how I have always looked at it. It's exhilarating in one sense and I have had some good experiences and made some good friends, but I have also had some of my worst experiences over there too. It's a bizarre place.

I've seen that country grow a hell of a lot since I first went over there to ride. It's definitely more civilised now than when I first went over there. They have more opportunities and the living standards have improved. On the whole I think the country has adapted remarkably well – especially when you consider how long they were under communist rule and influence.

Billy's 2003 season ended painfully when he crashed at Hull and broke his collarbone. Coventry missed his experience and influence as they just lost out to Poole in the play-offs for the League Championship. Hamill enjoyed being captain of a young team at Coventry that included some of the sport's up and coming stars like Lee Richardson, Andreas Jonsson and the young American duo of Billy Janniro and Ryan Fisher.

But, once again, rule changes in Britain gave him another winter of uncertainty. The BSPA decided to scrap the points limit and replace it with a new grading system that hit Coventry particularly hard. In an underhand effort to cut costs – it was argued that newcomers to the top flight, Swindon and Arena Essex, were concerned that they wouldn't be able to assemble a competitive team – the BSPA announced that no Elite club could have more than one rider from grades A or B. Coventry had three – Hamill, Jonsson and Richardson.

Colin Pratt, who had already had to decide between Billy and Hancock once before, now had to choose one from three. Would it be experience over youth? Englishman favoured over foreigners? Or would loyalty count the most? It was a hard decision to make and one that Pratt voiced his opposition over to anyone who would listen. Lee Richardson eased his dilemma when he signed for Peterborough following GP star Ryan Sullivan's departure from Alwalton. This meant that it was between Hamill and Jonsson. In late 2003, it was announced that Jonsson was their choice and Billy had been frozen out of the British League again.

After so long at Cradley, the first couple of years were a bit weird. But I would consider myself to be a Coventry rider now whereas before I was still a Cradley rider. I've been there awhile and I've been captain of Coventry for some time. I'm at home there. I've dealt with Prattie more than anybody so my working relationship hasn't changed. My race jacket has changed and my team-mates have changed through the years, but the last couple of years have been a lot of fun.

It's the third time that I've been in that position and it seems like a vicious circle. I wanted to ride in Britain and at one point they were trying to get Mark Loram's average re-assessed so I could sign for Arena Essex – but that was a no-go. I can't understand why this grading has been done, and I can't see what the long-term benefits are going to be. I don't want to hang up my steel shoe just yet.

When I'm at home I do miss England. There are certain things in England that you don't have at home. It's such a big part of my life because I've been over there for fourteen years. I like the pub atmosphere in England. Back home, if you go to the bar, it's because you want a beer or a drink, whereas in England it's more social. You can go to the pub in England just to hang out and I like that aspect of it and the pub meals – I enjoy all that. I do miss it when I go back to California especially that little village because it's a pretty close-knit community, which you don't have in the US. I've never experienced that sort of thing in California.

If you look at American Speedway, what bothers me is that it has been made into a hobby sport. It's not a professional sport anymore. I think that was done on purpose by Brad Oxley to make speedway pay at Costa Mesa. You can't make a living at it anymore over there.

When I left at the end of 1989, I was averaging around $800-$1,100 a week. If I wanted to retire from international racing and race at home I couldn't *do it; I would be lucky if I made $300 per week. It's not so much that I can't do it, it devalues the whole sport and that's what angers me more than anything. And it's been made that way on purpose.*

They do have tracks in New York, Indianapolis and Canada, but the sport has already taken that step. Costa Mesa was the flagship of American Speedway, but it's been devalued so much. It's probably a little bit unfair for me to say this, because as a rider I've got a different point of view from the promoters and I don't know all the reasons, but there is definitely room for some criticism. Daytona, or Daytona bike week, is huge and why speedway has never been there before I went there in 2003 is ridiculous. And they loved it, because we were throwing up more dirt and riding the outside, we were going in balls-out and grabbing a handful, and speedway bikes are designed to go round an oval so you can go in flat out. Whereas you can't do it with the Flat-Track bikes that they use, it's a lot harder and you have to pull on the brakes to slide – but you don't do that with a speedway bike and that excited everyone at Daytona. It would be great to go to Daytona bike week and put on a meeting – that would be so cool. But it hasn't happened yet…

I have mixed thoughts about when the time comes to retire. I just hope that I can find something to do. If I don't, I just want to devote my time to my wife and kids. Because of my racing schedule I've missed parts of my children growing up and it would be nice to be able to spend more time with them.

It's scary for me because speedway has been the thing that got me out of trouble and captured my interest. I hope that I can find something else that will still provide that feeling. Whether I will or not, I don't know – I think probably not. Everybody is looking for that, and I've found it with speedway and I'm hoping that I can find something that I am that passionate about.

I'd liked to stay in speedway if I can find a role, but I wouldn't do it just for the sake of doing it – I would need to find a niche. I think I would like to play more of a role in my children's development – and I'm not doing that at the moment. I'm there when I'm there, and it's a treat when I'm there and my kids feel like it's a treat – but the travelling doesn't allow me that much time.

It's becoming harder to keep everything level. Margi in particular is a bit older and she gets sentimental about leaving her friends, but Kurtis is not worried about that at the moment. Christina and I probably spend more time apart now than we did in our younger years because of our kids' schooling. California has one of the largest divorce rates in the world but we're still going strong, and she has always stood by me and supported me.

No doubt his retirement from a sport where danger is an occupational hazard will ease some of the worry for his family. As a speedway wife and parent, you are never free from the constant worry of injury that comes with all professional motorcycle racers.

'I don't worry about him when he's on the track because I have no control over what happens out there,' said his wife. 'I love it when he wins, but when something happens to him I feel it just as much as he does. But having kids too, you can't show that you're nervous at all – especially Kurtis, but Margi is really good. I just tell them everything will be okay. If he crashes, I don't go running down to the pits because I think if he wants me he will call me. I can't let Margi and Kurtis see me worry. We go to the races when he's in Sweden – in fact the whole town goes on a Tuesday night and they have big crowds there. I think that is because they get a lot of coverage in the local press – sometimes three pages.

'Billy's a hero in Eskilstuna. But Margi is still puzzled because when he takes her to school, all the kids in school want autographs, photos or whatever. She can't understand it because he's just her dad.'

Billy Hamill realises that he doesn't have too many years left as a professional speedway rider. As Craig Cummings has pointed out, his back injury has probably cut short his career.

Life as a top international speedway rider is not all glamour and glory. Long gone are the days when a rider could earn enough money from riding in one league, race on the European continent once a week and be able to pursue his World Championship dreams. Now, to fund an ambitious racing programme a rider is required to race in two or three leagues in Europe and also obtain reasonably lucrative sponsors. It is a punishing schedule and one that can only be maintained while the fires of ambition are still burning brightly.

When the hammer falls on Hamill's exciting and enthralling speedway career, he will not only join a select band of American riders who have won the World Championship, he will also be remembered as a rider who tried to elevate the sport that he loved. Billy is a speedway hero who lived a dream – and heroes never fade away.

Statistics

Racing Record

British League Averages

YEAR/CLUB	MATCHES	RIDES	1ST	2ND	3RD	UNPLAC.	POINTS	BONUS POINTS	TOTAL POINTS	CMA	MAX F	MAX P
1990 Cradley Heath	35	161	39	46	37	39	246	25	271	6.73	–	–
1991 Cradley Heath	37	179	74	64	28	13	378	23	401	8.96	–	–
1992 Cradley Heath	34	167	64	55	28	21	336	25	361	8.64	1	–
1993 Cradley Heath	24	137	57	45	25	10	286	22	308	8.99	–	–
1994 Cradley Heath	46	241	99	83	31	28	494	29	523	8.68	–	–
1995 Cradley Heath	44	228	170	42	8	8	602	20	622	10.91	11	5
1996 Cradley & Stoke	38	198	136	43	9	10	503	25	528	10.67	5	6
1997 Belle Vue	40	215	118	69	20	8	512	29	541	10.07	4	6
1998 Coventry	35	211	124	59	18	10	508	23	531	10.06	3	2
1999 Coventry	27	137	66	38	22	11	296	9	305	8.91	1	1
2000 Coventry	38	198	80	71	30	17	412	22	434	8.77	1	1
2001 Coventry	35	178	92	50	20	16	396	16	412	9.26	2	1
2002 Coventry	32	156	60	52	25	19	309	31	340	8.72	–	2
2003 Coventry	36	179	76	60	32	11	380	33	413	9.23	2	1
Career Total	501	2585	1255	777	333	221	5658	332	5990	9.27	30	25

CMA (Calculated match average) is the total number of points, divided by the number of rides, multiplied by four.

World Championship Record

World Final:

1991	Gothenburg, Sweden	6 points	12th
1993	Pocking, Germany	7 points	10th
1994	Vojens, Denmark	1 point	16th (reserve)

Grand Prix:

1995	80 points	5th
1996	113 points	1st
1997	101 points	2nd
1998	62 points	9th
1999	35 points	18th
2000	95 points	2nd
2001	61 points	6th
2002	95 points	9th

Grand Prix Appearances	52
Appearances in the final	18
Success Rate	33.33%
Wins	6
Runner-up	6
Third	4

Major Honours

World Individual Champion	1996
World Championship runner-up	1997 & 2000
World Team Champion	1990, 1992, 1993 & 1998
Third place in the World Team Cup	1991, 1995, 1999 & 2000
World Finalist	1991 & 1993
World Championship Semi-Final Champion	1991
Grand Prix Champion of Austria	1995
Grand Prix Champion of Sweden	1996
Grand Prix Champion of Denmark	1996
Grand Prix Challenge Champion	1999
Grand Prix Champion of the Czech Republic	2000 & 2001
Grand Prix Champion of Europe	2000
Third German Grand Prix	1995
Runner-up Italian Grand Prix	1996
Third British Grand Prix	1996
Runner-up British Grand Prix	1997
Runner-up Czech Republic Grand Prix	1997
Runner-up Polish Grand Prix	1997
Runner-up Czech Republic Grand Prix	1998
Third German Grand Prix	1998
Runner-up Polish Grand Prix	2000
Third Danish Grand Prix	2002
AMA US National Champion	1999, 2001 & 2002
SRA US National Champion	2002
Top AMA points' scorer	1989
Appearances for the USA	24

Club Honours

Finished top of the British League Averages, 1995, 1996 & 1997
2000 Craven Shield winner with Coventry
Runner-up in the 2000 Knockout Cup with Coventry
1995 Four Team Champion with Cradley Heath
1994 Runner-up in the Knockout Cup with Cradley Heath
1992 Danish League Champion with Fjelstad
1990 Premiership winner with Cradley Heath
1995 Runner-up in the Premier League Riders' Championship

Bibliography

Index

Bibliography

Books

Bamford, Robert & Shailes, Glynn, *A History of the World Speedway Championship* (Tempus Publishing, 2002)

Bruce Penhall's Stars & Bikes (Studio Publications, 1980)

Foster, Peter, *Heathens, Cradley Heath Speedway 1947-1976* (Tempus Publishing, 2002)

Hillenbrand, Laura, *Seabiscuit* (Fourth Estate, 2001)

Loader, Tony (ed.), *1990, Loaders Speedway Annual* (Privately Published, 1991)

Bibliography

– *1991, Loaders Speedway Annual* (Privately Published, 1992)

– *1992, Loaders Speedway Annual* (Privately Published, 1993)

Oakes, Peter (ed.), *1990 Speedway Yearbook* (Front Page Books, 1991)

– *1991 Speedway Yearbook* (Front Page Books, 1992)

– *1993 Speedway Yearbook* (Front Page Books, 1994)

Roberts, Gary, *California Speedway '97* (Sherbourne Publishing, 1997)

– , *Hamill & Hancock: World Speedway Champions* (Sherbourne Publishing, 1999)

Scott, Michael, *The 500cc World Champions: the Story of the Class of Kings* (Haynes, 2002)

Magazines

Speedway Star, Speedway Mail, 5-One, Speedway Magazine (USA), Speedway Now, Cycle World (USA), Speedway World (Australia).

Index

Index

Other Speedway Titles Available from Tempus

If you are interested in purchasing
other books published by Tempus, or in case you have
difficulty finding any Tempus books in your local bookshop, you can also
place orders directly through our website

www.tempus-publishing.com

or from

BOOKPOST
Freepost, PO Box 29,
Douglas, Isle of Man
IM99 1BQ
Tel 01624 836000
email bookshop@enterprise.net